THE GREAT TITANIC CONSPIRACY

Robin Gardiner

THE GREAT TITANIC CONSPIRACY

Robin Gardiner

Ian Allan PUBLISHING

The Great Titanic Conspiracy
Robin Gardiner

First published 2010

ISBN 978 0 7110 3496 9

Published by Ian Allan Publishing

an imprint of Ian Allan Publishing Ltd, Hersham, Surrey KT12 4RG.
Printed in England by Ian Allan Printing Ltd, Hersham, Surrey KT12 4RG.

Mixed Sources
Product group from well-managed
forests and other controlled sources
www.fsc.org   Cert no. SGS-COC-005526
© 1996 Forest Stewardship Council

Visit the Ian Allan Publishing website at www.ianallanpublishing.com

Distributed in the United States of America and Canada by BookMasters Distribution
Services.

Dedicated to Bruce Williams
Long time 'Devil's Advocate'

Died 2006

Contents

Acknowledgements

I would like to express my gratitude to all those writers and researchers whose works, published or otherwise, provided a mass of valuable information, and most of whom are mentioned in the Bibliography.

My thanks also to those who provided me with additional information from their own family histories or their own research or expertise, in particular Robert McDougall, for his generosity with his extensive research into Liverpool's maritime history, Captain Peter Carey, for his expertise and experience in the field of maritime insurance investigation, and Glyn Lancaster Jones, for photographic evidence.

Thanks again to friends and family for their continued interest and support, particularly my wife Lynn, for putting up with the mass of paperwork spread throughout our home and for her continuous editing of all my manuscripts.

Introduction

To understand why they sank the *Titanic* we first have to know that they didn't!

There are a number of good reasons to believe that the vessel that sank on the night of April 14/15 was in fact *Titanic's* slightly older, and very similar, sister ship *Olympic*. What follows is a brief rundown of those reasons, wherever possible in the order in which they occurred.

Olympic and *Titanic* were the first two of three sister ships, each intended to be about 850 feet long and weighing between 40,000 and 45,000 gross registered tons apiece. When completed they would turn out to be slightly more than 882¾ feet long and have a gross registered tonnage of 45,324 tons and 46,329 tons respectively. The third sister, *Britannic*, would be slightly larger at 887ft 9in long and 48,158 gross registered tons. *Britannic*, which never entered service with the White Star Line, played a very minor part in what happened to her sisters, except to show us the British Government's continued confidence in these vessels despite the fate of her sister. The '*Olympic*' class ships were intended by their owners to be the safest, strongest, most opulent and, by a comfortable margin, the largest vessels afloat, although by the time the first of them was launched that margin had been drastically reduced by German ambitions in the same direction.

The first two White Star vessels of the class, *Olympic* and *Titanic*, were constructed side by side at Harland & Wolff's Belfast yard from a single set of drawings. As launched, the two sisters were identical. *Olympic's* keel, Yard No 400, was laid on 16 December 1908, and that of *Titanic* 15 weeks later on 31 March 1909. Work on the first ship progressed more rapidly than on the second, with the consequence that by the time they were launched the time gap between them had opened to almost 32 weeks. *Olympic*, with her hull painted white, or light grey, to aid photographers, was launched on 20 October 1910, and *Titanic*, with her hull painted the more usual black, on 31 May the following year.

It has been said that *Olympic* was built with a bow-fronted wheelhouse, as is shown on plans of the ship published in *Shipbuilder* in mid 1911. However, a photograph taken from the top of the huge steel gantry specially constructed by Harland & Wolff to enable them to build the vessels shows this not to be the case. This photograph, taken immediately after the ship was launched, apparently shows a straight-fronted wheelhouse, exactly as it appeared on earlier drawings of the ship.

On the very same day that *Titanic* was launched, *Olympic*, after two days of trials, and public examination, was handed over to her new owners, the White Star Line. She left Belfast that afternoon for Liverpool, the line's home port, where she would be opened for public inspection the following day. She then moved on to Southampton, and again the public were allowed aboard before the vessel began to prepare for her maiden voyage, which would begin on 14 June 1911.

On schedule, under the command of Captain Edward John Smith, the White Star line's senior captain, *Olympic* set off on her first voyage to New York and back, via Cherbourg in France and Queenstown (now Cobh) in southern Ireland. She arrived in New York after a passage lasting 5 days, 16 hours and 42 minutes, having made an average speed of just over 21 knots. After an uneventful and otherwise successful maiden voyage, as she was docking her stern collided with the tug *O. L. Halenbeck*, smashing the smaller vessel's stern frame and rudder. It was not an auspicious beginning.

As *Olympic* was leaving Southampton water on 20 September 1911, at the start of her fifth voyage to New York and back, still under the command of Captain Smith but with Trinity House Pilot George William Bowyer effectively in control, she was rammed in the starboard quarter by the Royal Navy's old 7,350-ton armoured cruiser HMS *Hawke*. Both vessels were badly damaged in the collision. It would require a full two months' work back at the builders' Belfast yard to patch up the damaged liner well enough for her to resume service. During those repairs various spare parts were required that could only be obtained by cannibalising the second '*Olympic*' class vessel still under construction. We will look at the collision between *Olympic* and HMS *Hawke* and the repairs required by the liner in detail in Chapter 6.

In November 1911 the *Olympic*, with *Titanic's* starboard main propeller and shaft, left Belfast to resume her career, though not for long. As we now know, these ships were the largest and most opulent vessels built up to that time, but because of faulty workmanship they were anything but the strongest and safest. The hulls of all three vessels were of riveted construction, and for the most part a new technique, hydraulic riveting, was employed. This new technique, which took the place of the older system of hand-riveting with red-hot rivets, should have resulted in much stronger and more reliable joints. Unfortunately the workers at Harland & Wolff saw the coming of the new technology not as a labour-saving advantage but as a threat to their jobs (which in the long term it certainly would be). When building *Olympic* the workers adopted a somewhat Luddite attitude; instead of taking the care needed to position the new riveting machines exactly where they should be to do their work effectively, they didn't bother. Consequently many rivets were not put in straight or tight, and in some cases the holes drilled for them were stretched out of shape. To make bad matters worse some of the plating of the ship's hulls had been drilled before the plates were bent to shape. This had also badly distorted some of the rivet holes, particularly where the plates had been bent around the curve of the ship's bilges. Add to this the enormous stresses imposed on the hull by the *Hawke* collision and it is hardly surprising that large sections of this riveting failed within weeks of *Olympic*'s return to service, and the Board of Trade required the ship to be dry-docked in February 1912 for repairs.

Many rivets were drilled out and replaced, and steel strips were riveted over the joints to reinforce them. When the vessel returned to the yard in March 1912, ostensibly to have yet another propeller blade replaced, it was found that many more rivets had failed and much more reinforcement was carried out. (BoT reports at PRO.)

Even while repair work was under way on *Olympic*, conversion of *Titanic* into a reasonable twin of her sister must also have begun. After *Olympic*'s maiden voyage, J. Bruce Ismay, the managing director of the White Star Line, suggested certain improvements for incorporation in *Titanic*. These included the fitting of extra cabins on B Deck; this had been a promenade deck on *Olympic*, but would be completely turned over to cabins and public rooms on her sister. These alterations had been begun before the *Hawke* incident took place, at least as far as altering the window layout on B Deck and probably constructing the cabins there as well. Fortunately, these cabins were built of lightweight steel plates and it would not be at all difficult for Harland & Wolff to remove them again, which seems to be what happened. The open promenade areas at the rear end of B Deck on both ships were planned to be considerably longer on *Olympic* than on *Titanic*; so this too required conversion. The B Deck window layout, regularly spaced windows on *Olympic* and irregularly spaced ones on *Titanic*, and the length of the aft promenade area on B Deck, long on *Olympic* and short on *Titanic*, are important recognition features.

A Harland & Wolff photograph of *Olympic*, taken when the vessel was in the Thompson Graving Dock in 1911, clearly shows a vertical joint in her hull plating immediately forward of the port-side anchor hawse pipe. Photographs of *Titanic*, while still on the stocks and while fitting out in 1911, show that there was no similar joint in her hull plating just ahead of her port-side anchor. However, a picture of *Olympic*, taken during her 1912/13 refit following the *Titanic* disaster, shows this vessel not to have the telltale plating joint, proving quite conclusively that the hull pictured is that of *Titanic*, although the name *Olympic* is clearly visible on both sides of the bow.

Photographs taken of *Titanic* at Southampton shortly before her maiden voyage show a large area of discoloured plating, as if it had been newly painted with paint that did not quite match the original, in the same location as *Olympic*'s hull was damaged by HMS *Hawke*.

As previously mentioned, to make life easier for photographers *Olympic*'s hull was painted white, or very light grey, for her launch. *Titanic*'s hull was never painted light grey because, as the second vessel of the class, she was nothing like as newsworthy when it was her turn to enter the water. Curiously, where rust and marine life have flaked the top layers of paint from the hull of the wreck discovered by Dr Ballard in 1985, patches of what appear to be white paint are exposed. This white or light grey paint beneath the black topcoat of the hull means that, whatever ship the wreck is, it is definitely not *Titanic*.

Now we come to the very complicated but absolutely damning evidence contained in the gross registered tonnages of *Olympic* and *Titanic*. *Olympic* was first registered on 29 May 1911 at 45,323.82 gross registered tons (grt) and 20,894.2 net registered tons (nrt). These registered tons are not a measurement of weight at all, but a measurement of volume: 100 cubic feet equals 1 registered ton. The grt represents the total enclosed areas of the ship, including the superstructure, engineering and crew spaces, while the nrt is just the enclosed areas used by fare-paying passengers - cabins, public rooms and so forth. It is the gross registered tonnages that mainly concern us here.

Titanic was registered on 25 March 1912 at 46,328.57grt, a gross registered tonnage that was 1,004.65 greater than that of *Olympic*. The extra (roughly 1,000) tons were there because of the extra B Deck cabins, the Café Parisien and enlarged restaurant, while the same areas on *Olympic* were open-ended promenade deck but with large glass windows protecting passengers from the elements. Gross and net registered tonnages were not calculated at the last moment but from measurements taken by Board of Trade inspectors as the ship was being built. Board of Trade inspector Carruthers visited *Titanic* almost 2,000 times during construction. As the differences between the B Deck layout of the two ships was already largely in place by early September 1911, Carruthers would have already been well aware that *Titanic* would eventually finish up with a grt approximately 1,000 tons greater than her sister. Because harbour dues and such like were calculated on a vessel's grt, it was an offence to understate that tonnage. This presented White Star and Harland & Wolff with a problem. With the grt of *Titanic* already known to the Board of Trade, they could not pass off the sister ship without bringing her up to something like the same specification, but they simply did not have the time to properly convert the whole of B Deck to the same layout as that of *Titanic*. Nor could they leave *Titanic* with all of her cabins on B Deck if they wanted to pass her off as *Olympic*. Alterations to *Titanic* in order to make her the same in general layout and appearance as *Olympic* were not too much of a problem because the ship would remain in the yard from the time the decision to switch them was made in about October 1911 until the exchange actually took place in the first week of March 1912. It was not too much of a job to remove the alterations to *Titanic's* B Deck and convert it back to its original form. On the other hand, they would only have about a month to change *Olympic's* appearance to that of her sister, from early March 1912 until she was due to leave the yard, as *Titanic*, to prepare for her maiden voyage, during the first couple of days of April.

Because of the shortage of time the only alterations to *Olympic's* B Deck that could be completed were the two executive stateroom suites, the enlarged restaurant and the Café Parisien. As these alterations noticeably changed the outward appearance of the ship it was essential that they were done in the time available. We know that the rest of the alterations were never carried out because during the sinking a steward walked along B Deck, checking that cabins were empty and locked. As he was carrying out his duties he could see the swung-out lifeboats hanging from their davits two decks above, something he patently could not have done had there been cabins between the passageway he was in and the outside of the ship. To make up this shortfall of something like 700grt, the forward end of A Deck was enclosed. This work was actually carried out during the very last week that the vessel which sailed as *Titanic* was still at Belfast - after the 25 March registration. Only in this way could *Olympic* be made to match up with *Titanic's* known grt. The A Deck windows could not have been installed on *Titanic* at the last moment because they would have raised her grt to something over 47,000 tons.

To put it in its most basic form, you cannot add 1,000 tons to a 46,000-ton ship and end up with a 46,000-ton ship. The vessel that sailed out of Southampton on 10 April 1912 can only have been a 45,000-ton ship with the last-minute addition of 1,000 tons of grt in her B Deck public rooms and enclosed area on A Deck.

Titanic's registration document has an interesting hand-written note included in it, which says:

'Note 2. The undermentioned spaces above the upper deck are not included in the cubical contents forming the ship's registered tonnage: Open space in front of poop 16 feet long = 65.24 tons. Open space abaft 2nd Class smokeroom, 6 feet long = 15.84 tons. Open space on promenade deck, abreast windows, port side, 198 feet long = 343.27 tons. Open space on promenade deck, abreast windows, starbd side 198 feet long = 377.24 tons.'

Of course the spaces referred to are not above the upper deck at all but on A Deck. The document is dated 25 March 1912. The man responsible for forwarding this document to the Registrar is Harold Arthur Sanderson (White Star's manager). The registrar's signature is unreadable. The question is, why were these spaces not to be included in the grt of the ship? The only believable reason is that they did not actually increase the cubic capacity of the vessel, which in turn would mean that approximately the same cubic capacity had been lost somewhere else on the ship. Clearly this loss of capacity cannot have occurred within the hull of the vessel or it would not have affected the grt but only the nrt - but the removal of cabins on B Deck, turning that area into an open-ended promenade space, would have done so. That these spaces should have been included in the grt is shown by the fact that they appear on the document at all. Had they been truly open spaces such as the after part of A deck, they would not have merited a mention. As all sorts of charges were calculated on the ship's grt, it is completely unbelievable that the British Government would allow White Star to register a ship (any ship) at less than its true, chargeable, cubic capacity.

The explanation put forward for the addition of the A Deck screens was that Joseph Bruce Ismay thought they would protect promenading first-class passengers from spray. A Deck, by the way, was almost 50 feet above the water, with a raised bulwark along its outside edge to protect promenaders and prevent them from toppling overboard before these alterations were envisaged. One can't help wondering just what cosseted first-class passengers would be doing on deck in weather that would throw any appreciable amount of spray more than 50 feet in the air. Although *Titanic's* supposed sister ship sailed the North Atlantic, known for its violent storms, she was never fitted with these passenger-protecting screens, and she was the flagship of the White Star Line fleet.

Only a few items recovered from the wreck have any sort of identification at all on them. One of these, which in any way indicates that the ship might actually be *Titanic*, is a helm indicator from the stern, or docking, bridge. This does have *Titanic's* build number on it, 401, but could easily have come from any vessel of the class. Another is a slate slab supposedly from the stewards' lavatory on the port side of E Deck; unfortunately, detailed drawings of *Titanic* show that no provision for the fitting of any such slate slab was ever made. That Harland & Wolff mixed up parts from one ship with those of another is clearly illustrated by their still pricing items being fitted to *Olympic* to *Titanic's* account years after the sinking.

A section of hull plating recovered from the wreck does show an irregularity in the porthole layout on C Deck that should be peculiar to *Titanic*. The piece of plating comes from the side of the stewards' toilets and has one more small porthole than the corresponding section shown in photographs of *Olympic*. As we know, the builders were trying to make the external appearance of one ship as similar as possible to that of the other. This extra porthole was cut in the white-painted upper part of the hull and was very visible. As the transformation progressed a new porthole would have been cut as a matter of course. The already existing porthole in the real *Titanic* would have been sealed up, either during the week that the switch actually took place or during the ship's winter refit at the end of 1912.

Before the ship known as *Olympic* was broken up shortly before the Second World War many of her fixtures and fittings were sold off, including the panelling from most of her public rooms. The oak panelling from the first-class smoking room is now installed in the conference room of the Swan Hotel in Alnwick, for example. Other panelling from third-class areas of the ship now adorns a private flat in Wirral. This woodwork has the reverse sides clearly marked. On the panels the number 400 is stencilled, but on the frames the number 401 is clearly visible.

The one item recovered that should have been unmistakably marked, the vessel's crow's-nest bell, has no name or number on it at all. Normally one would expect to find the ship's name cast into a bell, and it is the recovery of these that is usually accepted as proof of identity. In this case it would be no more proof than the helm indicator, as such objects could all too easily be moved from ship to ship. Even to the present day the most common maritime insurance frauds involve changing the identities of ships.

Even the builders' model, which looks like *Titanic* but which began life as *Olympic*, and is now on display at Liverpool Maritime Museum, has the build numbers of both ships, 400 for *Olympic* and 401 for *Titanic*, on different parts. Until this model, which was actually constructed by Harland & Wolff, was converted into a *Titanic* lookalike on the museum's instructions, it had represented *Olympic*, although fitted with parts obviously intended for a model of her sister. At one time this model was even altered to represent the third sister ship, *Britannic*.

After the sinking of the ship usually known as *Titanic*, 13 lifeboats were recovered and taken into New York before being returned to Britain. While these boats were still at New York they had *Titanic's* name sanded off and the brass White Star badges and numbers removed, supposedly to deter souvenir hunters. While removing the names and other paraphernalia workers discovered the name *Olympic* carved into the gunwales. The old name had been filled with putty and painted over. Eventually the boats were returned to Britain and a dozen of them were reused by the White Star Line to help bring the number of boats aboard the second sister ship up to a level acceptable to the travelling public. Boat No 12, considered at the time to be an unlucky 13th, was not reused but lay at Southampton until the end of the First World War. Many local sea scouts had joined the Royal Navy on the outbreak of war, and some at least had given their lives for their country. By way of a thank you, the 13th lifeboat, No 12, was handed over to the sea scouts to use as a cutter. During the eight or nine years the boat had been laid up, its appearance had deteriorated somewhat, so the sea scouts set about tidying it up. They stripped off the old paint and there, cut into the gunwale of the old boat, was the name of *Titanic's* sister ship, *Olympic*. This boat was finally wrecked in a collision with the Gosport ferry at Portsmouth and taken by the Royal Navy to Haslar for demolition. However, for many years afterwards its port and starboard White Star insignia were used as prizes by a local sea scout group. It would appear that when the lifeboats were returned to Britain the badges that had been so carefully removed in New York were returned with them.

While making preparations for the blockbuster movie *Titanic*, the producer, James Cameron, paid a number of visits to the wreck. On one of those visits a small robot submarine equipped with cameras and powerful lights was sent deeper into the interior of the sunken ship than any other had been. The tiny submersible visited the special suite of staterooms that had been occupied on the fateful voyage by Joseph Bruce Ismay. Film taken by the robot showed the empire-style sitting room to be in a remarkable state of preservation, its cast iron fireplace with its veined marble surround still in place. Veined marble is a naturally occurring metamorphic crystalline limestone and, like snowflakes and finger prints, no two pieces are the same. However, the marble filmed on the wreck exactly matches that shown in a photograph of the corresponding stateroom aboard *Olympic*, taken in 1911. (*Titanic - Breaking New Ground*, 1998 TV programme.)

The question should perhaps be, 'Why did they sink the *Olympic*?', and perhaps more importantly, 'Why did the British and to a lesser extent the American governments help with the cover-up?' To find the answers - and they are many and varied - we must go back to well before the loss of the ship and look at the political situation in Europe and the quest of a certain American financier and industrialist for ever more gold.

Chapter 1

The search for *Titanic*

On 9 August 1953 a very interesting article, written by Victor Sims, appeared in the *Sunday Chronicle*. The headline reads 'Ship Seeks *Titanic* Millions' with the subheading 'Mystery explosions in Atlantic'.

It appears that the British Admiralty had chartered the 783-ton salvage vessel *Help* from the world-famous Southampton salvage company of Risdon Beazley in an effort to find the wreck of the *Titanic*. The wreck, as we now know, lies in more than 12,000 feet of water and is extremely difficult to reach, even with the technology available in the 21st century. Imagine how much greater that difficulty must have been more than 50 years ago. Only the fact that television had reached a point in its evolution whereby a camera could be sent down under the sea to the required depths made the attempt possible at all. Even though there were deep-diving submersibles available, such as the bathyscaphe *Trieste*, easily capable of reaching the extreme depth of the abyss, these were not employed because the Admiralty preferred to work in secret. Harbour pilots from Falmouth in Cornwall confirmed that the salvage vessel had called there in early August but had supposedly left hurriedly for Southampton, However, the harbour master at Southampton denied all knowledge of the vessel's movements, saying, 'She has not arrived, nor is she expected.'

The *Help* carried a 33-man crew and three civilians believed to be either scientists or Admiralty observers, under the command of Captain R. Bogart; all were sworn to secrecy. All wireless traffic with the *Help* was transmitted in naval code. Shipping officials suspected that the salvage ship was sending out decoy messages to confuse rival salvage companies as to her position. Nevertheless, an Italian salvage ship did head towards the general area where the *Help* was working, only to be turned away by ships of the Royal

Navy. All requests made through Land's End radio to speak to the master of the *Help* were ignored. Other vessels in the area where the White Star liner had foundered reported hearing repeated heavy explosions. Then, from St John's in Newfoundland, came the news that the wreck of the *Titanic* had been found.

On the evening of 8 August reports began to circulate that the *Help* would soon begin salvage operations to recover a cargo of gold and other valuables worth something in the region of £8,000,000 - a cargo that in all official records never existed, but the Royal Navy wouldn't have been there without some very compelling reason.

There is nothing unusual in a salvage company keeping its activities a closely guarded secret. The world of maritime salvage is extremely competitive and it is not unheard of for one company to attempt to hijack a wreck being worked on by another. However, in this instance Risdon Beazley clearly had the full support of the Royal Navy and therefore had nothing to fear from any rival company.

Since that newspaper report was published a smattering of further information has come to light, even though official records are still closed. In those days before the sophisticated sonar equipment of the present time was available, images of the deep-sea floor were generated by dropping explosive charges and measuring the shock waves that bounced back off the bottom. While this system may have lacked the finesse of the modern side-scan sonar, it did work and was accurate enough to have revealed a wreck the size of *Titanic*, even if it was 12,500 feet below the surface. Instead of dropping their explosive charges over the last reported position of the liner, 41°46'N, 50°14'W, the *Help* supposedly began her search some miles away. Of course we now know that the wreck does indeed lie some miles from that last reported position, which begs the question, 'How did the Royal Navy know that in 1953?' Only later did the *Help* change her position and begin dropping explosives over the coordinates given in *Titanic*'s distress calls. These later explosions were most likely intended to throw any observer off the scent, just as the maritime officials suspected.

In the 1950s deep-water salvage was a primitive affair, although Risdon Beazley was probably the best in the world at it. The company did hold the record for bringing up large pieces of salvage from deeper wrecks than anyone else. First a wreck would be located, then a camera would be lowered. Then, with the aid of a mechanical grab, explosive charges would be placed in order to blast open the remains of the ship. Once enough charges had been exploded to open up a route down through the sunken vessel to wherever the materials to be salvaged might be, the grab would be lowered in. A mechanical grab was not the most sensitive or selective of tools, so it was pot luck as to what would actually be recovered, if anything. Modern photographs of the bow section of the wreck show a hole in the hull alongside a forward hold. The plating surrounding the hole is bent outwards, indicating an internal explosion. Various fanciful explanations have been put forward to account for this hole, such as water trapped in the hold becoming pressurised when the ship struck the bottom. This might have been believable if only the pressure had not had a much easier escape route through the hold's hatch cover than through the inch-thick steel plating of the hull. The hatch cover is missing and may well have been blown off when the *Titanic* reached the sea floor. Interestingly, French experts who surveyed the wreck in the years following its rediscovery by Dr Robert Ballard's 1985 expedition concluded that the hole had been caused by an internal explosion. Could this be a result of the 1953 salvage attempt?

The stern section of the wreck is so badly smashed that it is barely recognisable as part of a ship at all, while the bow is relatively intact. Once again various whimsical explanations for this phenomenon have been put forward. One particular theory, which flies in the face of the laws of physics, seems to have gained fairly wide acceptance among those who should know better, perhaps because the alternative is embarrassing for them. According to this theory the ship broke into two main parts while still on the surface and the bow section planed away at an angle. This at least makes partial sense, as anything moving through water, or even air, takes the line of least resistance. The sharpest, smoothest part tends to lead, and with the bow section that would be the knife-edged stem of the ship. Provided that the torn section where the vessel had snapped in two was not a great deal heavier than the stem, this planing effect is precisely what one would expect. As the ship was sinking the rounded bottom of the hull would also tend to act as a leading edge, which is why most vessels that sink in deep water finish up sitting upright on the bottom regardless of their attitude when they left the surface. Exactly the same principles are employed in archery and darts: the smooth, heavy point leads and the lighter, rougher flights follow along behind. In the case of the *Titanic* the knife-edged stem provides the heavy point and the torn steel around the break acts as the flights. The application of physical laws does seem to have governed the bow section's journey to the bottom of the sea. However, if the generally accepted theory as to why the stern section is so badly smashed is to be believed, we also have to believe that those same physical laws were suspended for its last journey.

According to the received theory on the sinking of the stern section of *Titanic*, this part of the ship sank vertically and at great speed. Indeed, it was moving so fast that it drew a column of water behind it, like a slipstream. Eventually it crashed into the sea floor, doing a great deal of damage to itself in the process, only to then be crushed out of recognition by the column of fast-moving water that was following it. Sounds quite good at first glance, doesn't it? What a pity it doesn't work in reality. The laws of nature are not suspended for anyone, not even the *Titanic* or those that put forward this theory. Allowing that the ship broke in two on the surface, which I don't believe for one moment, then the stern section would have behaved very much like the bow. The curved stern, being a great deal smoother and sharper than the torn area around the break, would have led. The weight of the rudder and the propellers with their massive shafts would have ensured that the extreme rear part of the ship was the heaviest, adding to the tendency of anything moving through water to go smoothest, heaviest part first. Any air trapped in the stern would have been expelled before the section passed the 1,000-foot mark, or the water pressure would have crushed it into such a small area that it would not have materially affected the descent. The rudder would have been forced hard over to one side or the other and the whole stern section would have spiralled down to land on the sea floor in an upright attitude. There would have been no column of water to act as a gigantic sledgehammer and to pulverise the stern once it had come to rest. In no other example of a deep-sea wreck do we see any solid evidence of this crushing effect by a column of water following the ship down. Something else smashed the stern of the ship to the extent that it is no longer recognisable, and the most likely candidate has to be the repeated use of explosives to force a passage into the ship in 1953.

Clearly the 1953 expedition to the wreck of the *Titanic* was unsuccessful as far as recovering the bulk of any treasure was concerned. Nor was it entirely successful in locating the position of the wreck, because the Royal Navy had already known roughly where it was ever since 1912. British warships had been close enough to observe the sinking liner and record its exact position, even if they had declined to answer distress calls or go to her assistance. In November 2000 the Navy finally admitted that one of its vessels, the cruiser HMS *Sirius*, was in the area on the night *Titanic* foundered. As we shall see, the Royal Navy was being economical with the truth, and its presence was not the only naval one that night.

Whatever had drawn the Royal Navy to the wreck of the *Titanic* in 1953 was still there, or so they believed. Eight million pounds is a lot of money, and if that was the value in 1912 when the liner sank, the figure would grow dramatically with the passing of time. Such was the attraction that after a lapse of 25 years the Royal Navy would be back to try again.

The Royal Navy was not the only body interested in the ship. In that same year, 1953, Clifton Webb and Barbara Stanwyck starred in the film *Titanic*, based loosely on the disaster. Until then the ship and those that had been lost with her had been almost forgotten by all except those that knew of the fortune supposedly hidden away within her shattered hull. Most of those who did know about her cargo never expected there to ever be any chance of its recovery. Even Lloyd's of London, the famous maritime insurer, which officially owned the wreck, attached little or no importance to it. Thus, when in the 1950s Mr Douglas Faulkner-Wooley showed an interest in purchasing the wreck from the insurance company, Lloyd's was quite happy to let him have it for the princely sum of £1. Mr Wooley's intention was to raise the sunken vessel and bring it back either to Liverpool, the White Star Line's home port, or to Southampton, its port of departure on its maiden voyage. Once back in Britain the plan was to restore at least a part of the ship to something like its original condition and open her up as a museum. It is a curious fact that back in 1912 Lloyd's denied being the underwriters for the vessel and even went so far as to publicly announce that *Titanic* was not built to its requirements. To the present day, if one makes inquiries at the Guildhall Museum in London, where most of what remains of the official record covering the liner's insurance resides, one will be informed that the underwriters were not Lloyd's at all - but we will deal with the insurance question later.

In 1966 Mr Faulkner-Wooley, in association with Mr Philip Stone, formed the '*Titanic* Salvage Company', whose aim was to raise the wreck of the White Star liner and restore it to its former glory. The major stumbling block seems to have been raising the finance to begin the project, and little progress was made until 1972. Then Douglas Wooley, with Clive Ramsey and Joe Wilkins, formed the 'Seawise Salvage Company'. 'Aquatech' was also set up that same year by Mr Wooley and Mr Tony Wakefield. This time Douglas Wooley put together 'Monetary Investments Maritime Limited' to encourage investment in the other companies.

Over the years between 1966 and 1972 Mr Wooley had turned his attention to the burned-out wreck of the *Queen Elizabeth* lying in Hong Kong harbour. His intention here seems to have been to raise the *Queen Elizabeth* as a sort of practice run before making an attempt on the *Titanic*, although the problems posed by each vessel are in no way similar. As the 1970s wore on, the Admiralty began to openly show a little interest in Mr Wooley's plans for the *Titanic*, although it didn't mention its previous involvement. In 1978 some sort of agreement between Douglas Wooley and the Admiralty seems to have been reached whereby they would join forces to find and survey the liner, in conjunction with Le Fathom Line Limited. This is of particular interest because, as we know, the Admiralty already knew exactly where the ship was. The joint venture appears to have been code-named 'SOLLIS'.

At about the same time another potential partner for Mr Wooley seems to have entered the picture, Mr Blundell, a South African businessman who offered to put up £6.5 million to partially fund the expedition. For this Mr Blundell was promised 41% of the value of anything salvaged from the wreck, so Douglas Wooley handed over that percentage of shares in his *Titanic* Salvage Company. According to a report on the venture produced by Mr Robert McDougall, a maritime historian from Blackpool, no sooner did Mr Wooley hand over the shares than Mr Blundell and the £6.5 million evaporated, never to be seen again. Despite the sudden departure of Mr Wooley's financial backer, the Royal Navy continued with the project, and provided the survey vessel HMS *Hecate*.

This was no half-hearted contribution from the Navy. HMS *Hecate* was a deep-ocean survey vessel of the 'Hecla' class. She was 260 feet long with a beam of 49 feet and displaced 2,800 tons. She carried a crew of 121 including 13 officers and six scientists. The ship was capable of 14 knots with her three Paxman Ventura diesel engines and had a range of 12,000 miles at a cruising speed of 11 knots. Two small survey craft, a launch, a Westland Wasp helicopter and a Land Rover were among her standard equipment, together with two 20mm Oerlikon guns. She had joined the fleet, with two sister ships, *Hecla* and *Hydra*, in the mid-1960s, and would remain in service until 1990.

In 1977 the Royal Navy had carried out a series of experiments with a new deep-water sonar system intended to detect Russian nuclear submarines that habitually hid themselves in the deep waters of the North Atlantic in the same general area where the *Titanic* had foundered. The easiest way to test any underwater search equipment is to look for something of which you already know the exact location. The test was successful inasmuch as the sonar detected the two large sections of *Titanic's* hull on the ocean floor. Understandably, because the Royal Navy didn't want the Russians to know that they could find and therefore destroy submarines hiding in deep water, they classified the whole operation. Only the Americans were made privy to any of the information gathered.

In 1978 everything appeared to be going swimmingly for Mr Wooley, right up to the time he was ready to join the expedition. At the last moment, even though he had provided detailed plans and had been otherwise instrumental in bringing the project to fruition, Douglas Wooley was excluded and the *Hecate* sailed without him. From what information is available, almost 30 years after the event, the only person on the expedition with any real connection with Wooley was Commander John Grattan of Le Fathom Line Limited.

In 1978/9, shortly before the joint venture to find the *Titanic* began, Now magazine published an article describing Commander Grattan as the Royal Navy's senior diver, and explained how he, Seawise and *Titanic* Salvage, a company formed by Wooley and others to undertake the project, expected make the search during that summer. Interestingly, the article also stated that Grattan had revealed the exact location of the wreck to the publishers, although they were going to keep it secret until after the expedition had taken place, which confirms that the Navy already knew its precise position. According to the magazine, Dave Berwin, the world's leading expert in underwater photography, had been engaged to help and to raise the necessary finance. A feasibility study had supposedly been carried out by Commander Grattan's Le Fathom Line, which operated as a diving consultancy. Grattan had started out in the Fleet Air Arm (the Royal Navy's air force) but had been grounded after he broke his spine in an inter-service skiing contest. He qualified as a diver in 1956 and enjoyed it so much that he went on to become a specialist in the science. By the time he became involved in the Sollis Project, Grattan was earning his living as a diving consultant for various oil companies, but his great love was wreck diving, especially if there was a profit to be made. There was certainly the prospect of a healthy return for whoever managed to salvage artefacts or gold from the *Titanic*.

The results of the trip by HMS *Hecate* in the search for the wreck of the *Titanic* have never been released by the Royal Navy. However, we do know that the Navy did find the wreck again, and this time they managed to take some photographs, two of which have somehow become public. One of these pictures shows a ship's cranes and could hardly be described as conclusively from the White Star liner. The other shows a section of the forecastle deck with the massive anchor chains still in place. This second picture is definitely of an 'Olympic'-class ship and is fairly conclusive evidence that the expedition did indeed reach the wreck of the ship we know as the *Titanic*.

In fact the Navy has denied that the expedition ever took place, but then it has denied a lot of things over the years that we now know happened. For example, according to the Royal Navy it had no surface vessels or submarines operating in the North Atlantic in 1978 or 1985. Despite this denial we know that the Royal Navy was deeply involved in the NATO exercise 'Ocean Safari', which was seen from the Wood's Hole expedition vessel *Knorr* on 1 September 1985, the day after the wreck of the *Titanic* was officially discovered.

To finally substantiate the fact that the Royal Navy already knew the exact location of the wreck of the *Titanic*, we need only look at the London edition of the *Sunday Observer* for 31 August 1985. One day before Dr Robert Ballard actually discovered the wreck, the newspaper ran an article by Alan Road proclaiming that the ship had been found. Mr Road, acting on information received from a Mr John Pierce, had contacted the Admiralty, which had confirmed the discovery before the article had been written. Dr Ballard later said that he had no explanation for the Royal Navy's knowledge that the ship had been found a day before it actually had been, unless the Royal Navy was using psychics. Once more the Royal Navy was not telling the whole truth, or even telling outright lies, something it had a habit of doing whenever the subject concerned events surrounding the loss of the *Titanic*.

There was no need whatsoever for the Royal Navy to employ supernatural means to be relatively sure of when and where Dr Ballard would find the *Titanic*. It was watching every move he made and already knew the position of the wreck, as did Dr Ballard in all probability. The American and British navies had been collaborating with one another in policing the Atlantic Ocean ever since the Great War. Since the end of the Second World War and the beginning of the Cold War that collaboration had been fairly close. There can be little doubt that the information gained during the HMS *Hecate* expedition in the search for the *Titanic* was passed to the US Navy. The wreck of a large vessel, especially one in deep water, was extremely useful to nuclear navies such as those of America, Britain and Russia because it provided an ideal hiding place for a submarine. The mass of metal that made up the wreck threw off detection apparatus, making it practically impossible to tell the wreck from a submarine or a submarine from the ocean floor.

Dr Ballard was, and may still be, a US Navy reserve officer who would have been made aware of the findings from the 1977 and 1978/79 expeditions. His interest in the *Titanic* was well known within informed circles at the time, and in October 1977 he had persuaded the Wood's Hole Oceanographic Institute, part of the United States Navy, to put up some funding for an expedition to find the ship. The expedition failed through lack of adequate funding and because the equipment available to the US Navy was simply not up to the task.

One other party seems to have been made privy to the information gathered in the 1977/78/79 expeditions, 'Cadillac' Jack Grimm. Jack Grimm was a multi-millionaire Texas oilman who happened to collect Cadillac motor cars, hence the nickname, and he was also something of an eccentric. Over the years he backed a number of unusual projects such as looking for the Loch Ness monster, searching for Noah's Ark in Turkey, searching for a hole at the North Pole and seeking the Abominable Snowman. In his own way Grimm wanted to leave his mark on the world, to be remembered in the history books. Like all extremely wealthy men he was also interested in making more money. In the summer of 1980 he mounted his first expedition to find the wreck of the *Titanic*. Despite being given rather dubious advice as to what equipment he would require for the search by the experts he employed, Grimm still managed to survey about 500 square miles of the ocean floor in the same area as that visited by the Royal Navy in 1953 and 1978/79. Fourteen possible targets were identified by sonar, several of which could have been the wreck. Unfortunately, faulty equipment and foul weather forced him to abandon the expedition before any definitive identifications could be made.

On 28 June 1981 Grimm's second expedition left Wood's Hole, that same US Government establishment, for another stab at finding the liner. Thirteen of the previously discovered targets were examined, none of which could be positively identified as *Titanic*, although Jack Grimm believed he had found the wreck and publicly said so. Newspapers all over the world carried the story that the most famous liner in the world had been found. Unhappily for Grimm, the pictures taken of the wreck were of too poor a quality to confirm his claim. Since at least one of Grimm's sonar targets was within 200 yards of where the ship lies, it is only fair to accept that the Texas oilman did find the ship, but as he couldn't prove it he would have to try again.

In 1983 he returned to the site of the sinking but could accomplish nothing because the weather was too bad and the expedition had to be abandoned. Despite being the first to publicly announce the discovery of the wreck of the *Titanic*, Jack Grimm sadly failed to win his place in the history books.

So what is it about the wreck of the *Titanic* that has repeatedly caused the most powerful governments in the western world to expend vast sums of money on trying to reach it? What do they believe the sunken ship contains that is worth so much effort? Can it be as simple as £8,000,000-worth of gold and other treasure, now probably worth more than a billion pounds? It is a good reason, but is it good enough? After all, everything that went to the bottom of the North Atlantic with the ship belongs to somebody, and he or she might well appreciate its return.

There is evidence to suggest that at least one other item might have been meant to go down with the ship - an item that perhaps the then leaders of the western world would prefer remained lost, and which they certainly would not want to fall into the hands of any private individual who might make it public. Is it possible that something was placed aboard *Titanic* in 1912 with the intention that it spend eternity on the bottom of the sea? At the time, before the Great War, the mere idea that something could ever be recovered from 2½ miles beneath the Atlantic Ocean would have seemed preposterous. If we carry this line of questioning a step further, we must ask whether there might be something aboard the ship that is missing. Once the ship had gone, who would ever know?

If either of the last two questions is valid, then the sinking of the *Titanic* was not an accident at all.

Chapter 2

Enter John Pierpont Morgan

By 1901 many shipping lines were struggling to make ends meet. Waiting in the wings for just this situation was the American financier, banker and captain of industry John Pierpont Morgan. Morgan already owned most of America's steel industry and all of the railway rolling stock on that country's eastern seaboard. It seemed a logical step to both control a major outlet for his steel production and to extend the routes available to fare-paying travellers at the same time. Isambard Kingdom Brunel had done much the same thing in Britain half a century earlier when his Great Western Railway Company had built the first Atlantic passenger steamship. It should have been obvious that Morgan would do something along the same lines, but the European ship-owners were caught napping. J. P. Morgan began by buying up the American Line, then the Red Star, Dominion, Atlantic Transport and Leyland lines, and forming the combine International Mercantile Marine. The ships of the IMM lines continued to sail under their own house and national flags because under American law only ships actually built in America could fly the 'Stars and Stripes'. Anyway, seamen's wages aboard ships sailing under the US flag were considerably higher than those of the vessels of other nations. Having swallowed up the small fry, Morgan turned next to the major Atlantic passenger lines, Cunard, White Star, Hamburg Amerika and North German Lloyd. The two German lines managed to fight off Morgan's takeover bids by coming to an agreement with him to fix fare prices, share routes and profits, and to cooperate in a number of minor ventures. Cunard also avoided being swallowed up, but only with British Government help. The British at the time owned the largest mercantile fleet in the world, as well as the largest and most powerful navy. They were afraid that if Cunard fell into the American's hands, they would lose control of the North Atlantic shipping routes and perhaps even the ability to transport goods and persons to and from the outposts of the empire.

The British Empire, the largest the world has ever seen and upon which the sun never set, stretched all around the globe, so Britain had long known the value of sea power. Until Tudor times the navies of the world had consisted of merchant ships, pressed into service as and when required. This haphazard policy had proven inadequate for the British and they had begun to build ever larger and more powerful dedicated warships. As ever, the problem with any dedicated fighting force is that it costs a fortune to maintain and only actually earns its keep in time of war. In order to obtain value for money from their armed forces the British fought an almost continuous series of colonial wars right up until the end of the 19th century, steadily expanding their empire. Colonising armies could be kept relatively small, and armies of occupation, by treating subjugated people well, could soon win over a civil population so that the majority were truly proud to be a part of the British Empire.

As a continuation of this policy the British Government's offer to Cunard was that if the company would build a series of new super-liners in such a way that they could in the event of war be easily and quickly converted into armed merchant cruisers, the government would subsidise a large part of the cost of building and running them. As an added bonus, the government would throw in a contract to transport the mail from Britain to America, which would guarantee an income of £150,000 a year for Cunard. These not inconsiderable benefits for the Cunard Line would only be made available if the management guaranteed that the line would remain British for at least the next 20 years. Not surprisingly, the people at Cunard agreed to the government's terms. The new ships, which would not come into service for another five years, were the *Lusitania* and *Mauretania*, and they would shortly be followed by a third sister, *Aquitania*. Even as they were being built, the new Cunard super-liners, and the rest of the Cunard fleet, were probably assessed as insufficient should there be a major war, which seemed more than a faint possibility.

The rapid deployment of ever larger colonial armies had its own problems. Although J. P. Morgan was probably regarded by both the British and American governments as uncontrollable, they would have been well aware that he did have the wherewithal to produce troopships large enough for any foreseeable contingency. If he could be persuaded to build those ships, and if the British Government could obtain some sort of agreement that the ships would be made available should the need arise, then perhaps he should be encouraged to take control of the other major British transatlantic liner fleet. The problem in dealing with anyone as powerful as J. P. Morgan lay in the fact that all of the major powers were aware that his money and influence could prove decisive in a European conflict. Should either Britain or America try to control him by threat or force, there was nothing to stop him lending his financial assistance (something with which he was familiar) to another rapidly growing military and maritime power - Germany. How then could the financial ogre that Morgan might easily become be kept in line? The short answer, of course, was that he couldn't. While the governments of Britain and America fondly believed that they were persuading the financier to do what they wanted by letting him have his way with White Star, he was, in fact, only doing what he had planned all along. Consequently, on the understanding that the ships of the White Star fleet would be made available to them in the event of a European war, the British Government did not support the White Star Line in its attempt to fight off the American financier's takeover bid.

It had always been a policy of Morgan to offer more for a company than it appeared to be worth when he moved to take it over. He offered White Star's shareholders ten times as much as the line earned in 1900, which had been an exceptionally good year because the British Government had been obliged to charter so many ships in order to transport troops to South Africa to fight the Boer War.

The war, which had officially broken out in 1899 and had been engineered by the British Government with the able assistance of Cecil Rhodes and his lieutenant Dr Jameson, had undoubtedly been a mistake. A few thousand Dutch farmers had defied the might of the British Empire for three long years, and had embarrassed more than a little the supposedly invincible British Army. The British Government of the time, as always greedy to obtain anything and everything belonging to anyone less powerful than itself, had begun the war in order to gain control of the South African gold and diamond resources, but it had not allowed for the immense size of the country, or the resolve of the peoples it was about to subjugate. The Dutch settlers, the Boers, adopting the guerrilla tactics of 'hit and run', proved a tougher nut to crack than anticipated. Not until the British had assembled an army of more than two million men were the Boers forced to surrender. However, the British had learned a valuable lesson from the encounter, something that they should have learned from the Crimean War 45 years earlier - that it is vital in times of distant conflict to be able to transport large bodies of troops to wherever they were required, en masse. In that lesson lay at least part of the motivation behind the *Titanic* disaster.

Colonial wars were one thing. A major European or world war was something else again. Towards the end of the 1800s the technology of warfare had begun to advance apace. Instead of the single-shot rifle the British were equipped with bolt-action repeating weapons and the machine gun had made its appearance on the battlefield. Heavy and light artillery, previously only present in relatively small numbers because of transportation difficulties, now played a dominant role in large set-piece battles. Most important of all was the coming of the railways, which allowed large armies with their supplies and equipment to be transported overland very quickly. Armies in continental Europe that had previously taken weeks or months to prepare for a battle could now take the field in a matter of days. Another consequence of this new ease of overland transport was that much larger armies could readily be gathered together. From the latter part of the 1800s onwards wars would not be fought by armies numbering in the thousands but in the millions.

The problem for the British, the largest imperial power of them all, was that Britain was a small group of islands and therefore her armies, for whatever conflict, could not be transported to any foreign field by rail. They had to be moved by ship. To make matters worse, the British Empire, which her army had to police and defend, stretched right around the globe and was vulnerable to attack from any neighbouring country at short notice.

Winston Churchill, who served in the Boer War as a humble lieutenant but was to go on to become Britain's most prominent politician, had himself seen at first hand how massive was the requirement for transporting troops to achieve victory. It was a lesson he did not forget.

To return to J. P. Morgan's takeover of the White Star Line, 75% of the shareholders were for accepting his offer of £10 million, as it would give them a substantial profit on their original investments. Even William James Pirrie, the managing director of the Belfast shipbuilders Harland & Wolff and J. Bruce Ismay's friend, was for selling out, if only because he confidently expected all of the lines making up IMM to come to him for any new vessels. Morgan clinched the deal when he offered to keep Ismay on as managing director, and chairman, of the White Star Line.

By May 1902 agreement had been reached, and on the 17th the last Annual General Meeting of the Oceanic Steam Navigation Company, the White Star Line's parent company, took place. Five days later the agreement between John Pierpont Morgan and the White Star Line was signed. All the shareholders had been paid by 1 December 1902 and the White Star Line belonged to J. P. Morgan as part of the IMM group.

By the time the takeover was agreed only two of the original partners in the Oceanic Steam Navigation Company were to remain with IMM and White Star, Joseph Bruce Ismay and Harold Sanderson. Ismay and

Sanderson had become friends in 1886, and in 1895 Ismay had invited Sanderson to join Ismay, Imrie & Company; he was made a partner in 1900.

Initially Morgan wanted Albert Ballin of the Hamburg Amerika Line to run IMM, but changed his mind when his plans to take over the two leading German lines fell through. Instead, although Ismay was still chairman and managing director of the White Star Line, Morgan decided that he was the man to take over as president of IMM as well. Initially Ismay refused, but the financial inducement of £20,000 a year was enough to make him change his mind, and on 21 February he wrote to Charles Steele, Morgan's deputy, accepting the position as president of IMM.

From the moment the memo was signed, J. Bruce Ismay was in total charge of everything that happened within IMM, except the spending of Morgan's money. Not only did he control everything, but he would also have been kept informed, one way or another, of everything that was going on within the company, and there was a lot going on.

On the other side of the Atlantic the American Government, which had some years earlier made an agreement with the rulers of China not to prohibit Chinese immigration, broke that agreement. In 1902 it made permanent the exclusion of Chinese immigrants from the United States, which had already been provisionally in effect for 20 years. Unfortunately, although it had made the entry of Chinese labour illegal, the Government did not manage to stop the immigrants themselves. The White Star Line had always played its part in transporting these Chinese labourers to America and continued to do so even after the practice had become illegal. It should perhaps be remembered that the American railroad system was constructed with a largely Chinese labour force and that it was principally Chinese workers who toiled in Mr Morgan's steel mills. He would not therefore have seen this flouting of the law as anything detrimental in the shipping line.

J. P. Morgan never explained his decisions or sought publicity. A true autocrat, he gave orders and expected them to be obeyed. Only rarely would he express an opinion, and he seems to have taken the advice that appeared on a small white enamel plaque on the mantelpiece of his private study: 'Pense moult, parle peu, écris rien' ('Think a lot, say little, write nothing') - advice that suited every major successful criminal throughout history as well as it suited J. P. Morgan.

If British greed had been the cause of the Boer War and would play its part in the loss of the *Titanic*, then Belgian and American greed would be there as well.

Not long after Morgan gained control of the White Star Line, another little plum fell into his lap. The Belgian King, Leopold, had decided that the time was ripe for the exploitation of the Belgian Congo and that, as the Americans didn't appear to want to establish an African empire of their own, he should call on their assistance. He first approached Henry Cabot Lodge, who suggested that he talk to Nelson Aldridge. Aldridge, the chairman of the American Senate Finance Committee, was another multi-millionaire and a card-playing partner of J. P. Morgan.

Leopold impressed Aldridge and a few other influential Americans by promising them a share in the loot from the colony. One of those impressed by the financial prospects was Thomas Fortune Ryan, another close associate of J. P. Morgan. Leopold's plan was simple. He intended to open up a strip of territory right across the Congo and allow American businessmen to help themselves to whatever they wanted, in return for a percentage of the take. Once the Americans were established he believed that he would have nothing to fear from the major colonial powers like Britain and France. The King, in an effort to ingratiate himself with Morgan, gave more than 3,000 Congo artefacts to the American Museum of Natural History, knowing that Morgan was on its board. He need not have bothered as Morgan, through his associate Ryan, was already interested in the prospect of acquiring access to the Congo's natural resources of copper, cobalt, diamonds, gold, tin, manganese and zinc. As a major steel producer, the American needed cobalt for the production of high-grade steels for tools and, hopefully in the near future, armour plate. Copper, tin and manganese were useful when it came to making tough bronze for such items as the propellers for his ships, and he was always interested in laying his hands on gold and diamonds. King Leopold's timing could hardly have been better.

Leopold's enthusiasm to involve J. P. Morgan in his schemes is understandable when one realises just how influential the banker was. In the 19th century the American economy went through a crisis about every 10 or 20 years - 1819, 1837, 1857, 1873, 1884 and 1893. After the crisis of 1893 J. P. Morgan spent most of the rest of the decade reorganising (Morganising) bankrupt railroads and industrial companies. Reorganising under the Morgan system usually meant that the financier ended up with a controlling interest in a company. By this time J. P. Morgan was so rich and powerful that when the American Government almost ran out of gold in 1895 he raised $65 million worth of the precious metal and bailed them out. In saving the US from bankruptcy Morgan had effectively bought the government of that country.

European bankers and statesmen were more than happy with Morgan's performance as it kept America from reneging on its debts. The United

States economy didn't become self-supporting until 1914. Had the country been unable to pay its debts, or had gone off the international gold standard, foreign financiers would have withdrawn their money, crippling the economy and preventing any further expansion. As it was, during the earlier part of the 1890s European investors had anticipated the coming crisis, sold off $400 million worth of American assets and sent the gold home. This would have inevitably slowed the growth of the American economy, but it didn't stop it. By the time Leopold sought Morgan's involvement in what has become known as 'The Rape of the Congo', the banker's financial muscle and political influence was sufficient on its own to allow him to complete his plans.

Even though Morgan had spent the better part of a decade reorganising the American financial system at the end of the 19th and into the early 20th centuries, it still left a lot to be desired. In 1907 another crisis struck and the banker was forced to act again. Once more his intervention saved the US economy from total collapse. At that point he had reinforced the fact that he owned the government, or at the very least that it could not manage to regulate the financial establishment without his help. Although such a concentration of power went against the grain of the American masses, it would take six years and a change of government and president, and the decline of J. P. Morgan's health, before his grip loosened. The financier's power to control the actions of the American Government, to a greater or lesser extent, meant that he could be sure that any inquiry into his part in what was about to happen on the North Atlantic would not ask too many pertinent questions.

·

Chapter 3

A dual role

By the latter part of 1907 it seems that J. P. Morgan, possibly with an eye to the profitability of long-distance large-scale troop transport in war, which he had learned all about when he moved to take over the White Star Line, decided to have a finger in both the peace and war enterprises that were then gaining momentum. Big ships were clearly going to be a good investment for him, especially as they are built of steel for which he needed new outlets after the American railroad building boom came to an end. After all, he was among the world's largest steel producers, and ship owners.

William Pirrie, at Harland & Wolff, had already begun modernisation of the Belfast yard to enable the construction of the world's largest ships, which would not have happened without the agreement of Morgan, at least in principle, that those ships should actually be built. Major alterations to British docks and shipyards at that time also required the agreement of parliament, which is another indication that the British Government recognised the coming need for some exceptionally large vessels. J. P. Morgan and the management of the White Star Line would also have been aware of the British Government's future need for large transports when the inevitable European war broke out, and would have wanted to be the people to supply them, at a price. If some sort of British Government subsidy could be agreed, White Star would be more than happy to have the world's largest liners built for use by themselves on the profitable North Atlantic route in peacetime, and for the Government to utilise in time of war. This would be an ideal arrangement for Morgan and White Star, as the already existing agreement with the British Government meant that the line's vessels were at the latter's disposal anyway, if the worst came to the worst, so any new agreement would merely reinforce the existing one.

At the same time the British Prime Minister, David Lloyd George, and his familiar, Winston Churchill, must have seen an opportunity of acquiring some large troop transports or hospital ships at a reduced rate. However, from a military viewpoint there was an obvious snag: how well would vessels as large as those envisaged for the White Star Line withstand damage inflicted by enemy action? Could the 5,000 or so troops they were comfortably capable of carrying be evacuated in an emergency? Large warships were unlikely to pose any great threat to the new liners because of their high speed. The guns of smaller vessels were limited in size and would only be able to inflict minimal damage before the liner's own armaments could be brought into play. With the submarine an untried weapon, mistrusted by the Admiralty, the only way a small warship could be expected to stop a huge liner was by ramming it. Any new vessel intended to carry a significant part of the British Army at any one time would have to be tested so that the planners could be reasonably sure it could survive such an encounter. If that same test could also be used to demonstrate to J. P. Morgan and others that they were not necessarily cock of the walk, so much the better. However, such a test was still a little way away into the future, and other factors would come to have a bearing.

In 1898 Guglielmo Marconi, long accepted as the inventor of wireless even though he wasn't, fitted the *St Paul*, a 554-foot-long American Line luxury liner, with a temporary wireless installation in order to show potential financial backers that the system was viable. (The first wireless patent had been granted by the American Government to one Mahlon Loomis more than 20 years before Marconi claimed wireless as his own invention.) The advantages of wireless at sea are all too obvious to us now, but at the end of the 19th century ship owners were not easily convinced that it was worth the expense. The Germans, however, were so impressed that they fitted the *Kaiser Wilhelm der Grosse* with Marconi equipment in 1900. This was the first permanent Marconi wireless installation afloat.

With his eye to the maritime application of 'his' invention, Marconi took a house on the Hyde side of Southampton Water. By this time many major shipping lines, particularly those sailing on the Atlantic routes, were operating out of the Hampshire port and had offices there.

The potential spread, on a worldwide scale, of the new invention may not have had the mass investment attraction that the Internet and video phone communications have for today's smart money. Nonetheless, there was almost certainly a core like Lloyd George, Sir Rufus Isaacs (the Attorney General) and his brother, and a few other influential characters in the British political hierarchy, who were keen to see the commercial arteries expand, as they stood to make a lot of money by investing in the new technology. On top of that was the possibility for exploitation by the intelligence services of practically all the major powers, a possibility they were not slow to appreciate. Just as with computers today, there was no such thing as security. The only way to protect information was to encrypt it, and code-breakers have always delighted in deciphering the most complicated of riddles. During that first decade of the 20th century there was enough going on to warrant every government having a militant intelligence arm dedicated to the gathering of what was known as wireless intelligence, now referred to as 'SigInt'. Most of them had rather more than one.

The main British example of this new branch of intelligence-gathering operated out of a single room in the Admiralty building, the now famous Room 40. Room 40 eventually grew into what we now know as GCHQ. As a consequence of this preoccupation with gathering wireless intelligence, as well as the convenience of being able to communicate with ships at sea, and for those ships to be easily able to communicate with one another, warships of all the major powers were soon equipped with the most powerful up-to-date versions of the new invention. While at sea the warships of the Royal Navy kept a constant watch on all wireless traffic coming from any source within range, in the hope of overhearing something useful.

Wireless was by no means the only enormous technical development to manifest itself during those early years of the 20th century. Not least among the remainder was the evolution of liquid fuel to replace coal as the main source of energy aboard British warships. Winston Churchill and his mentor, Jackie Fisher, were behind the Royal Navy's policy of building new super-dreadnoughts fuelled by oil instead of coal, despite the fact that Britain had any amount of coal but no oil. To ensure an adequate supply of the precious fluid Churchill turned his attention to the massive oilfields of Persia/Iraq, the same oilfields that are being fought over today. At the time Churchill steered the British Government into a move to take over control of the oil in Iraq even though he actually had no direct influence over British naval policy. However, he did have plans to gain control of it before many years had passed. He knew that the British Empire's most potent weapon was still the all-powerful Royal Navy. Admiral Fisher had already explained to the politician how, if ships could be refuelled at sea or at least very quickly in harbour, then because they could be at sea for a greater percentage of their time the effective size of the fleet would automatically increase.

April 1908 was not a particularly good month for the Royal Navy. The cruiser HMS *Tiger* was rammed while on manoeuvres south of St Catherine's Point on the Isle of Wight during the first week of the month. Then, about three weeks later, on the 25th, HMS *Gladiator*, another cruiser, was rammed by the American liner *St Paul* (which we have already come across) during a snow squall off Great Yarmouth. The *Gladiator* had to be beached to prevent her from sinking. Twenty-seven lives were lost. The Trinity House Pilot aboard the *St Paul* at the time of the collision was George Bowyer, who would also be acting as pilot aboard *Olympic* when she was rammed by HMS *Hawke* in September 1911, and who would be on the bridge of the *Titanic* when she departed Southampton at the start of her ill-starred maiden voyage on 10 April 1912, when she almost collided with the American liner *New York*.

Meanwhile the construction of White Star's and the British Government's new giant ships was moving steadily forward. As early as October 1908 models of the new ships were under construction in the Model Office in the Belfast shipyard of Harland & Wolff. There were two half models (ie, the hull was split in half from bow to stern, so that only one side of the ship was visible), which were respectively a quarter-inch-to-the-foot working model and an eight-inch-to-the-foot model. It was intended that the ships would be identical, so a single *Olympic/Titanic* model would suffice. (For the chequered careers of these shipbuilders' models see Appendix 1.)

The first of the White Star Line's new super-liners, *Olympic*, went down the slipway and into the water on 20 October 1910. At almost 900 feet long, the huge ship was the largest man-made moving object on earth. (For a detailed description of the construction and layout of the '*Olympic*' class liners see the author's earlier works *The Riddle of the Titanic* and *Titanic - The Ship That Never Sank*). Even at this early stage it would have been clear to any observer, particularly those on the other side of the English Channel, that these new 'Olympics' were not designed to operate solely as passenger liners to challenge Cunard. Because of their watertight bulkhead arrangement, which did not include any longitudinal subdivision of the hull, they were doubtless designed as troopships right from the outset. They were constructed in such a way that they would remain on a relatively even keel no matter how badly they were damaged, allowing boats to be lowered from both sides of the boat deck. Another powerful indicator of these ships' potential purpose lay in the lifeboat arrangement. As passenger liners they would be equipped with just 16 real lifeboats and four collapsible ones, but the specially built lifeboat davits were intended to handle at least 64 boats, and were capable of dealing with a great number more. (The original design drawings show this class of ship with 64 real wooden lifeboats.) These ships were designed to be loaded and unloaded quickly, possibly without benefit of a proper dock or quayside; survivability took a secondary place. The ability to load and unload a passenger ship quickly is not a prime consideration for designers of large passenger liners. However, for a troopship that might be embarking or disembarking large numbers of military personnel in hostile water, perhaps within sight of an enemy, speed would be of the essence.

Even when operating as passenger vessels the new ships would be much too big to enter some of their normal ports of call, like Queenstown in Ireland and Cherbourg in France. In those circumstances fare-paying passengers would join or leave the ship in much smaller purpose-built vessels known as tenders. Troops would not always be afforded the luxury of a proper port or tender and would have to leave the ships by their own boats. This loading and unloading of men and materials, including horses, was something that was regularly practised by captains and crews of ships likely to be requisitioned by the military. Some captains, for example Captain Stanley Lord of the Leyland Line's passenger cargo ship *Californian*, proved to be very much more adept at the operation than others. Lord was so good at it that if anyone wanted to evacuate a large vessel on the high seas he was an obvious choice either to command that vessel or to be on hand to receive its people. By coincidence, the Leyland Line was one of those that belonged to Morgan's IMM company.

Almost as if the owners, Marconi and the British Government didn't care who knew about the possible military future role of the 'Olympic' class ships, they took no particular pains to hide it. Initially both *Olympic* and *Titanic* were allocated standard civilian wireless call signs; *Olympic* was allocated MKC and *Titanic* MUC. Then the call sign of the second vessel was altered to MGY, but the alteration was not immediately made public. In those early days of wireless communication there was no shortage of available call signs or any obvious need to reissue ones that had been used before. Nevertheless, MGY had been previously allocated to an American vessel, the troopship *Yale*.

Chapter 4

1911: Agadir and Egypt

As the first decade of the 20th century drew to a close the political situation in Europe continued to deteriorate, as to some extent it did throughout the world. The British, who considered themselves to be fairly secure in their island fortress, looked on as Germany and France bickered with one another. They had fought each other 40 years earlier, a war that Germany had won easily, making the British take notice of this rising power. At the end of that relatively minor conflict France had been forced to cede the territories of Alsace and Lorraine to Germany, something that had rankled ever since. Not that there was a whole lot that France could do about the situation as, since the Franco-German war of 1871, Germany had grown into the most powerful military force in Europe, with the possible exception of Britain, which had the resources of her empire to call upon should the need arise. Unfortunately for France there was no guarantee that Britain would come to her aid should the all-powerful German Army invade; after all, Britain and France were hereditary enemies who had been at each other's throats for the better part of a thousand years. Anyway, at the time Britain had her own problems, most notably Ireland, to do more than keep an eye on the squabbling between her neighbours.

Ireland, then as now, was a divided country, under British rule. The majority of the Irish population wanted independence and Home Rule, but there was a large faction very much in favour of remaining under the control and protection of Britain. Winston Churchill, at the time a member of the Liberal Party, had always been against Home Rule for Ireland, as had his father. However, following the election of January 1910, when the Liberals were returned with just two more seats than the Tories, and needed the support of the 82 Irish and 41 Labour seats to remain in power, he conveniently changed his mind. He told the Irish Nationalist leaders that it was the ambition of his life to bring in a Home Rule Bill for Ireland. It should have been apparent to all and sundry then that Churchill only had two major objectives, political power and personal renown.

Following his miraculous conversion to the Irish Home Rule cause, Churchill was invited to speak in Belfast. He would address the people of

Ulster at Belfast's Celtic football ground. The police warned him that he was not popular with the general population, that revolvers were being taken out of pawn, and that thousands of bolts and rivets had been stolen from railway yards. To insure the politician's safety 10,000 troops were massed in Belfast. The speech went off without incident, at least partly because of the pouring rain, which helped dampen the crowd's ardour and kept many of them away. Immediately after the meeting Churchill was quickly driven to the station, where a special train carried him to Larne before the Ulster Unionists learned that he had fled.

The Unionists in the British Government were so alienated by the Irish 'Home Rule Bill' (the military hierarchy later threatened to resign) that many who prided themselves on their patriotism began to plot against the elected body. There had long been organised gun-running into Ireland for the benefit of both the Unionists and the Irish Liberation Army, but the scale of this increased dramatically. Not least among those engaged in supplying arms to the Irish factions were the Americans, one of whom was a close associate of J. P. Morgan, Thomas Fortune Ryan. Ryan was also heavily involved in stripping the Belgian Congo of whatever raw materials and minerals were available, much of it destined for Morgan's steel companies. There can be no doubt that the British authorities were aware of what was going on but, in view of the likelihood of a European war, a direct confrontation with Morgan or his associates was to be avoided if at all possible.

To make bad matters worse, the situation in Britain, as far as labour relations was concerned, was also in a parlous state. On 20 June 1911 (two days before the Coronation of King George V), seamen at Southampton went on strike. They were quickly followed by seamen and dock workers at Liverpool, Cardiff and Hull. On 1 August the London Docks warehouses went up in flames, 20,000 men were on strike, and 20 ocean liners were unable to sail as a result. It looked to Winston Churchill, who, as Home Secretary, was responsible for keeping law and order, like the beginnings of a general strike. There was clearly the danger of a railway strike. In August the crisis came, and there was talk of revolution and civil war in the air. Churchill decided that troops were needed as, he estimated, there were 50 places in the country where violence might erupt at any moment, but he ordered the troops to fire over the rioters' heads.

On 13 August the rioting began in earnest, in Liverpool. The 'Riot Act' was read and troops were used in an effort to restore order. Initially the troops did only fire over the heads of the crowds, but inevitably there were casualties. When two officers and 32 men escorting a Liverpool prison van were attacked, the soldiers fired and one civilian was killed. At Llanelli, in Wales, there were more riots, and two men were killed when troops repelled an attack on a train.

Even King George V took an interest. He didn't like the half-hearted way the troops were being used and thought that the military should be given a free hand to restore order, and the mobs should be made to fear them. Not surprisingly the situation continued to worsen. On 18 August two-thirds of the nation's railway workers went on strike. Churchill saw it as a potential disaster; nothing like it had ever happened before. Already there had been at least six attacks on stations, many signal boxes had been damaged, trains had been stoned, telegraph and signal wires had been cut, and there had been nine attempts to wreck trains. On 19 August Churchill, still in his capacity as Home Secretary, gave the military authorities instructions that amounted to martial law.

'General Officers commanding the various military areas are instructed to use their own discretion as to whether troops are, or are not, to be sent to any particular point. The Army regulation which requires a requisition from a civil authority is suspended.'

In the meanwhile he was deploying 50,000 men as a vast strike-breaking force. Over the next couple of days Churchill issued a series of disastrous bulletins that exasperated the unions. With the benefit of hindsight it appears that he was trying to bring about a confrontation between the unions and the authorities, just as Margaret Thatcher was to try in the 1980s. This characteristic disregard for the wellbeing of others was almost a hallmark of Churchill's early career and was never far below the surface later. Fortunately the Prime Minister, Lloyd George, realising that such a confrontation could 'bring open warfare in the streets', stepped in and used his remarkable powers as a negotiator to settle the rail strike in just two days. It was all over by 20 August. 'I'm very sorry to hear it,' Churchill told him. 'It would have been better to have gone on and given these men a good thrashing.'

In the House of Commons on 22 August there was an outcry against Churchill led by Labour Party leaders Ramsay MacDonald and Keir Hardie: 'The Department which has played the most diabolical part in all the unrest was the Home Office.' Keir Hardie charged Churchill with unlawfully instituting martial law and using armed force to intimidate the workers and support the railway companies.

There was a lot happening in the rest of the world in 1911 to give the

British Government further cause for unease, despite its preoccupation with domestic matters. Not only did the Japanese, still flushed with their successes against the Russians six years before, launch their first dreadnought battleship, but civil war erupted in China, finally putting an end to the feudal system of government there and making the country at once an emergent power to be considered.

There was no possible way that Britain could maintain a standing army of sufficient power to contain the threat posed by all of her possible enemies at any one time. She would perforce be obliged to deal with them piecemeal. Although the Russian armed forces amounted to more than 13 million men, France to more than 4½ million, and Italy 4 million, still the most obvious threat to Britain, in 1911, came from Germany and Austria, which had more than 14½ million men under arms. The only, and obvious, thing for the British to do was prepare for a war in Europe while also establishing the facilities necessary to fight in the Far East or Africa should the need arise, which hopefully it would not.

The Kaiser's speech of 1911 when he proclaimed his country's right to a 'Place in the Sun' not only threatened European domination but hinted at German expansion in South Africa as well. The British, with more overseas possessions to consider than anyone else, took notice. The Germans were well placed to threaten Britain. They had a very strong mercantile fleet with Blue Riband-class transatlantic liners and a navy that, although vastly inferior to that of Britain's, was the second most powerful in the world. With a budding U-boat arm equipped with wireless, the German Navy was in a position to threaten Britain's merchant fleet, a point that some in the Admiralty appreciated even if others didn't consider the submarine a serious weapon of war. Moreover, the Germans had the vital staging posts, at Cameroon, Togoland and Tanganyika, and the infrastructure was in place in South West Africa, a rallying ground for disgruntled Boers, to allow invasion of British South Africa, or so the British believed. In reality Germany's colonial ambitions were more directed towards North Africa, where they would hopefully not come up against the British. Following the Italian's lead, the Germans began to make tentative imperialist manoeuvres in North Africa, most notably at Agadir, bringing Europe to the brink of war three years before it finally happened and setting in motion a train of events that would inexorably lead to the sinking of the *Titanic*.

The major colonial powers had been dividing the world between themselves for years. For example, Britain gave France a free hand in North Africa in exchange for the same treatment in Egypt. France quickly gained control of Algeria, then turned her attention towards Morocco. Germany, which had until then stayed out of the scramble for North Africa, now began to show some interest in the area. When a French expedition was sent to occupy Fez in 1911, the Kaiser responded, on 1 July, by sending a warship, the *Panther*, to Agadir, ostensibly to protect the interests of German merchants there. This example of gunboat diplomacy set alarm bells ringing through the chancelleries of Europe, focusing attention on Germany's growing sea power and ambitions; she did not respond to repeated requests for an explanation from the British Foreign Secretary, Sir Edward Grey.

The question at the time was, as far as the other world powers were concerned, if there was a war between Germany and France, what would Britain's position be? For a while no solid indication came from the Foreign Office. Then, on 21 July, Lloyd George used the annual dinner at the Mansion House, given by the Lord Mayor of London to the bankers in the City, to make Britain's intentions clear in his speech. This was the key passage:

'…if a situation were to be forced upon us in which peace could only be preserved by the surrender of the great and beneficent Britain has won by centuries of heroism and achievement, by allowing Britain to be treated where her interests were vitally affected, as if she were of no account in the Cabinet of Nations … then I say emphatically that peace at that price would be a humiliation intolerable for a great country like ours to endure.'

The warning was clear: if Germany went to war, she would find Britain against her. To drive the point home, a British warship was dispatched to Agadir, to lie practically alongside the *Panther*.

The Kaiser's sabre-rattling at Agadir in 1911 was a serious crisis, which led to a World Power Conference. France managed to keep its hold on Morocco only by handing some of its West African possessions to Germany, such as Cameroon and Togoland. Germany's possession of these areas considerably increased the threat to Britain's South African holdings, which in turn would have caused no little alarm to British leaders like Winston Churchill. Churchill, it should be remembered, had personal experience of Britain's struggle to wrest control of South Africa from the Boers little more than ten years earlier. Worse still, the Agadir incident had convinced Churchill that war with Germany was not only inevitable but imminent.

The incident was a serious enough threat to the peace of Europe that the British Government began to make preparations to meet a possible invasion. In 1911 the normal complement of troops on the Isle of Wight was about 800, but in September of that year War Department contractors on the island were asked whether they would be ready to supply food for about 4,000 troops should they be called upon to do so.

There were rapid, concerted reactions by bankers, as the Agadir crisis snowballed from 1 July 1911, to get gold out of the threatened war zone in Europe and across the Atlantic to the safety of the United States. To allay public fears that war might be imminent, many of these gold shipments were made in secret. Nevertheless, the flow of gold would continue right up until war finally broke out in 1914, and for some time afterwards.

20 September 1911, a critical date in the *Titanic* story, falls well within the time frame of the panic over what was happening in North Africa. J. P. Morgan, together with many others, was more than a little alarmed at the Agadir crisis and began to ship large quantities of antiques and museum pieces back to America where they would be safe. As Morgan owned quite a lot of what was on exhibition at the British Museum and the Victoria & Albert Museum, these began to look a little bare, which did nothing to endear the financier to the museum authorities. Quite naturally much of what J. P. Morgan wanted to move across the Atlantic was carried aboard his own ships, and often the most valuable objects went aboard what he believed was the cream of those vessels, *Olympic*.

As a result of Morgan's defeatist attitude, as the British Government saw it, in removing his treasures, it began to make life difficult for him. Customs officers closely inspected everything he sent aboard ship. As Morgan's organisation was shipping not only his own artefacts but almost certainly large quantities of contraband such as industrial diamonds and cobalt gleaned from the Belgian Congo, this Customs attention was rather more than an inconvenience. It didn't take the financier long to make his displeasure known to the British. The latter, in their turn, realising that war was all but inevitable and that they would need Morgan's financial muscle, began to look for alternative means of curbing the magnate.

The national museum authorities are, of course, just another tentacle of the Government octopus, and the Government was always interested in what Morgan and his colleagues were up to. A Trustee of the British Museum was dispatched to America to meet with Mr Morgan. This is recorded in the Trustees' Minutes (British Museum) Index entry for 14 August 1911, wherein it appears that Sir Charles Hercules Read was given an extra 12 days' leave to visit America. Read left London on 9 August for Liverpool, where he joined a ship. He would not return until 9 September, a full month. Clearly the trip by Sir Charles was of some consequence to Morgan because he set time aside from his demanding schedule to meet the representative of the British Museum and escort him from London to New York. The entry in the Museum Trustees' Minutes reads:

'The Directors having informed the Trustees that Mr Read proposed to pay a visit to America which might be indirectly advantageous to the museum, but that he could not take all the time required out of his ordinary leave, the Trustees granted Mr Read additional leave to the extent of twelve days, if required, during the current year.

Read a report by Mr Read, 9th October, stating that he had taken the additional leave (12 days) granted to him to visit America (during August) and had specially inspected the Metropolitan Museum at New York and the Widener collection. The Trustees approved.

The Director reported that Mr Read had become a resident officer of the British Museum, having succeeded on the 26th December to the house given up on his retirement by Sir George Warner.'

On his return to Britain, Sir Charles reported to the British Museum by letter dated 9 October 1911:

'My dear Kenyon,

As the Trustees were good enough to allow me extra leave for a fortnight, in consequence of my proposed visit to America in August last, it seems to me fitting that I should report that I was able to avail myself of the privilege thus granted.

I left London with Mr Pierpont Morgan on 9th Aug. and arrived at Liverpool on my return on 9th Sept., an absence of exactly 28 working days.

Although, as was to be expected, most people were in the country or in Europe, I was able to see the recent acquisitions of the Metropolitan Museum, an institution now conducted on admirable lines, and by no means deserving of the damaging judgement passed upon it recently by Lord Carson.

The newly installed Egyptian department is most interesting, and it is astonishing to see monuments of such size and weight transported to New York with such apparent facility. This department of the Museum is admirably manned and is making very rapid progress.

At Philadelphia I passed an interesting and useful morning in Mr Widener's house, which is full of fine works of art of other kinds besides pictures. I also saw Mr Gordon of Pennsylvania University and had from him a detailed account of a recent robbery in the Museum there, and another in the Field Colombian Museum in Chicago.

In New York I was fortunately able to be of some use to Mr Morgan in his collection, an attention he greatly appreciates.

Yours very truly, C. H. Read.'

Read's trip to America at this time, and particularly his friendly relationship with J. P. Morgan, is curious to say the least. The major British museums were being put to considerable inconvenience by Morgan's hurried shipping of his artefacts to America, the British Museum itself in particular. There has to be a reason, and it is not difficult to find.

The Tutankhamun Deception by Gerald O'Farrell demonstrates that Howard Carter and Lord Carnarvon had been quietly removing treasures from Tutankhamun's tomb for more than a decade before its official opening in November 1922. One of the chief beneficiaries of this looting was Morgan's Metropolitan Museum in New York.

The millionaire Theodore Davis, who had earlier employed Howard Carter on his concession ground in the Valley of the Kings, had, in 1909, given artefacts to Herbert Winlock (later to become director of the Metropolitan Museum) to ship to New York. Winlock did not examine these closely until 1921 when he was amazed to find some of them bore the seal of Tutankhamun and the royal necropolis seal, proof that they had been interred in the Valley of the Kings. It would appear that not all of the artefacts filched from the tomb were shipped, sight unseen, to the Metropolitan Museum. Some at least were held back by the excavator and his patron, which, after all, seems only reasonable as they had done all of the spade work and incurred all of the expense in finding the tomb in the first place. Among the items squirreled away was a papyrus scroll. Not of any great value in itself, what the scroll contained was political dynamite.

In essence the ancient papyrus recounted the second book of the Bible, Exodus, but with a difference. The scroll told, as a matter of record, that the Jews were not God's chosen people but a mongrel race descended from Egyptians and slaves. The scroll tells how a group of disaffected Egyptians left Egypt to preserve the religion founded by the heretic pharaoh Akhenaten, with his blessing and under the guidance of his trusted advisor Moses. In short, the old Egyptian document had/has the potential to destroy the foundations of the Christian and Jewish religions.

Lord Carnarvon had a contact at the British Museum in the person of Assistant Keeper Wallace Budge. Through Budge the scroll was offered for sale to the museum, but at a price that was outside their budget. Had they gone to the government it is likely that the funds could have been found, the scroll purchased and suppressed, and the threat removed. Unfortunately, they didn't, and it wasn't. Instead Charles Hercules Read talked to J. P. Morgan about the inflammatory document.

By 1911 the existence of the scroll was known to any number of serious collectors and governments, who recognised its importance, although few had actually seen it. The British in particular, who had only recently become aware of the provocative nature of the historical document, had a vested interest in ensuring that it remained hidden for the foreseeable future. When Howard Carter tried to bring a court action against the Egyptian Public Works department for political reasons, it was the British Government, with the assistance of the Rothschilds, who headed him off, for fear of the scroll's message becoming public.

The British Government, with its not wholly secure hold on power in this part of its empire, had to tread carefully. Anything that came to light that could be exploited to destroy the stability of the Middle East, which rested on the cornerstones of respective religions, could have disastrous effects on the vital oil for Britain's new battleships. And stability has never been a noticeable quality where the Middle East is concerned. The contents of the scroll could all too easily destroy that shaky stability and plunge the whole of the Middle East into war.

It is hardly surprising, then, that J. P. Morgan managed to find the time to spend with Charles Hercules Read. Morgan's focus of interest in antiquity and religion embraced how the Christians evolved from Judaic law and what the Jews inherited from the earlier civilisations of Egypt and Sumeria. He personally travelled great distances year after year, in discomfort, seeking anything related to the connection between the Christian and Judaic philosophies. That he put up with this hardship and privation time and again indicates that his interest was almost obsessive. As it happened the scroll would not only support Morgan's interest in the Christian/Jewish connection but would also serve as a club to keep his Jewish financial rivals in order. To the British it was a threat to their Middle Eastern oil supplies, as war in that area would have been inevitable if the contents of the scroll leaked out. It wasn't until early in 1912 that Morgan paid £80,000 for the Coptic manuscript, which had first been offered to the British Museum.

Chapter 5

Preparations for war at sea

Despite Lloyd George having made Britain's position over Agadir clear, the political situation continued to decline throughout August 1911. This was not because the differences between the major European powers were irreconcilable but simply because nobody knew what to do about it. Then on 23 August Prime Minister Asquith convened a secret meeting of the Committee of Imperial Defence to discuss what action Britain should take if France was attacked. The meeting, which lasted from 11.30am to 9.00pm, was an eye-opener. Sir Henry Wilson opened the proceedings by outlining the Army's role in the event of a European war. Standing by an enormous map, he revealed the British Army's plan for helping France. Following the Clausewitz theory of supporting the largest allied force engaged against a common enemy, a British Expeditionary Force would be prepared. Six infantry divisions and a cavalry division, about 160,000 men in all, would be sent across the Channel as soon as war was declared. This force, or 'contemptible little army' as Kaiser Wilhelm was to describe it, would eventually prove its worth when war finally came. The Army, it seemed, was ready. Now what about the Navy, which would have to carry these troops to France?

Admiral Sir Arthur Wilson, the First Sea Lord, considered by some to be the greatest figure the Royal Navy had produced since Nelson, was the next to spell out what he saw as his service's role. Sir Arthur, who was almost 70 years old, had won the VC fighting on land against the Dervishes. He was popular with the men of the Royal Navy and was regarded as a sturdy old sea dog, known throughout the fleet as 'Tug' Wilson. What this distinguished sailor had to say caused dismay in the Cabinet. The Navy was not ready for war with Germany and could not spare a single man, a single officer, a single ship to assist the Army. Every vessel the Admiralty could muster, in home waters, would be required to keep the enemy confined within the North Sea.

General Sir William Nicholson, Chief of the Imperial General Staff (CIGS), was stunned. He said that he had always presumed that the Army could count on the ungrudging assistance of the Transport Department of the Admiralty. He had presumed wrongly, Sir Arthur Wilson replied, uncompromisingly. The Navy could not furnish any ships. Reginald McKenna, who was still the First Lord of the Admiralty but was soon to be replaced (although he didn't know it at the time), supported his First Sea Lord. No assistance could be given during the first week of war. The Navy would be fully occupied in transporting its own personnel and mobilising itself. McKenna added that the Admiralty had already actually recorded in a Committee of Imperial Defence paper its inability to guarantee the transport of troops on the outbreak of war.

General Sir Henry Wilson emphasised that the dates fixed for embarkation of a British Expeditionary Force (BEF) were from the second day of mobilisation to the 12th day. It was expected that the Germans would deploy 84 divisions against 66 French divisions, so the French would need assistance from the outset.

Asquith agreed that the simultaneous mobilisation of the French and British armies, and their immediate concentration in the theatre of war, was absolutely essential. Winston Churchill, still then Home Secretary but manoeuvring his way towards the First Lord of the Admiralty's job, agreed with the Army view that the BEF would be needed by the French within days of war breaking out. He expressed his opinion that the Germans would attack through Belgium and that they should be halted there. In the event, he was absolutely right.

Admiral Sir Arthur Wilson explained that he thought the expeditionary force was a poor idea anyway. In his opinion the smallness of its numbers would be a considerable disadvantage, as would the difference in language and training between the French and British forces. Over and above that, the differences in arms, ammunition and equipment would cause almost insurmountable logistical problems. In his way the old admiral was also right, but he had seriously underestimated the fighting ability of the relatively small but highly trained and efficient British Army.

Churchill, with a certain amount of justification, was worried about what might happen to an expeditionary force if the French Army retreated. General Sir Henry Wilson's opinion was that, as long as the British had command of the sea, the British Army would be able to operate from whatever base it chose. In other words there should be no chance of the Army being trapped in France. General Wilson's whole line of reasoning was based on the idea that the Royal Navy would be able to dedicate itself to the support of the Army, and the Navy had already made it clear that this was not going to happen, at least not in 1911 or 1912.

Churchill wasn't convinced by General Wilson's logic. He was worried about the Army being forced to retreat into the French interior, away from its own country, because of the lack of naval support during the early days of any war. Before an expeditionary force could be sent to France, provision would have to be made to extricate it if the French collapsed, and that provision would have to be reliable.

Admiral Sir Arthur Wilson, whose grasp on reality was not quite as secure as it might once have been, had a somewhat exaggerated opinion of the Navy's capabilities. He was opposed in principle to the idea of the Army sending an expeditionary force. He believed that if the greater part of the Army was sent to France on the outbreak of war then the British civil population would panic about home defence. In his view the Navy could handle the situation, practically on its own. In Admiral Wilson's assessment the Navy would immediately on the outbreak of war blockade the whole of the German North Sea coast. Then, if the Army would supply the Navy with troops, he thought that landings on Heligoland and in Germany itself would be a good idea. For the Heligoland adventure the Admiral thought that just one division, supplied by the Army, would suffice. Haldane pointed out that the Germans defending against the landings in Heligoland and their home country would have the benefit of the railway system to move troops into any threatened area. Before any bridgehead could be established the British troops would find themselves confronted by at least ten times their number of Germans.

Admiral Wilson never got around to explaining quite how his army divisions were going to get to Heligoland and Germany, or how they might be supplied if they did manage to get there in the first place. He had already told the committee that there were no ships to spare for the transportation of troops. He would have known about the troop-carrying capabilities of the new White Star 'Olympics', although they were untried. Perhaps the very existence of the first of these ships had convinced the old admiral that there was no need for the Navy to supply ships for the transportation of troops.

Admiral Wilson's assessment of the way in which a war with Germany should be conducted convinced Churchill, and Haldane, who effectively controlled the Army, that naval thinking was about a century and a half out of date. Admiral Wilson had clearly failed to grasp the fact that a war with Germany would, at least in the first instance, be essentially a land war, and that hopefully it would be fought in France or Belgium. Haldane was of the opinion that the Navy's first priority must be to transport troops to where they were needed, then to keep them supplied. Haldane, who in his five years at the War Office as Secretary of State for War, had completely reformed the Army (and given it a brain), decided that he wanted to take over at the Admiralty. Straight after the committee meeting he told Prime Minister Asquith that he wanted to take over the Navy, but the Prime Minister had other ideas. Asquith didn't want to move Haldane to the Admiralty for two reasons. The first was that he was too useful where he was, and the second was that a transfer of such a famous 'new broom' would cause considerable friction with the admirals. Anyway, he already had someone else in mind to take over at the Admiralty, although he wasn't yet ready to make any announcement. For a month he appeared to be turning the problem over.

While Asquith seemed to be thinking things over, Churchill, who had also made it plain that he wanted the post of First Lord of the Admiralty (and had been promised the position by Asquith), began preparing the ground by running down Admiralty operations to his colleagues, and pointing out Admiral Sir Arthur Wilson's shortcomings. At the end of September 1911 Asquith officially offered the Admiralty to Churchill, who had been well aware of what was in the wind and had been expecting the announcement to come at any time since the meeting of 23 August. Churchill and Reginald McKenna would simply swap jobs. McKenna, who was First Lord of the Admiralty until Churchill's appointment and unaware of his rival's designs on that position in the Government, was bitter about being moved to the Home Office and resisted the transfer for as long as possible. Behaving like a true British politician, he delayed the drafting of a new Admiralty Warrant for almost a month, during which time he drew the salaries of both Home Secretary and First Lord of the Admiralty, while Churchill drew no salary at all.

Asquith's appointment of Churchill was a little ironic. Just two years earlier he had almost brought down the Government with his fanatical resistance to the construction of eight new battleships. Now, of course, he couldn't get enough of them. Like McKenna and the others that attained high office in the British Government, Churchill fulfilled all of the prerequisites of a successful politician. He would embrace any policy that would bring him fame, popularity with the voting public (whom he detested), and personal gain. As the Spectator reported:

'We cannot detect in his career any principles or even any consistent outlook upon public affairs. His ear is always to the ground, he is the true demagogue, sworn to give the people what they want, or rather, and that is infinitely worse, what he fancies they want.'

Without doubt the gist of the Committee of Imperial Defence meeting would have reached the ears of J. P. Morgan and it would have done nothing to reassure him of the safety of his treasures and investments in Europe in general and Britain in particular. With the threat of war imminent and armed with the knowledge that Britain was by no means ready for it, Morgan would have moved decisively to safeguard his investments. Much the same ideas must have occurred to those in authority at the British Treasury, so together with Morgan's artefacts British bullion began to secretly leave for America where it would be safe.

Churchill, who was preparing to take over control of the Navy for at least a month before he actually did so, had one further important task to perform before he left his post as Home Secretary. Very shortly after the Committee of Imperial Defence meeting he chaired another committee. This one had been specially formed to review and amend the existing Official Secrets Act. Until this point the Act had only really covered military installations, but under Churchill's guidance draconian changes were made. From 1911 the Act not only covered military installations but docks, harbours and shipyards as well. The Act came into effect on 22 August 1911, only a few weeks before Churchill moved from the Home Office to the Admiralty. Its new provisions made it simple to keep what went on over the next few years a secret, and made it possible, because they came and went via civilian docks, to control what British seamen said about anything that happened while they were serving afloat.

When Churchill received his appointment to the Admiralty, Parliament was in recess, and so were the higher echelons of the Royal Navy. As far as those who generally staffed the Admiralty were concerned, this was holiday time and they were all off hunting, shooting and yachting. Churchill immediately complained that, should the call to arms come, there would be no one in place to answer it. (One assumes that Asquith was aware of the situation at the Admiralty, which explains his readiness to remove McKenna from control there.)

Clearly the situation was intolerable and would have to change. In short order the new First Lord made sweeping changes; from then onwards the Admiralty was in a state of war readiness with, for the first time in years, officers on duty 24 hours a day, seven days a week.

Churchill, after hearing what had been said at the Committee of Imperial Defence meeting, understandably had no confidence in the present First Lord, Sir Arthur Wilson, and if he had been given a free hand he would have replaced him with the recently retired Admiral Fisher as head of staff. However, Fisher had left the service under something of a cloud, so bringing him back presented difficulties. Fisher's age, his bad temper and, above all, King George V's dislike of the old admiral all worked against him. He had been a favourite of King Edward VII but not the new King, who, as an ex-naval man, took a personal interest in the affairs of his old service.

Nevertheless, Churchill realised that the Navy desperately needed reform and that to bring it about he would have to create a Naval War Staff. Unfortunately he hadn't got the faintest idea how to go about doing so. All of his previous military experience had been with the Army and had little bearing on naval requirements. He needed help, and there was only one man whom he believed knew all there was to know about the Navy. While he was still at the Home Office Churchill, despite knowing full well that the King and most of the Government would oppose his doing so, had secretly contacted Jackie Fisher, who was enjoying his retirement as Baron Fisher of Kilverstone at Lucerne. Fisher, who had been First Sea Lord until his retirement in 1910, agreed to help Churchill. The politician and the sailor held a three-day meeting at Reigate at the end of October, staying up half the night talking as Fisher outlined his programme of reforms. He also gave Churchill a few pointers about managing the Navy, such as 'Armour is vision', 'Never rely on an expert', 'The secret of successful administration is the intelligent anticipation of agitation', and 'Somebody must be hung for every little thing that goes wrong'. The new chief of the Admiralty took in everything Fisher had to say. Fisher also explained that Churchill needed the right men on his naval staff. Those right men were, of course, men that Fisher either liked or could control. The Navy was officially controlled by a board of four Sea Lords under the supervision of the First Sea Lord. The First Sea Lord was responsible for war preparations and the distribution of the fleet; the Second Sea Lord was responsible for manning the ships and training the men; the Third directed naval construction; and the Fourth saw to stores and ammunition. All of the existing Sea Lords would have to be changed if the Royal Navy was to be ready to fight a war against Germany, which Fisher had long been sure would start on 21 October 1914. In a remarkable example of professional foresight he was only about seven weeks out in his prediction. Most important of all, Fisher's recommendation was the appointment of Admiral John Jellicoe as the new First Sea Lord. If Jellicoe was in command of the home fleet on the outbreak of war, Churchill would have nothing to fear, Fisher insisted.

The 70-year-old ex-First Sea Lord also explained to Churchill the need for bigger and better battleships. The new ships should be fitted with 15-inch guns and should burn oil instead of coal, which would not only dramatically reduce the manpower needed to operate the ships but would also reduce the amount of smoke created by the ships at sea, making them harder for the enemy to find. It would also mean that they would spend less time refuelling and more time at sea, effectively increasing the numbers of available vessels.

As a frightening example of how ready Churchill was to take risks, the following takes some beating. Late in 1911 the new Admiralty supremo ordered the construction of five new, fast oil-burning battleships, *Queen Elizabeth, Warspite, Barham, Valiant and Malaya.* As Fisher had advised, the new ships were to carry 15-inch guns, none of which had ever before been made. Normally a prototype weapon would have been built and tested, but that would take a year, much too long to suit Churchill. True to type, the First Lord of the Admiralty was taking a tremendous gamble with the country's safety, as the new guns might turn out to be useless, in which case so would be the ships that carried them.

To guarantee fuel for the new oil-burning 'Queen Elizabeth' class battleships, Churchill had earlier decided that Britain would nationalise the Anglo Persian Oil Company, which brought in oil from the huge fields of what is now Iraq. (Short-sightedness on the part of the politicians who handed control of the oil back to the Iraqis must be one of the most obvious causes of the recent war in the Middle East, which was supposedly fought to remove non-existent weapons of mass destruction from the hands of Saddam Hussein.)

When Winston Churchill had moved from the Home Office to become First Lord of the Admiralty late in September 1911, he was already aware of the disappointment that the new Cunard liners had turned out to be as far as the Navy was concerned. Although they had been built to Admiralty specifications and under Admiralty supervision, the new Cunarders were completely useless for their intended role as armed merchant cruisers. They were too big, much too expensive to run and, above all, much too fragile to tangle with an enemy warship no matter how small. (This conclusion would be powerfully reinforced during the first month of the First World War when *Lusitania* sank in just over 15 minutes after being struck by a single torpedo from U-9.). The Royal Navy was big and powerful enough to manage without the liners, but the Army, in the light of the Committee for Imperial Defence meeting, could not make do without reliable troopships. It was already apparent that the first of the new White Star liners was not as well built as she should have been. The *Olympic*, which had sailed on her first transatlantic voyage on 14 June, was already in need of extensive repairs to her hull-plating where riveted joints were failing. This defective workmanship would have its part to play in later events.

Clearly the British Government and the Army could not take the new White Star ships on trust, particularly when events at Agadir almost plunged Europe into a premature war. The vessels would have to be tested, and if that test could also for a time discourage J. P. Morgan from shipping his ancient artefacts out of Europe, so much the better. As a bonus the test envisaged would also provide an opportunity to try out the ram bows that were still being built into British warships as a matter of course, although almost all other navies had discontinued the practice.

Chapter 6

Olympic and *Hawke*

Everything at Southampton seemed much as usual on the morning of 20 September 1911 as *Olympic* prepared to depart on her fifth round trip to New York, via Cherbourg and Queenstown in Southern Ireland. Until that morning there had only been a skeleton crew aboard the ship to look after the everyday routine work that had to be done even when the vessel was in port - jobs such as keeping a couple of boilers working to provide steam power for the ship's electrical systems and cranes. Dockyard workers, together with members of the crew, had seen to the hard work of filling the ship's bunkers with about 7,000 tons of coal and bringing the cargo aboard. Cargo stowage was the responsibility of the ship's second officer, who would have prepared a plan showing exactly what cargo was stowed in what hold so as to maintain the balance of the vessel. Employees of the White Star Line would have seen that the ship was fully provided with clean linen and enough food and drink to keep a small army satisfied for the six or seven days that the ship was expected to be at sea.

As this was sailing day a full crew would be required, so most of these had been signed on for the voyage during the previous couple of days. Even in those far-off days, when the British merchant fleet was by far the largest in the world, ordinary seamen and stokers were signed on for a single voyage at a time, out and back. There was no such thing as security of employment, but once a seaman had signed on for a voyage he could confidently expect to be paid for the full duration of it, barring catastrophic accidents such as the ship sinking. From early on the morning of 20 September ordinary seamen, stokers, coal trimmers, stewards and the like began to arrive and prepare the ship for sea. More boilers had to be lit and brought up to their full working pressure of 215lb per square inch. Cabins were prepared to receive their passengers. The ship's senior officers began to arrive and check that all was in order, including the captain, Edward John Smith, Commodore of the line and the highest paid seaman afloat.

However, not all of the ordinary sailors who joined the ship that morning remained aboard throughout the preparations. It was normal practice for some of them to slip ashore for a last pint or two in the local hostelries once their particular tasks were completed, only rejoining the ship at the last possible moment. It was not uncommon for some of these men to misjudge just what was the last possible moment and miss the sailing of their ship altogether. Extra men were signed on as a matter of course to cover this eventuality.

As usual before the sailing of an immigrant ship - a ship that carried large numbers of usually third-class passengers intent on starting a new life in another country - Board of Trade inspectors arrived. They were there to check that equipment such as lifeboats and accommodation was in order before signing the necessary documentation allowing the ship to leave port. Another requirement for a liner leaving Southampton was a Trinity House pilot to guide the ship through the tricky waters of the Solent. For this voyage Captain William Bowyer was the pilot.

As the morning wore on the passengers began to arrive. Many first- and second-class came by boat train, which delivered them to the quayside right alongside the huge liner. Third-class passengers were not so well provided for and generally made their own way to the ship. No matter what class passengers were travelling, as soon as they went aboard the ship they were met by a steward and were taken or directed to their cabins or dormitories.

While the preparations were being made on and around *Olympic*, preparations of another sort were also well under way. HMS *Hawke*, one of six 'Edgar' class cruisers, had already put to sea from Portsmouth. The 360-foot-long 7,350-ton warship had, even by 1911, long since been outdated by more modern designs. With her backward-raked bow, seen in profile, she looked to modern eyes as if the extreme forward end of the vessel had been fitted upside down. The obsolete cruiser was armed with two 9.2-inch guns, ten 6-inch and 17 smaller ones. More up-to-date warships, ever since the appearance of HMS *Dreadnought* in 1906, tended to carry an all-big-gun armament, with just a few smaller weapons for self-defence. As one would expect, knowing of the Navy's inbuilt resistance to change, an important design feature of the 'Edgar' class of ship was a steel beak projecting forward beneath the water, from the bow. This armoured ram was soon to prove how effective it could be.

HMS *Hawke* left the Royal Naval Dockyard at Portsmouth at about 7.30 that morning, ostensibly for some speed trials. Even when she was new the obsolete cruiser couldn't quite have managed 20 knots, something that everybody with any connection with her would have been well aware of. Speed trials for a vessel whose best speed was already a matter of record seems the tiniest bit surplus to requirements but, nonetheless, that is the reason given by the Royal Navy for *Hawke's* excursion.

At about 11.30 that morning *Olympic* cast off her moorings and moved out into Southampton Water. Her fifth voyage had begun, a voyage that would prove to be another major factor in the loss of the ship we know as *Titanic*.

Very slowly *Olympic* made her way down Southampton Water heading for the Solent, where she would turn into the eastern channel, passing the northern coast of the Isle of Wight, on her way out into the English Channel. In fact, she moved so slowly down towards the Solent that it seemed as if she was barely under way at all. It took her more than an hour and a quarter to cover about 10 miles. Modern-day car ferries cover the same stretch of water in much less time. By the time *Olympic* began her turn into the Solent, HMS *Hawke*, which had supposedly been off St Catherine's Point on the southern tip of the Isle of Wight at the time *Olympic* cast off, was fast approaching her from the west, at least as fast as the old cruiser could manage. *Hawke* had apparently travelled more than 30 miles in the time it had taken *Olympic* to cover 10, and half of that 30 miles had been through the heavily congested and notoriously hazardous Needles Channel between the mainland and the Isle of Wight.

The Naval Dockyard at Portsmouth lies a little to the east of Southampton Water, and *Olympic* would pass the entrance on her way out into the English Channel. *Hawke* was on her way home and initially travelling considerably faster then the liner. On clearing the sandbanks at the mouth of Southampton Water *Olympic* made a sweeping turn to port and began to pick up speed.

According to the received, official version of events, the cruiser attempted to overtake the accelerating liner on her starboard side. This placed the warship between *Olympic* and the Isle of Wight. As the *Hawke*, which was initially travelling faster than the liner, reached a point somewhere about abreast of the White Star ship's second funnel, the liner matched then surpassed her speed. By this time *Hawke*, trapped between *Olympic* and the land, was running out of sea room. Commander Blunt, on the *Hawke*, then decided to abandon his attempt to overtake and instead turned out into more open water by passing close under the liner's stern. As the smaller ship came closer to *Olympic* she was caught up in the suction effect, caused by the passage of the huge White Star vessel's hull moving through the water, and was drawn inexorably into her side. By way of explanation for the accident, Commander Blunt later said that his helmsman had turned the ship's wheel the wrong way and before the mistake could be rectified the helm had jammed, which hardly supports the suction effect theory. Again according to Commander Blunt, immediately after the accident *Hawke's* helm freed itself and was once more operating normally. The story is, of course, nonsense. *Hawke's* steering gear, specifically designed so as not to jam, was operated by hydraulics, which cannot jam unless the pressure within the system fails. This can only happen if a pipe bursts, a seal fails, or the pump ceases to operate. If the system does not lose hydraulic pressure, mechanical failure of the steering gear will inevitably result because of the tremendous forces applied by the hydraulics. In any event the cruiser's steering would have been useless until it had been properly repaired. It would certainly not be operating normally immediately after the collision, as Blunt claimed.

Hawke's bow was badly distorted and torn in the collision and the iron ram that formed part of it had been completely torn off, or so the Navy claimed. However, although somewhat mauled, *Hawke* was able to make her way slowly into dock at Portsmouth, unaided.

Olympic had not fared so well. She had a huge hole in her side. Two of her aft compartments were flooded. She was down by the stern, and her starboard main and centrally mounted turbine engines were out of commission. She was going nowhere very quickly in the immediate future.

Olympic, although badly damaged, was in no danger of sinking, so she was brought to a standstill and the anchor was dropped. While a quick assessment of the damage was made, Captain Smith cut off all passenger communication with the outside world. Nobody was allowed to send wireless messages or to leave the ship. With his vessel now drawing rather more water than she had previously, Smith was obliged to wait until the following day and a favourable tide before *Olympic* could return to Southampton for a more detailed inspection. However, it was immediately apparent that the liner was too badly injured to continue her journey to America.

In the evening the Southampton & Isle of Wight Company's passenger steamer *Duchess of York* took off about 100 of *Olympic's* passengers who wanted to go to London, and took them to Southampton. Mr Phillip C. Curry of the White Star Line was among them. He said that the rest of the passengers were quite happy about remaining aboard the damaged liner.

The following day *Olympic*, assisted by tugs, managed to make her way back to Southampton and the Harland & Wolff repair yard, where a proper assessment of the injury could be made, and the crew released. The visible damage to the ship above the waterline was impressive but was as nothing compared to that below. *Hawke's* armoured bow, which had struck the liner about 85 feet from her stern, had smashed a huge hourglass-shaped hole more then 25 feet high and 10 feet wide. The ram had penetrated far enough into *Olympic* to bend her starboard propeller shaft and fracture the crankshaft of the engine. The cruiser had also damaged all three blades of the starboard propeller, as she had disinterred her bow from the liner's vitals. For some reason never given, the collision had made the turbine engine, situated on *Olympic's* centre line immediately above her keel, inoperable as well.

On that same day, 21 September, White Star issued a writ against Commander Blunt, it being impossible to sue the Royal Navy, to recover the costs of repairing *Olympic*. This was immediately countered by a writ from the Navy against White Star to recover the costs of repairing its cruiser.

On 22 September the Royal Navy convened an inquiry into the collision between *Olympic* and *Hawke*, which is done after all serious collisions involving naval vessels. At this inquiry only naval personnel were called to give evidence, so it should come as no surprise that the *Hawke* was found to be in no way to blame for the affair.

The judgement of the naval court of inquiry into the incident was delivered on 19 December 1911, as follows:

'The president [Sir Samuel Evans] accepted in all material respects the evidence from the *Hawke* and found that the collision was solely due to the faulty navigation of the *Olympic*.'

Although the White Star Line would appeal against that verdict all the way to the House of Lords in 1914, they never managed to get it overturned.

Everybody makes mistakes, but this inquiry was more than merely mistaken - it must have been an intentional cover-up, a travesty. In order to accurately fix the position of the collision, the Navy said that it had recovered *Hawke's* armoured ram from the sea bed where it had settled after being torn off as the cruiser reeled away from *Olympic*. In reality *Hawke's* ram had not been torn off at all but had survived the collision without any appreciable damage. The ram, clearly still in excellent condition, had still been attached to the cruiser when she returned to Portsmouth Harbour. There is a crystal-clear photograph of HMS *Hawke* in dry-dock for repair after the incident, the undamaged ram firmly in place on her otherwise badly mauled bow. During the so-called repairs to the cruiser the armoured ram was removed and the whole front end of the ship replaced with an ordinary, more modern-style bow. The local newspapers covered the event and *Hawke's* subsequent inspection.

'*Hawke* was placed in the dock at Portsmouth Dockyard on Thursday morning, for inspection. Below the waterline the injury appeared even worse than above it. The formidable ram was completely shattered, the whole projection being pushed round to Starboard and the plates shattered and buckled in all directions, many of them folding back and covering the hawse pipes. It is certain that a completely new bow will be necessary before the cruiser will again be ready for sea.'

Clearly the Royal Navy was not telling the press the whole truth.

The whole story of how the so-called accident happened is, of course, balderdash, an obvious attempt to cover up what had really occurred. The official explanation for the collision, that the smaller vessel, *Hawke*, was drawn into the liner's side by suction, a phenomenon brought about by the water pushed aside by the movement of such a large hull and returning to fill the space left as it passed on, is unlikely to say the least. In reality, no naval captain, unless otherwise instructed, if he valued his career would approach anywhere near such a huge vessel as *Olympic* while she was moving at high speed. Anyway, had it been the suction effect that caused the collision between *Olympic* and *Hawke*, the two ships should have been drawn together practically broadside to one another. In that case the damage to the larger vessel would have extended over a larger area of her side, but would not have caused all of the internal injuries

As we have seen, the Navy had supposedly established the exact position of the accident by recovering from the sea bed *Hawke's* iron ram, which it was claimed had been torn off in the collision, a claim that we now know to have been a blatant lie. The Royal Navy also confirmed that HMS *Hawke* was out that day on speed trials and that she was at the Nab Buoy at 7.30am. She ran at 96rpm for 4 hours and reduced speed to 82rpm off St Catherine's Point at 11.30am, and then proceeded through the Needles Channel. This could not be the truth as *Hawke's* best speed would not allow her to make the necessary distance in the time available. A knot is about 15% longer than a statute mile. At her top speed *Hawke* could cover about 22½ miles in an hour, or just over 28 miles in the time available. The distance from St Catherine's Point to where the collision occurred, making no allowance for turning around the Needles or negotiating past Hurst Castle (guarding the entrance to the western end of the Solent) was something slightly more than 30 miles, very close to the distance she could have covered in the time available, steaming all out. Once any sort of allowance is made for sea room to clear the Needles, Hurst Castle, or any other ships that might conceivably get in her way - and, as we shall shortly see, at least one vessel did get in the way - the figures make even less sense.

It appears that up to the time the Nab Channel was dredged, in 1910/11, the dangerous Western Solent was sometimes used by the Royal Navy's larger vessels entering or leaving Portsmouth. Once the Eastern, or Nab,

Channel was dredged, the western route was all but abandoned. Presumably the Nab route was dredged to accommodate the new giant liners using Southampton or the Royal Navy's new super battleships coming and going from Portsmouth. We can be sure that dredging a channel that was so important to both commercial and military interests would certainly have required Government permission and probably funding. By 1911 it was usual practice for both naval and larger civilian vessels to use the eastern channel between the Isle of Wight and the mainland when entering or leaving Portsmouth or Southampton. To this day Royal Naval vessels still use this route, and they probably have every year except in exceptional circumstances such as wartime. The western channel was, and still is, avoided because of its heavy commercial and pleasure traffic, and for its tricky sandbanks. Given that the newly dredged deep-water channel was available, why did HMS *Hawke*, an armoured cruiser drawing 23 feet of water, use the more hazardous Needles Channel when returning from a routine excursion?

So what really happened? Well, according to eye-witness reports, *Hawke* did come up from behind *Olympic*, on her starboard side, and did appear to be attempting to overtake. However, from that point onwards the received version of events is demonstrably untrue. In *Hawke*'s path was the brand-new South American patrol vessel *10 de Octobre*, which had just been completed by White's Southampton shipyard and was out for its initial trials. The presence of the foreign warship meant that Commander Blunt had to alter course towards the Isle of Wight in order to pass between her and Cowes, somewhat limiting his room for manoeuvre. *Hawke*, after going around the new patrol boat, then turned 90 degrees to port (left), which would have taken several hundred yards, and slammed into *Olympic*'s side at right angles. Hardly the collision one would expect if the smaller naval ship had been accidentally drawn into the liner's side by the 'suction effect'. Unfortunately, the *Hawke* could hardly have caught the liner in a more vital spot. Nor could the angle of attack when the cruiser's bow had sliced into *Olympic* have been calculated to do more damage. The *Hawke*'s bow only remained wedged in the liner's side for seconds before the race of water along the side caused by Olympic's momentum twisted the cruiser's hull through an ear-shattering arc. The tremendous twisting movement would perhaps have sheared off *Hawke*'s underwater ram as she wheeled away if it had been severely damaged in the collision, but we now know it wasn't. Luckily, or perhaps as a result of careful planning, the accident had happened at lunchtime when all of the passengers were in the dining saloons, so there had been nobody in the second class cabins destroyed by

Hawke's bow. Nobody was seriously injured in the accident.

As *Hawke's* shattered upper bow withdrew from *Olympic* it dragged a lot of cabin furniture and some luggage out of the liner. Among the detritus was a leather bag containing clothing, surgical instruments, diploma, medical books and other things belonging to Dr Downton. The bag was picked up by a boatman, who it seems just happened to be on the spot, and was handed to the Customs officers at Cowes.

Before *Hawke's* bow tore free, the tremendous leverage exerted on the liner's hull would have stretched the starboard side of the ship, twisting her keel. Had the riveting of *Olympic's* shell plating been up to standard, it is just conceivable that the ship might have withstood the colossal forces involved in the impact; but we know that the riveting was not up to standard.

The collision was so violent that *Olympic's* stern was pushed around by something more than 45 degrees, which indicates that the cruiser's engines were still at full-ahead when she struck the liner. The force of the collision and the fact that *Hawke* was specifically designed to sink large ships by ramming them argues that the damage sustained by the White Star ship would be rather more than that described above.

The circumstances of the *Hawke* incident raise the question as to whether the collision was an accident at all, or a planned event. Three points argue strongly that this incident was no accident. The first, that no Royal Navy Captain would have taken his ship anywhere near a liner the size of the *Olympic* in the confined waters of the Solent without direct orders to do so, should be enough to convince anyone. The second point, that Commander Blunt had to go around a foreign warship that he would not have expected to be on the scene in order to reach *Olympic*, should arouse more than a little suspicion. The third point, that *Hawke* had no business to be in the Needles Channel at all, without orders, must clinch the matter beyond all doubt. Commander Blunt on the *Hawke* was almost certainly carrying out specific orders from his superiors. This is supported by the fact that, instead of receiving any sort of reprimand for his part in the collision - and he must have been at least partly responsible just by being where he had no business to be - Commander Blunt was rewarded by being given command of a larger cruiser.

Once *Olympic* had been brought to a halt, a quick assessment of the damage was made and all passenger communication with the shore was suspended. Only signals approved by the Captain were allowed to leave the stricken liner. Even though *Olympic* was noticeably down by the stern very shortly after the collision, no preparations were put in hand to evacuate the liner.

Despite Captain Smith's apparent lack of concern, some passengers were prepared to make their own arrangements to either get a message away or to leave the damaged ship. Immediately after the *Hawke* collision Captain Smith issued orders that nobody, except White Star officials, was to enter or leave *Olympic*. (It was not unusual for a security clampdown to be put into effect aboard White Star vessels that were involved in any serious incident. However, this one was applied with more expedition than was normal even for the White Star Line.) In this instance the security measures adopted were not particularly effective. Mr Magee, of San Francisco, an American passenger, who was particularly anxious about getting back to New York, succeeded in getting off the ship. He hailed a boat that was being rowed by a young fellow called Spencer and, sliding down a rope that was passed out of a porthole, he managed to reach the boat and was taken ashore. He rewarded Spencer with a couple of sovereigns.

On reaching Cowes, Magee made straight for the shipping office of W. T. Mahey and telephoned from there to try to book passage to New York on the *Adriatic*, which was sailing from Liverpool on Thursday evening. He was unable to complete the arrangements and left by passenger steamer for Southampton. Mr Magee explained his hasty departure: 'The fact is, I wanted to see my baby at home, and seeing that the *Olympic* was out of commission, I thought I had better look out for another ship.' He had dangled, up to his waist in the water, for 4 or 5 minutes before Spencer had rescued him. Once he had reached Southampton he went to the White Star office 'and booked my three berths on the *Adriatic*'. He was only just in time as there were only seven berths left on that ship when he booked. He would be two days late in seeing his baby. Who really was the American passenger on *Olympic* who was so desperate to get off the ship after the *Hawke* collision? His explanation that there was a child he must see is a little unlikely, to say the least, but he was so desperate to reach America that he was prepared to risk his life, and to pay for a three-berth cabin on the *Adriatic*.

Another enterprising American on the *Olympic*, probably a journalist, threw overboard a watertight container attached to a piece of wood. It was picked up by Mr Ernest Kirk, a photographer, and found to contain a cable message to the *Boston Herald*, briefly reporting the collision and stating that while there were many narrow escapes all were safe on board. Although no money was enclosed, Mr Kirk dispatched the cable at a cost of some £2.

That a passenger had to get a message away by putting it in a bottle and throwing it overboard confirms that Captain Smith had stopped the transmission of any messages from the damaged liner. It also argues that the American passenger was prepared for what happened, as was Mr Kirk. Is it really believable that Kirk would have sent this telegram at his own expense unless he had been pre-warned that the necessity might arise? After all, £2 was a considerable sum of money in 1911, the equivalent today of a week's wages for an ordinary working man.

There was no shortage of small boats on hand to collect anything that came from the damaged liner. There was even one, at least, with a cameraman aboard who managed to get a picture of the collision. The picture is not very clear and has not withstood the passage of time particularly well, but it does show that *Hawke* did strike *Olympic* at an angle of about 90 degrees. Perhaps the cameraman was simply there to get a shot of the world's largest liner leaving port.

The damaged liner returned to Southampton the following day so that the damage might be examined at Harland & Wolff's repair facility there. It was soon apparent that *Olympic* was very badly damaged indeed and that any further planned voyages, for the foreseeable future, would have to be abandoned.

Consequently, the White Star Line refused to pay *Olympic*'s crew for the remainder of the aborted voyage after 22 September, justifying that decision by claiming that the ship was a wreck; only in these circumstances were the owners entitled to stop the crew's pay. If the vessel was merely damaged, the seamen were due payment for the complete voyage for which they had signed aboard. Not unexpectedly, the crew were not happy with this decision and consulted their union officials at the earliest opportunity. As was only to be anticipated, the seamen's union contested the owner's decision to stop its members' wages and the first court case began on 29 September. It was initially heard at the petty sessions of the Southampton County Court, but the magistrates were unable to come to a verdict, so on 11 October they referred the whole thing to the Admiralty Court. The date set was in March 1912, and a determination was arrived at on the first day of April. The court found in favour of the owners. They agreed that following the *Hawke* incident *Olympic* was a wreck. Still not satisfied, the seamen took their grievance to the Court of Appeal, basing their case on Section 58 of the Merchant Shipping Act of 1894:

'Where the service of a seaman terminates before the date contemplated in the agreement [of service], by reason of the wreck or loss of the ship... he shall be entitled to wages up to the time of such termination, but not for any longer period.'

The word 'wreck' within this section [of the Act] means something less than total loss. Any damage to a ship from a cause for which neither the master nor the owner, on the one side, nor the seamen, on the other, is actively responsible, which damage does not constitute loss of the ship, but of necessity renders her incapable of carrying out the maritime adventure in respect of which the seamen's contract was entered into and so terminates the service of the seaman, will render the ship a 'wreck' within the section.'

The appeal failed.

The Appeal Court hearing the seamen's claim that their wages should not have been stopped following the collision between *Hawke* and *Olympic* would have been aware that the accident, according to the Naval Inquiry, had been entirely the fault of the liner. They knew that the owners and master had been found responsible. As the accident had been judged to be the responsibility of the owners, there can only be one justification for the court upholding their decision to terminate the crew's wages. *Olympic* really was a wreck following her brush with HMS *Hawke*.

Indeed, the liner was very badly damaged. From the available photographs we can see the large hourglass-shaped hole punched in the side of *Olympic*, supposedly about 8 feet deep, extending from D Deck down through E, F and G Decks, well below the water line, about 86 feet from the stern. The White Star Line, for reasons of its own, claimed that the cruiser's armoured bow had only penetrated about 8 feet into the interior of the liner. The 8-foot-deep-gash story must have been an attempt by *Olympic's* owners to play down the full extent of the damage.

HMS *Hawke* had not escaped the encounter unscathed. Photographs of the cruiser following the collision show that at least 15 to 20 feet of the cruiser's bow was damaged, which argues that it penetrated at least that far into the interior of the liner. Armed with that knowledge it is easy to understand how the liner's centrally mounted turbine engine and probably also her keel could have been critically damaged.

It took Harland & Wolff's repair yard at Southampton two weeks to patch up the damaged liner well enough for her to even attempt the voyage back to Belfast for proper repairs. A gigantic patch, not unlike a big sticking plaster, made of heavy timbers above the waterline and steel plates below it, was placed over the damaged hull plating to seal up the hole. For the trip back to the builders, which began on 3 October, *Olympic* was obliged to steam on just her port main engine, which tells us that the centrally mounted turbine really was damaged and unusable, together with the starboard reciprocating engine. Under normal circumstances this turbine could operate on the exhaust steam from one or both of the main engines. By the time the ship made it back to the Belfast yard the patch on her hull had failed and the same two aft compartments were once again flooded, which argues that the hull was no longer rigid and that the flexing had loosened the patch.

What might have been the motives for the attack by the Royal Navy on an American-owned, British-registered White Star liner, which were to set in motion a chain of events that would culminate in the most famous shipwreck in history? It has been suggested to me that as the new government-funded Cunard liners had failed to live up to their planned capabilities as armed merchant cruisers, the Army and Navy were concerned that the new White Star vessels might prove to be no better. What could be more natural, given the facts as they emerged at the 23 August meeting of the Committee of Imperial Defence, than that the new troopships should be severely tested? After all, the safety of the whole British Empire rested on the ability of the mercantile marine to move troops around the world, or so the government believed at the time. As well as the need to test the new ships, the British were faced with another dilemma. Could they allow the Coptic scroll, described in Chapter 4, to fall into the hands of J. P. Morgan without at least showing him that Britain was not a force to be trifled with?

As we have seen, ever since the Germans had triggered off the Agadir incident, Morgan had been shipping artefacts, formerly on display in prestigious European museums, to relative safety in America, much to the displeasure of men like Churchill and Lloyd George. From the British point of view this evacuation of treasures under the public gaze was defeatism and would have to be curbed. What better way to achieve this than to physically prevent one of Mr Morgan's shipments from leaving? That the British Government was itself secretly shipping gold to America and safety should war come was completely beside the point as far as it was concerned. As it was to turn out, this slap on the wrist for Mr Morgan was not the brightest move that could have been made. Until then a great deal of what Morgan was up to was being done relatively openly. He made no secret of the fact that he was moving his treasures across the Atlantic, out of the way. After the *Hawke* incident Morgan had his own Customs officials sent over from America so that anything he wanted to send home could be packed up in Europe, under the eye of his own men, and be sent to America without any further inspection by European Customs officials. This peculiar Customs arrangement meant that Morgan could ship anything he wanted to without the consent or knowledge of the governments involved. Anything he did choose to send wasn't checked on its arrival in America either, but went directly to the Metropolitan Museum before the crates were opened. Morgan owned the Metropolitan and paid the wages of all who worked there. This unusual Customs arrangement was to stand Morgan in good stead when, a little over six months later, perhaps he recouped his losses on *Olympic* due to the *Hawke* incident and returned the slap on the wrist with interest.

Chapter 7

The switch

When *Olympic* reached Belfast for repair following the *Hawke* incident, having taken three days on the short journey from Southampton, the only dry-dock in the world large enough to hold her was already occupied by her slightly younger sister ship *Titanic*. Harland & Wolff, thanks to the Marconi wireless equipment aboard the liner, must have already known that there was no great hurry to dry-dock *Olympic*, simply because it couldn't even be attempted until at least some of the water had been pumped out of her. Eventually this was done and the damaged liner was hauled in for a proper inspection and for repairs, such as they were, to begin. A gigantic and very confusing game of musical chairs had commenced.

Once the water was removed from the dry-dock the full extent of the damage to the ship seemed obvious. Large sections of three or four of the massive frames comprising the vessel's skeleton had been smashed and would have to be repaired or replaced, together with plating over more than a third of her full hull length. Plating on the starboard propeller tunnel would also require replacing. More seriously, the starboard engine crankshaft, propeller and propeller shaft would also have to be renewed as they were all damaged beyond repair. The crank, prop shaft and propeller presented a slight difficulty as there were no spares readily available. As *Olympic* was at that time the world's largest steamer and was practically brand new, the need for spares had not been anticipated. The only other existing parts that could be fitted to *Olympic* were those waiting to be fitted to the second sister, *Titanic*. With no other option open to them, Harland & Wolff decided to cannibalise the necessary spares.

Only after the work had begun did it become clear to them that the liner had suffered far more serious damage than had first appeared. As we know, the centrally mounted turbine engine, which was normally run on the low-pressure exhaust steam from one or both of the main engines, had been put out of commission by *Hawke*. While this engine was being repaired it must have been discovered that it had been moved slightly in the collision. Even then, with no obvious break in the ship's keel, the rectification work would continue. However, the mere fact that this engine needed any repair at all should have told the people at Harland & Wolff that the damage extended at least as far as the centre line of the ship. This fact, allied to the way that the temporary patch on the vessel's hull had failed during the short voyage from Southampton to Belfast, would in its turn tell them that the hull was no longer rigid and would have to be stiffened. While hull plating was removed to allow access to the engineering spaces in the ship, such as the main engine rooms, it was not an insurmountable task to fit what amounted to an extra bulkhead or two. These new bulkheads would of course have to run longitudinally, which rather turned the whole design concept of the vessel on its head. We already know that when Dr Robert Ballard was exploring the wreck of the ship we know as *Titanic* in 1985 and 1986 he discovered a bulkhead within the vessel that did not appear on any of her drawings. This bulkhead must have been fitted as an afterthought and surely was intended to stiffen up the hull - there is no other believable reason. Judging from later events, the hurried repairs and stiffening failed to do the job.

Harland & Wolff was under a considerable amount of pressure to complete the repairs to *Olympic* as quickly as possible. The ship had cost the White Star Line about £1,500,000 to build (to gain some idea of how that figure relates to today's prices you have to add a couple of noughts), and the company was losing between £4,000 and £5,000 a day in lost fares, freight charges and builders' costs while the ship was laid up. So without further ado the crankshaft and propeller shaft intended for *Titanic* were fitted in place of *Olympic's* own bent and twisted ones. Then it was time to fit *Titanic's* starboard main propeller to her damaged sister; still bearing *Titanic's* build number 401, it is clearly visible in the wreck, showing that the ship is in fact *Olympic*. Only at this point did it become apparent to all concerned with the repair that they were wasting their time.

Between the front face of the propeller and the rear face of the huge stern frame of the ship there should be a massive thrust bearing, a large bronze ring that stopped the propeller rubbing directly on the frame and prevented the stresses imposed by the thrust from the propeller being transmitted directly to the engine's crankshaft. Without this bearing the life of the engine would be dramatically reduced. When they came to fit that bearing they discovered that there simply was not enough room for it. The propeller shaft, even though both *Titanic* and *Olympic* were supposed to be identical as far as their engines, transmission and steering gear were concerned, was not long enough. *Hawke's* bow, acting as both a wedge and a lever, had stretched the starboard side of *Olympic's* hull. Because of the sheer size of the ship and the extra stiffening that had gone into her, it was impossible to bend her hull back into shape. Luckily for the shipbuilders there was another set of thrust bearings part way along the propeller shaft, but these were not enough on their own to absorb all of the stresses. Nevertheless, they would have to manage for a while because there was no way on earth that the original thrust bearing could be refitted. To compound the builders' problems, *Olympic's* starboard propeller had continued to turn for as least one full revolution after coming into contact with *Hawke*. Even one revolution of the bent propeller shaft would have effectively destroyed the bearing through which it ran in the ship's stern frame. These bearings were never intended to be a replaceable part and were meant to last the full life of the ship. There is, then, every possibility that the huge frames at the rear end of the liner had been damaged by *Hawke* and the replacement of such frames had never been done before. Not for another 20 years would a large ship have her stern frame replaced after its hull had been plated.

Under normal circumstances, at this point the ship would either have been written off as beyond economic repair or the decision to completely rebuild the aft part of the hull would have been taken - but these were not normal circumstances.

Harland & Wolff was short of money and could not afford to do a proper repair job on *Olympic* without extracting a large percentage of the cost from White Star before the work was completed. Unfortunately White Star was also experiencing something of a cash crisis. It had already paid out for one new ship, and was in the process of paying for a second. The line's owner, J. P. Morgan, had for the time being invested as much as he was prepared to in his shipping cartel. As far as Morgan was concerned, if White Star could not solve its own financial problems, it would just have to go. It wasn't as if White Star was the only shipping line he owned, and, if it did go under, his other lines would buy up the best of its ships at knock-down prices. As no real money would actually change hands, this scenario would have caused Morgan no concern at all.

Joseph Bruce Ismay, the man actually running IMM, was concerned about the fate of the White Star Line. Until White Star had been taken over in 1901/2 he had been the owner of the company, which had been built up by his father. Ismay was not about to sit idly by while his father's shipping line went under. The quick answer to the problem was already at Belfast, fitting out. What could be easier than sending the second sister to sea in *Olympic's* place?

There is no record of a conversation between Ismay and Pirrie, the head of Harland & Wolff, about the possibilities of swapping the damaged *Olympic* with her still incomplete sister ship, nor would we expect there to be, even though the conversation must have taken place. To switch the identities of ships without informing the relevant authorities is illegal. However, I am informed by a retired marine insurance investigator that switching vessels' identities is still, and always has been, the most common of maritime frauds.

As far as Harland & Wolff was concerned, there would be no great problems in the switch because the two vessels had been built from the same plans and were in most respects absolutely identical. As previously mentioned, some minor changes had been incorporated into the second sister, after she had been launched, on the suggestion of Ismay, who had sailed across the Atlantic aboard *Olympic* on her maiden voyage. On that voyage Ismay had noticed that the B Deck promenade was not used a great deal and, in his opinion, could be usefully converted into first-class cabin space. The first-class restaurant at the aft end of B Deck, on the other hand, had proved extremely popular and ought to be enlarged. A new feature, a Café Parisien, would also be incorporated to one side of the restaurant. None of these changes was of a major nature as far as the builders were concerned, as they were all built into the ship's superstructure and constructed from much lighter plating than the vessel's hull. By the time of the *Hawke* incident and *Olympic's* return to Belfast, at least the outer, visible, parts of these alterations had been carried out. They would have to be changed back to their original layout, but as anyone who has ever done anything practical will know, it is much easier to take something apart than to put it together.

At the time the decision to switch the ships was made, the second sister was still some way from being ready for service, but it would still be a lot quicker to complete her than to properly repair *Olympic*, even if a proper repair was possible.

Once the decision to switch the ships had been made the immediate problems were somewhat simplified. All that was required was that *Olympic* be patched up well enough to return to service for the time it would take to alter and complete her sister as a reasonable doppelgänger. In the same time, hopefully, the parts to effectively make good *Olympic* could be obtained, parts such as a slightly longer starboard propeller shaft or an aft bearing of reduced thickness. Nothing, of course, could be done about the stern bearing. They would just have to accept the fact that the starboard engine and shaft would vibrate and that the bearing would for evermore allow a certain amount of water to enter the ship. All ships leak to a lesser or greater degree, which is why they have pumps, so this was a problem they could cope with.

Even without doing a proper repair, it still took the full might of Harland

& Wolff two months to patch up *Olympic* well enough for her to return to service for the limited period they needed. During those same two months work began to alter *Titanic* back to her original layout as a lookalike for her sister, as well as continuing to complete her normal fitting out. The alterations to *Titanic* again presented no particular difficulties for the shipbuilders. However, they realised that it would take a little longer to do the alterations and to complete the ship than it would have done to simply continue as they had been doing, so they announced a postponed completion date. By way of explanation they said that the repairs to *Olympic* had drawn manpower from the second ship, thus delaying her completion. This explanation was plainly an excuse.

The work needed to patch up *Olympic* was of a major structural nature, such as removing and replacing heavy steel components and 30 feet by 6 feet, 1-inch-thick hull plates, while the work needed to complete *Titanic* was such as carpet fitting, installing wooden panelling, putting in the electrical fittings, and so forth. Even in 1911 riveters did not put in wooden panelling and electricians did not install propeller shafts. Completely different groups of workers were needed for whatever had to be done aboard each sister ship, which was why they had been built with one progressing a few months ahead of the other in the first place. For the repairs to *Olympic*, steelworkers must have been seconded from other ships being constructed in the yard or brought in from outside. *Olympic's* repairs could not have materially affected the progress in completing *Titanic*. Only altering the layout of the ship at the last moment provides a believable explanation for the postponed completion date.

Harland & Wolff had a little less than five months to alter *Titanic* back to her original layout, or at least something like it. As long as they could fool everyone for a couple of months they were in the clear. After that, any differences could be explained away as minor improvements, done while the ship was lying in port between voyages or during one of her not infrequent returns to the builders' yard.

It had been the intention of the owners and builders to make *Titanic* even more luxurious than her older sister. She was to have been *Olympic* perfected. These improvements, such as carpets in public rooms where *Olympic* had linoleum tiles, were of a very minor nature. Extra small portholes that had been cut to allow more natural light into toilets would have to be sealed up. Again this was obviously no problem to the workforce at Harland & Wolff, as the number of portholes on various vessels changed throughout their lives. The extra cabins on B Deck could all be removed and the promenade area reinstated without any major problem except for a large pipe that, on *Olympic*, had run along the ceiling (deckhead) of the promenade. On *Titanic* this pipe had been re-routed to run along the outside of the hull beneath the overhang of the superstructure and not through the new cabins. Working on the assumption that this pipe was pretty well out of sight anyway, it was ignored.

The White Star Line and Harland & Wolff did have one apparently serious problem, however - secrecy. Obviously they could not allow the whole world to know what they were doing, which is where Mr Churchill's draconian alteration to the Official Secrets Act came in remarkably handy. Under the Act anything that happened within the shipyard was an official secret, if the company wanted it to be. As a result, although just about everyone living in Belfast knew about the switch, nothing about it ever appeared in the newspapers. Local gossip remained just that, and still does. As late as the 1950s schools in the Republic of Ireland were still teaching pupils that the *Titanic* disaster was an insurance fraud, which was at least partly true. Stories of the switch still circulate throughout what was Northern Ireland's shipbuilding capital, and also spread to other parts of the British Isles; they were a regular topic of conversation in the pubs of Liverpool and Southampton, where many seamen who would sail on the ships actually lived.

In fact, the secret of the change in identities of the two vessels was no secret at all - the story just never appeared in the newspapers. The Official Secrets Act was a powerful tool in the hands of a Government that had a vested interest in keeping the switch under wraps. It was its high-handedness that had brought the event about in the first place. In the second place it had another use for the crippled *Olympic*, so as long as the ship was available for its purposes, and didn't actually cost it anything, the Government didn't mind what White Star and Harland & Wolff got up to.

Back at Belfast the new *Titanic* slowly began to take on the appearance of her sister. Only when the botched-up repairs to *Olympic* were complete and the ship had left the builder's yard would a large enough workforce become readily available to push the job forward. On 20 November *Olympic* was as ready as she ever would be to return to service. Her port main and turbine engines seem to have been operable within normal parameters, but the battered starboard engine still vibrated badly at anything more than a few revolutions per minute. Consequently, it was decided that the vessel should for the foreseeable future operate at reduced speeds. The reduction in stress would also go some way towards relieving the strain on the weakened hull and keel. By way of an excuse White Star explained that the slower cruising speed of the ship was an effort to conserve coal. As there was a great deal of industrial unrest in Britain at the time, and both miners and dock workers were either threatening to strike or had already downed tools, this excuse seemed reasonable enough. For westerly crossings the excuse might even have had an element of truth in it, but coal was readily available in New York. Even so, *Olympic* still only cruised at 20 knots on her homeward passages.

The speed reduction, as it turned out, was not enough on its own to prevent the patched-up hull from rapidly deteriorating. The North Atlantic, in winter time possibly the roughest sea in the world, did nothing to help. Before many crossings had been completed the ship's hull began to fall apart, so it was back to the yard for a few hundred rivets to be replaced and a little more reinforcement.

Then it was back to sea for another couple of voyages, still at reduced speeds. To reinforce the excuse that this slower cruising speed was a result of the steadily worsening coal shortage, *Olympic* began shipping extra coal from America in some of her cabins. While this might have convinced some people that the excuse was genuine, it should have had exactly the opposite effect. Coal produces extraordinary amounts of dust that would creep into every nook and cranny of the cabins being used as storage space on these voyages. It also has a very distinctive odour that permeates practically everything and is almost impossible to eliminate. Old railway bridges and tunnels, at least 30 years after the last steam trains passed under or through them, still have the unmistakable smell of coal about them. That same smell would have rendered cabins on *Olympic* completely unusable as passenger accommodation for years after the last of the coal had been removed. Obviously the White Star Line was not concerned about the loss of cabin space, which is entirely understandable if it was planning on losing the ship itself in the near future.

By the end of February 1912 Harland & Wolff had just about completed the conversion of *Titanic* back to her original configuration as a passable copy of her older sister. It was time to bring *Olympic* back to the yard and make the switch.

At 4.26pm on 24 February, at position 44°20'N, 38°36'W, during an eastbound crossing, *Olympic* supposedly ran over some uncharted underwater obstruction. The vessel shuddered violently, a condition that Captain Smith and his engineers appear to have been able to bring about at will. (Violent shuddering that would shake the entire vessel could easily be induced merely by suddenly running the main engines full astern while the ship was still moving forward at a respectable speed.) The story that the ship had apparently lost a blade from her port main propeller was circulated aboard. Whether or not *Olympic* had really lost a propeller blade is open to question, as the ship continued on her way and arrived at Southampton on time. A missing blade from the huge 27-foot-diameter propeller would have meant that it was so badly out of balance that the engine would have to be stopped. Had the propeller continued to revolve the vibration caused would have literally shaken the ship to pieces in short order. If the engine was stopped, *Olympic*, steaming on just her questionable starboard main and turbine engine, would have struggled to maintained her cruising speed and arrive in port on time. The conclusion is obvious. The ship did arrive in Southampton on time, therefore the starboard engine was not stopped, therefore it had not lost a propeller blade. The incident, including the violent shuddering of the ship, was all part of the excuse for her to return to Belfast for the switch.

After discharging her passengers at Southampton, *Olympic* departed for Belfast, arriving there in the afternoon of 28 February. The replacement of a propeller blade would normally be a one-day operation for the workforce at Harland & Wolff's Queen's Island yard, so we would have expected *Olympic* to have left on the 29th, 1912 being a leap year. As it turned out, the BoT inspector at the yard discovered that about 300 more failed rivets below the waterline of the liner had needed to be replaced and another 200 or so needed a little work. Perhaps another day's work was needed, making two days in all. In fact *Olympic*, or a ship pretending to be her, didn't leave until 6 March, a full seven days after her arrival. Any lingering doubts as to whether or not the switch was needed would have been amply dispelled by the failure of this latest batch of rivets in the shell plating of the ship, most of them in the area around the point where she had been rammed by HMS *Hawke*. The ship that quietly sailed out of Belfast on 6 March 1912 was not *Olympic* at all, but her sister *Titanic*.

During the preceding week, all of the major conversion work having been carried out over the last five months, the last-minute transfer of minor items like linen, headed notepaper and envelopes, menus, lifeboat nameplates and the rubber stamps from the ship's post office were moved from *Olympic* to *Titanic* and vice versa. Inevitably items were overlooked, among them at least one of the rubber post office stamps. Letters bearing *Titanic*'s postal stamp did leave the ship we now know as *Olympic* at Cherbourg in the period between 6 March 1912 and when *Titanic* first began her maiden voyage 35 days later.

The name *Olympic*, cut into either side of the bow of the older sister, was replaced with that of *Titanic*. The same operation, although in reverse order, was carried out aboard the new *Titanic*, which for the next 23 years would sail as *Olympic*.

The cutting patterns for the new names had been made in something approaching secrecy, over the preceding Christmas holiday period, by a Mr Williams. Williams's reward for surreptitiously making these patterns was extra holidays with pay, promotion to a better job with the guarantee of employment for life if he wanted it, and new accommodation close to the yard at the company's expense. When the White Star Line was absorbed into Cunard in the early 1930s Mr Williams was absorbed along with it.

It now appears that during the time the alterations to the ships were ongoing, a keen amateur photographer recorded at least some of what was happening. John Rochford Waters worked as a harbour master at Ardglass, just south of Belfast, during the relevant period. On his days off, because of his interest both in photography and ships, he regularly made the trip up to Belfast. On a vantage point on the opposite side of the River Lagan from the Queen's Island yard, John Waters set up his camera. He continued as harbour master at Ardglass right up until the eve of the Second World War. Over the years he told his family about what he had seen and that he believed 'there was something odd about the whole business of the loss of the *Titanic*'. Unfortunately John Waters is no longer with us, but he does have a single surviving family member who apparently still has the photographs.

Chapter 8

Finishing '*Titanic*'

With *Titanic* gone from the yard, Harland & Wolff was faced with the prospect of converting the battered *Olympic* into something they could pass of as a brand-new ship. Time was short because the date for the vessel's supposed maiden voyage had already been set. The ship was due to leave Southampton on 10 April, so, allowing for the fact that sea trials and provisioning at the Hampshire port would have to be included, the yard had little more than three weeks to complete the work, a seemingly impossible task even for the finest shipbuilders in the world.

Accepting the fact that a complete conversion could not be accomplished in the available time was more than half the battle. The work would be kept to a minimum and only what was absolutely essential would be done. Because views of the exterior of the ship had already been made public, those conversions would have top priority. A couple of small extra portholes were cut in a crew toilet on E Deck, as these would be clearly visible to the general public when the ship reached Southampton. The same applied to the cabin windows along the outside of B Deck, but as the superstructure was built of steel only half as thick as that used on the hull proper, this wouldn't take very long to do.

Constructing and fitting out the cabins themselves was a different matter. It would take months to fit all of the plumbing, electrical wiring and wood panelling in what was supposed to be a first-class area of the ship. Anyway, it would be a terrible waste of costly materials if the ship was to be scuttled on her maiden voyage, and Harland & Wolff didn't have money to waste on unnecessary trivia. The extra cabins were omitted; only the windows along the promenade deck were changed. Towards the forward end of B Deck a small number of cabins had been built when the vessel was originally constructed (see the plans), and these were retained.

As already described, we know that the cabins that should have been all along the outer edge of B Deck on *Titanic* were absent because, while the ship was sinking, a steward, Edward Wheelton, walked along B Deck checking that all the cabins there were empty and locked. While he was doing so he met Thomas Andrews, the manager of Harland & Wolff, and one of the designers of the 'Olympic' class ships, doing the same thing. While he was on B Deck the steward noticed that boats 5, 7 and 9 were no longer hanging from their davits but had already left the ship. However, boat 11 was still loading because Wheelton could see it from the deck he was on. For the steward to be able to see whether the lifeboats were there or not he would have to be able to get close to the windows and look out of them, as the boats were loading two decks above him. Quite obviously he would not have been able to do this if the outside of B Deck was cabins, particularly if those cabins were locked. As boats 5 and 7 were sited at the forward end of the boat deck, while 9 and 11 were among those kept at the after end, we can be sure that Wheelton was able to walk almost the full length of B Deck and look out of the windows as he went. B Deck can only have been an open promenade area.

One advertised difference on B Deck between *Olympic* and *Titanic* was the inclusion on the latter of what were known as the two millionaire suites. On the *Titanic* these suites had their own private promenade decks partitioned off from the first-class public promenade space, whereas on *Olympic* they did not. In other respects the two millionaire suites were the same on both vessels. All the shipbuilders needed to do was partition off the necessary section of B Deck to fool anybody into believing that part of the ship was as it should be. To be sure that nobody looked too closely, they would put their own men in the suites for the voyage.

When James Cameron was making the blockbuster movie *Titanic* he made a number of descents to the wreck. Unlike the dives carried out by Robert Ballard's team and those of the French IFREMER organisation, James Cameron was not financed by any government, so he could look at whatever he wanted to. Cameron had another major advantage over other explorers of the wreck inasmuch as the small, remotely-operated vehicle that he took down with him was regarded as nothing more than a film prop and therefore expendable. Other explorers had taken their own ROVs (remotely-operated vehicles) with them, but as these midget self-propelled submarines are expensive they had taken no chances with them. With no such constraints James Cameron sent his ROV deeper into the wreck than anyone else had dared to go. His little remote-controlled vehicle descended through two decks in order to reach the millionaire suite on the port side of B Deck. This suite, B52, slightly larger than its counterpart on the starboard side, had been supposedly designed for the use of J. P. Morgan, but was actually occupied by J. Bruce Ismay on the maiden voyage. The ROV found its way into the once palatial sitting room of the luxury suite. The foundering of the vessel and almost 80 years beneath the North Atlantic had taken their toll.

Little remained of the opulence that once had been, except for the marble fireplace surround, which was still firmly fixed in place, as described earlier.

With the forward part of B Deck well in hand, Harland could turn its attention to the alterations required at the after end. Much had been made of the fact that *Titanic* was to have a first-class restaurant that was somewhat larger than that of her sister. Along the starboard side of the enlarged restaurant there was to be a whole new feature, the Café Parisien, which occupied space that had been promenade on *Olympic*. These did present a problem for the builders. They had to be there or somebody was bound to notice; and they had to look right, because first-class passengers would be using them. The problem was not in the structure of the alterations as, like the rest of B Deck, it was built of relatively lightweight steel sheet. The problem was with the floor covering. On *Olympic* the public rooms had linoleum tiles on the floors, which are not easy to lift or re-lay. It would be a time-consuming exercise to make good the flooring so that it would not be obvious to the casual observer, and time was something the builders were short of. Once again the answer was simple - carpet.

Rather than trying to make good the tiled floors, they would be roughly patched up and carpet would be laid over the top of them. It is very much quicker to lay carpet than to lay tiles under the conditions facing shipbuilders. Another point in favour of the carpet is that it would cover up any small blemishes such as cigar burns or scuffs from boots and shoes, which would otherwise be impossible to disguise. Nobody in their right mind would lay floor tiles then carpet over them without a very good reason. The wreck of the ship we know as *Titanic* is surrounded by hundreds of linoleum floor tiles exactly matching those in *Olympic's* public rooms shown in photographs taken aboard *Olympic* before she entered service, and in artists' impressions made while the older sister was still under construction. The White Star Line explained this change from tiled floors to carpet by claiming that *Titanic* was *Olympic* perfected.

The name on the bow and stern of the vessel was altered in exactly the same way that it had been on *Titanic* a few weeks earlier. The old incised name on the bows was filled and new lettering cut using Mr Williams's patterns. The stern nameplate was a slightly different proposition inasmuch as it was proper plating with raised lettering spelling out 'OLYMPIC' and, in smaller letters underneath, 'LIVERPOOL'. For this they simply ground off the original name and replaced it with '*TITANIC*'. Because the ship was not intended to last for any length of time, the attachment of this nameplate was botched. While the ship was on her way to the bottom of the sea it fell off. There is no name on the stern of the wreck.

There were a myriad other small alterations to make, such as cutting a couple of extra portholes in the starboard side of the ship's forecastle Deck C, as this was a readily visible recognition point, which had been overlooked when converting the real *Titanic* into a lookalike of her sister. When *Titanic* as *Olympic* had left Belfast in early March she had 16 portholes in this deck where she should only have had 14. The ship's crow's-nest bell seems to have been another item that was overlooked during the first part of the switch, although *Titanic's* original bell has never turned up. There was plenty of time to change it during the next 25 years or so that the ship remained in service, or perhaps the name that would have been cast into it was simply ground off when the identity of the vessel was changed. The crow's-nest bell from the wreck has been recovered and there is no ship's name on it.

Minor items such as the ship's name on cast nameplates fixed to the bows of the lifeboats were no problem whatsoever. It was simply a matter of unscrewing the plates from the boats aboard one ship and fixing them to the boats on the other. In this way the boats would pass a casual inspection. However, a closer look would identify the ship from which they came. After the sinking 13 wooden lifeboats were recovered from the ship we know as *Titanic* and were taken to New York. This episode will be dealt with later, but for the time being we should know that while at New York the name 'Olympic' was found to be carved into the gunwales. The incised names were quickly filled with putty and painted over. The whole operation was witnessed by a retired captain who had taken a job in the docks to supplement his income. For whatever reason he kept quiet about what he had seen for almost 40 years before telling his story to a reporter from the *New York Times*. His story might have been regarded as apocryphal were it not substantiated by events on the other side of the Atlantic, recorded a few years later by an Admiral of the Royal Navy. As mentioned, this part of the story will be dealt with in some detail when we explain what happened to the lifeboats recovered by the rescue ship *Carpathia* after the disaster.

By the middle of March 1912 the vessel lying in Belfast had begun to look very much as she should have done if she was really *Titanic*. A quick coat of paint on the hull and superstructure would go a long way towards completing the illusion that this was a new ship, at least when viewed from the outside. Only someone who knew the ships intimately would notice that a cowl vent on the port side of *Olympic's* forecastle deck, which should not appear on *Titanic*, was suddenly there for all to see. Vents immediately behind the bridge had also apparently moved from ship to ship, but who was likely to notice?

Inside the engineering areas of the ship problems were beginning to mount up. Boiler furnaces that had been worked hard for three-quarters of a year could not be made to look brand new. Hot steel rusts at an alarming rate and stokers' shovels would inevitably leave scars on furnace doors and around the mouth of the furnace itself. Any experienced fireman would know immediately that the furnace he was feeding with coal was anything but new, no matter how thoroughly it had been cleaned up. With a new coal-burning ship nearing completion, some boilers would be fired up to provide heating and electrical power, but only a limited number, and they would hardly have been overworked. There would be no comparison between boilers that had been fired in the builder's yard and those that had been fired to provide the motive power for a large ship battling a North Atlantic storm. As a master mariner explained to me, 'Only an idiot would not know that he was dealing with furnaces that had seen considerable service.'

This simple truth could well be the explanation behind a curious happening soon after the ship left the builders. For her sea trials a special team of firemen was brought across the Irish Sea from Liverpool to feed the hungry furnaces with coal. After the trials the same team fired the ship for her trip from Belfast to Southampton. It should be remembered that there was a major coal strike going on at the time and many ships were languishing in port because there was not enough coal available for them to put to sea. Consequently there were a lot of firemen, and other seamen, out of work and looking for employment on any ship with enough fuel to leave harbour. The crew of firemen that brought the ship known as *Titanic* down from Belfast, with just one exception, Thomas McQuillan, deserted the vessel on her arrival at Southampton, despite the difficulties they were bound to encounter in finding alternative employment. The White Star Line had to recruit a complete new gang of firemen and trimmers for the *Titanic's* maiden voyage. Of course, the new gang would believe that they were working in stokeholds that had at least seen some hard work as the ship steamed at high speed from the builders to the line's Hampshire terminal. Even so, the firemen who signed on at Southampton must have thought that the gang who had brought the ship down from Belfast were an incompetent bunch to have done so much damage in so short a time. The engine room crews who also signed on at Southampton were mostly men who had served on *Olympic* before, and although the engines had been cleaned up they must have known that they were not new. Still, any signs of wear could be explained away as the result of testing and the short haul from the builders.

While the ship was still in the hands of the builders the Board of Trade inspector overseeing the construction and reporting back on all plan changes to his superiors was confronted by the dramatic drop in gross registered tonnage due to the alterations to B Deck. This could hardly be reported without serious questions being asked. Because the extra cabins had actually existed, the BoT was aware of what the grt should be, and would already have calculated what harbour dues would be when the ship entered service. As far as it knew the ship would be inspected by its own representative at Southampton and by his American equivalent in New York. The discrepancy would be immediately apparent. The only way forward was to bring the enclosed areas of the ship back up to the same figure as that known to the BoT and American authorities. As always, the problem was time. There was no way that the cabins could be built in the time available, but it was possible to fit windows to the forward end of the A Deck promenade space. This is how the problem was solved. So as not to confuse the BoT's book-keeping, the extra enclosed area on A Deck was listed on the registration form as not to be included as grt, but of course the Americans would not see that document. As far as they were concerned the grt exactly matched the figures they had been given.

By the end of March the conversion was all but complete except for a few carpets that still needed laying and cabins that still required some fitting out. It will come as no surprise to learn that these unusable cabins were those that had recently been used as extra coal bunker space. In that case they really would be unusable for the foreseeable future - not that that would have been any worry to White Star under the circumstances. Anyway, it was not enough of a problem to stop the ship completing the task the owners had in mind for her. Then, according to the usual accounts of events surrounding the short career of the *Titanic*, potential disaster struck.

Fire supposedly broke out in coal bunker No 10 at the aft end of the forward boiler room. This fire, if it really existed, could easily have been dealt with either before or immediately after the ship's trials, which were something of a joke in their own right. There was not a great deal of coal in the bunker at the time, so it could either have been removed or water could have been poured in until it was submerged. Either way the fire would have ceased to be a problem. Nothing was done and the bunker was allowed to continue to burn unchecked. Any secondary school student should know that coal gas, predominantly explosive hydrogen, is obtained by heating coal in an enclosed container, which is exactly what was happening in bunker No 10. That same student should also know that in the presence of coal gas only a spark is required to set off an explosion. Any number of coal-burning ships were destroyed by coal-bunker explosions, not least among them the third of the 'Olympic'-class vessels, *Britannic*. The danger attendant to a coal-bunker fire was well understood in 1912, so it appears incomprehensible that the builders or owners would allow such a fire to continue to burn when it was so simple to extinguish it. One possible reason is that the fire never really existed at all but was an invention to cover up something else that was going on. Could the bunker be being used for some purpose other than that which was originally intended, such as an extra trimming tank to correct a list or stern-down attitude in the ship caused by water entering the vessel further aft? We know that the original repair to the hull, carried out at Southampton following the *Hawke* incident, failed after less than two days at sea under ideal conditions. If the second repair, intended to be permanent, had failed to some extent, we have need for an extra trimming tank. There is another possible explanation for pretending that the ship had a bunker fire aboard when she left the builders, especially if there was the possibility that the ship might break up or sink on her way to Southampton. The blame could be laid at the door of the bunker fire. Nobody would question a ship sinking as the result of a coal bunker explosion, so the insurance companies would make good the loss.

To sink the ship on its way from Belfast to Southampton can never have been part of the plan with *Titanic*. She was a big ship, almost 900 feet long and 90 feet wide. The Irish Sea was not large enough or deep enough to permanently hide the wreck. Somebody would manage to reach it, probably to raise it for its scrap value if nothing else. If that happened the secret would be out and White Star would have some explaining to do. Should the vessel founder in the Irish Sea, the White Star Line would have to foot the bill for the salvage operation themselves in order to keep control of events. The bunker fire was just the company's own form of insurance.

The plan to dispose of the ship had already been hatched. The ideal place to lose it was on the main east-to-west shipping lane south of the Grand Banks, where there was 12,500 feet of water. In 1912 it cannot have been foreseen that anybody would ever be able to dive to that incredible depth, and certainly no sort of salvage operation could be mounted within the lifetimes of the people involved in the scheme. The site chosen to lose the ship also suited J. P. Morgan, but not for quite the same reasons as White Star. Mr Morgan had his own agenda.

Chapter 9

Belfast to Southampton

While Churchill and other members of the British Government had seen Morgan's removal of artefacts to safety in New York as defeatist, they did not view the removal of large quantities of Britain's gold reserves to the same safe haven in quite the same way. In their view they were merely being prudent. Since the Agadir incident had almost plunged the world into war, large quantities of British gold had found its way across the Atlantic, much of it aboard Mr Morgan's ships. So as not to depress public morale or the stock market, or invite the attention of the criminal element in every community, these shipments of gold were sent in secrecy. Another large shipment was due to leave Southampton during the second week of April 1912.

Although the British were well aware of the White Star plan to stage a fictitious accident with *Olympic/Titanic* some time during the ship's next voyage, they also believed that the ship, despite her somewhat bruised condition, was all but unsinkable and that she would complete the journey to the new world, one way or another. This belief that the ship was actually safe was bolstered by the fact that J. P. Morgan himself was supposedly making the crossing aboard her. He was booked to travel in one of the special millionaire cabins, designed and fitted out specifically to meet his tastes. Over and above that, many of Morgan's ancient artefacts and statues were also reputed to be making the crossing. As far as the British Government was concerned there was no danger at all of the ship failing to arrive in America, so there was no reason at all, given that Morgan and his treasures were going to be aboard, why it should not send its gold on the same ship. Arrangements had already been made and the officers of the White Star Line informed of the Government's intentions. Inevitably the information would have found its way back to J. P. Morgan, which was probably why he had booked his cabin well in advance, even though he had no intention whatsoever of being aboard the liner when she sailed.

Despite the best efforts of the workforce at Harland & Wolff, the vessel we know as *Titanic* was not ready for her acceptance trials on, ironically, All Fools' Day, as planned, so a spell of atrocious weather provided a ready-made excuse to postpone them until the following day. The trials, when they did take place, were something of a joke. *Olympic's* acceptance trials had taken two full days and the ship had really been put through her paces. She was run at 20 knots for her turning trials, when it was found that she could turn through 90 degrees in about three times her own length. An emergency stop from the same speed was tried and the vessel came to a standstill in about 800 yards, less than half a mile. Slow-speed handling tests were conducted, and the ship behaved perfectly. For those two days people ashore watched the gigantic new liner as she twisted and turned in the confined waters of Belfast Lough. Only after these extensive and exhaustive trials was the new ship accepted by the White Star Line. The trials of the second vessel, the ship we know as *Titanic*, were somewhat less thorough. For half a day the ship cruised leisurely up and down the lough. There was no attempt to find out if this vessel behaved in the same way as the one that had been so fully tested 10 months earlier. Of course, if this was the same ship there was no need to do any extensive testing, as it had already been done. Anyway, there would have been no point in subjecting an already damaged vessel to more stress than perhaps she could survive. Assuming that the BoT inspector, Carruthers, was even aboard for the tests, we have to wonder why he didn't insist on them being carried out properly, unless he was aware that a switch had taken place. After the so-called acceptance trials, and even though the ship had an uncorrectable list to port, and a reputedly uncontrolled fire raging in one of her forward coal bunkers, Harold Sanderson was only too happy to accept the ship on behalf of the White Star Line.

Olympic disguised as *Titanic* left Belfast on 2 April and, according to her papers for that voyage, headed for Southampton. All large ships are obliged to file papers covering their intended route and destination, and a crew list signed by the master. The captain himself was supposed to sign for the ship. In this instance the required paperwork was filed but with a noticeable inconsistency where the name of the master was concerned. According to the documentation the captain for this short voyage was not Edward Smith at all but Captain Herbert Haddock. At the time Haddock was listed by the owners as master of the *Olympic*, which adds a certain amount of curiosity value to the fact that his name appears on the crew list for *Titanic's* first and only successful voyage. However, Captain Haddock was fully occupied at the time at Southampton preparing the other sister ship for an Atlantic crossing. He and his vessel would depart from the Hampshire port only hours before the second sister arrived with Captain Smith in command. It would have been no problem at all for Captain Smith to have corrected the glaring mistake in his ship's paperwork before he left Belfast; after all, he had to file the crew list and other papers, if he was actually at Belfast at the time. The excuse given was that he forgot, which is hardly believable when one considers the fact that on any ship's crew list the master's name appears at the top. A possible explanation might be that Smith did not file the paperwork himself, that task being performed by another of his officers. There is some evidence to support this conjecture inasmuch as the captain could not have signed for the ship at Belfast because he was not there.

It was usual for any new White Star ship to visit Liverpool, the line's home port, and be opened to the public before heading for Southampton, where she would again be open for public scrutiny. Before the public were allowed aboard for their inspection tours on these occasions they had to purchase a ticket, the revenue from which went to support local hospitals. Even *Olympic*, when she had first left the builders, had followed this practice, although she was much too big to use the port on a regular basis, but not this time. Instead, the ship known as *Titanic* left Belfast and headed at high speed out into the Irish Sea. Supposedly she was going straight to Southampton, but there is some evidence to show that she stopped off at Blackpool Bay on the way, dropping anchor off Burbo Bank, Liverpool. Liverpool, as a major transatlantic seaport, though in decline because the River Mersey had a nasty habit of silting up and therefore limiting the size of vessels that could enter the docks, had its own Board of Trade officials. These officials were noted for their thoroughness, which is one reason why the ship was not calling there to pick up Joseph Bruce Ismay and his deputy Harold Sanderson. Instead of waiting for her in Liverpool they had spent the previous night in the North Euston Hotel in Fleetwood and had then taken the tender *Magnetic* out to meet the ship. (Curiously, while being questioned by Senator William Alden Smith during the American Inquiry into the loss of the *Titanic*, Ismay stated quite plainly that he had joined the ship at Liverpool.) It has also been suggested that Captain Smith joined the ship at the same time as Ismay and Sanderson. If this was the case, it could explain some of the curious events that occurred during the rest of the ship's voyage to Southampton, specially if Captain Smith had been unaware of the fact that he was taking over the botched-up *Olympic* and not a brand new vessel until he boarded her. Under those circumstances Captain Smith could be forgiven for taking umbrage. It would even be understandable if he did everything within his power, short of throwing his pension away by resigning, to prevent the coming transatlantic voyage from taking place at all.

Regardless of whether or not the liner stopped off at Liverpool we know that she did steam at her best speed for a good part of the voyage to

Southampton, which means that she should have been able to complete the passage in about 24 hours. During that voyage her magnetic compasses, which would have been adversely affected by the vast amounts of metal all around the ship while she was at Belfast, were calibrated and her wireless installation was checked. The wireless worked extraordinarily well. The Marconi set had a reputed daytime range of something like 350 miles, but at night that would automatically improve because of atmospheric conditions. During the hours of darkness the wireless signals might be expected to reach out as far as 1,000 miles. However, during the trip from Belfast to Southampton the vessel we know as *Titanic* established radio contact with Tenerife, more than 2,000 miles away, and Port Said, a distance of more than 3,000 miles. The wireless equipment was operating at almost ten times its advertised efficiency, which leaves one wondering if perhaps it had been significantly upgraded in preparation for the coming event, when it might be called upon.

The wireless wasn't the only thing that appears to have been working more efficiently than usual. The ship's supposedly brand-new engines also seem to have been performing exceptionally well. Although the vessel only needed to steam at about 18 knots in order to reach Southampton on time, if she stuck to the route she should have done and no detours were taken, at one point in the journey she was slicing through the water at almost 24 knots, 25% faster than she needed to move. During the early part of the 20th century, and indeed up until the 1980s, all new machinery had to have a running-in period when it was run lightly loaded. In the days before computer-controlled machine tools, this was to allow parts that rubbed together to gently wear away any tight spots and to ensure that a film of oil separated them. Under no circumstances would a brand-new engine be run at maximum power and revolutions per minute unless the operator was intentionally trying to destroy it. This leaves us with two alternatives: either Captain Smith wanted to damage the engines so that he could not take the ship to sea, or those engines were not brand new and had already been run in.

Titanic, as we shall call her for the sake of convenience, arrived at Southampton at just before midnight on 3 April, about 30 hours after departing from Belfast. This begs the question, why did the short voyage take 25% longer than it should have done? A stopover at Blackpool would provide an explanation.

When the liner did finally reach the Hampshire port she was met by no fewer than five Red Funnel Line tugs, which would assist in reversing the leviathan into her berth at the Ocean Dock. Again, contrary to the usual White Star Line practice, once the ship had arrived at Southampton she was not opened up for public inspection. Nor was the press allowed access to the vessel even though, as '*Olympic* perfected', newspaper articles and photographs would have been very good advertising. The excuse given was that there was still a lot of work going on aboard, which was true, and that time was desperately short. While this excuse might have been valid as far as the general public was concerned, it doesn't stand up with regard to the press, who could have been conducted to those parts of the ship that were completed. Instead, preparations for the coming voyage began immediately.

As we already know, the black gang - stokers recruited in Ireland and Liverpool who initially were completely unfamiliar with the ship but had worked in the boiler and engine rooms during the trip down from Belfast - might have signed on for the supposed maiden voyage. Perhaps because they had become all too aware that the boilers they were feeding with coal were anything but brand new, all but one of them neglected to do so. Or perhaps it was simply because the officers had not run the ship as if she was brand new on the short voyage. In consequence of this high-speed run, the firemen would have been worked much harder than they expected to be.

Because of the labour unrest, in particular the coal strike, there were many ships in Southampton without enough fuel to make an Atlantic crossing, several of them belonging to J. P. Morgan's IMM company. Consequently there were a lot of unemployed seamen, among them many experienced firemen and lookouts, all looking for a job. There was no welfare state in 1912 - if a man didn't work, he and his family did not eat.

There was not enough coal on hand to supply the new White Star liner, as her sister had taken most of it before she left just a day before the new ship arrived. Somehow the newcomer's bunkers, one of which was supposedly on fire and had been ever since her ridiculously short sea trials two days before, had to be filled quickly if she was to depart on time. To accomplish this, what fuel was available was scavenged from the bunkers of all the other IMM vessels in the port. Nothing was done about the fire, which still burned out of control in No 10 bunker. Instead, about 400 tons of coal were poured into the bunker on top of the fire, banking it up. Captain Smith and his senior officers would have been well aware of the danger posed by a coal bunker fire, and under normal circumstances would have moved heaven and earth to extinguish it. To have dealt with the fire while the ship was at Southampton, with all the labour available to him, would have been the captain's obvious course of action. Instead, the fire was fed with more fuel. There has to be a very compelling reason for Captain Smith's cavalier attitude to this fire, if it truly existed. The chances of the ship completing an Atlantic crossing without such a fire causing serious problems, perhaps actually sinking the vessel, were so slim as to be not worth consideration. Of course, there might not have been any bunker fire at all, so pouring coal into No 10 bunker would not have been the suicidal folly it first seems.

Normally an 'Olympic' class ship at the time would have a loaded draught of about 35 feet, meaning that the lowest part of the vessel's bottom would have been 35 feet below the water line. Photographs of *Titanic* leaving Southampton at the start of her supposed maiden voyage show her to have been drawing only about 33 feet. Under normal circumstances a ship would be at her heaviest right at the beginning of a voyage with her bunkers full of coal, provisions for her passengers and crew, and cargo in her holds. Clearly this ship was not fully laden, which makes perfect sense if she was only to steam a limited distance. Why would they go to all the trouble and back-breaking labour of lifting unnecessary amounts of coal from the bunkers of other ships and transferring it to their own vessel? At the very best of times coaling a ship was considered to be by far the worst task faced by a crew, and having to first remove that coal from the bunkers of four or five other vessels would have made the job infinitely worse.

To return to what was happening at Southampton as the White Star liner prepared for what was presumed to be her first transatlantic voyage, even as carpenters and painters put the finishing touches to cabins, and carpets were laid over the tiles in the public rooms, bed linen, towels, food and drink, and all the other paraphernalia needed aboard a ship to make life comfortable during a six-day Atlantic crossing were supposedly put aboard and stored away.

Cargo began to be lowered into the ship's holds, much of it perishable goods that could only realistically be transported aboard an express liner, but otherwise it was of no great intrinsic value; after all, why would White Star put valuable items aboard this ship when there were other, more reliable, vessels available? Cargo was not just put anywhere but was placed in the ship's holds according to the second officer's carefully worked-out plan so as not to upset the vessel's trim. Then there was Mr Morgan's shipment, which had to go aboard and probably be stowed in No 5 hold, in the aft part of the ship. As previously mentioned, Morgan had his own Customs arrangements. His shipments were inspected by his own tame Customs man, Mr Nathan, before being sealed and transported to the docks. They were not opened again by Customs officers on either side of the Atlantic, but were to be taken directly from the ship when it arrived in New York to the Metropolitan Museum, so we have no way of knowing what was in any crate being shipped. In this instance most of Mr Morgan's crates, instead of containing valuable artefacts and statues, might well have been filled with heavy valueless rubbish, but nobody outside his organisation would have known that.

The liner was a hive of activity as the work to get the ship ready for sea went on apace. It is hardly surprising that none of the dock workers noticed that the ship they were working on wasn't the brand-new *Titanic* at all, but her older sister in disguise. They did not have the run of the ship but were only allowed access to the parts of the vessel where their services were required, such as the upper decks and holds. Just as now it was not unheard of for items of cargo or even ship's fittings to mysteriously disappear while a vessel was being loaded, so some security arrangements were in place to prevent, or at least minimise, this unfortunate tendency.

As it happened, Easter weekend fell right in the middle of *Titanic's* preparations for sea. Easter Sunday was a national holiday and nobody worked. The dockyard was unusually quiet on that Sunday as *Titanic*, dressed with flags in her rigging, rode at the quayside. Despite the seeming urgency to get the ship ready, nothing much was done in that respect. However, not everyone had taken the day off. There is some evidence to suggest that early that morning a couple of vans belonging to the Dominion Express Security Company arrived on the quayside and unloaded their cargo of wooden crates and small barrels. Under the watchful gaze of the ship's First Officer the crates and barrels, which were all unmarked, were quickly lifted aboard and stowed in No 5 hold together with Mr Morgan's cargo. The British Government's gold shipment had arrived, all £8,000,000 of it. Of the ship's company, only the three most senior would be aware of what the crates contained. Without further ado, Mr Murdoch would have signed for the consignment and the vans would depart as quietly as they had arrived. There was nothing unusual about any of the procedure. Neither the owners nor the shippers wanted to advertise the fact that there was a large quantity of gold aboard the ship. Its anonymity was its best safeguard.

Chapter 10

Carpathia and *Californian*

With all of the unemployed seamen looking for a berth at Southampton, the White Star Line should have been able to put together a top-class crew of picked men for the coming so-called maiden voyage with very little effort. Instead they signed on a crew largely made up of inexperienced men who had never been to sea before or who had never worked aboard a first-class express liner - men who would be unlikely to realise that the vessel they were serving aboard was not what she pretended to be. For example, it was White Star company policy to only take on experienced lookouts who had recently passed an eye test. For this particular voyage that policy was suspended. At least one of the lookouts employed had never taken the eye test and on his own admission could judge neither distance nor speed. To make bad matters worse that same lookout was also incapable of judging the size of anything he might see from the crow's-nest. When the time came, this was the senior man on lookout duty and on whose ability to perform his allotted task depended the safety of all aboard the liner. As it turned out the lookout was a model of efficiency, but he was let down by the ship's senior watch officers.

To support the scratch crew, some men were signed on who had actually served on *Olympic* before, together with others who had worked aboard different vessels in the fleet, men who knew how to do what they were told. Officers were drafted aboard who had also served on *Olympic* previously, including a Chief Officer who, as we shall see, seems to have wanted nothing to do with the vessel. The senior officers signed on were Henry Tingle Wilde as Chief Officer, who came directly from *Olympic*; First Officer William McMaster Murdoch, also straight from *Olympic*; Second Officer Charles Herbert Lightoller from *Oceanic*; Third Officer Herbert Pitman from *Oceanic*; Fourth, and Navigating, Officer Joseph Groves Boxhall from *Arabic*; Fifth Officer Harold Godfrey Lowe from *Delphic*; and Sixth Officer James Moody from *Oceanic*. So we have a situation where the only three senior officers with any experience of managing the huge new liners were concentrated aboard just one of them.

Captain Herbert Haddock had taken over from Captain Smith as skipper of what he had been told was *Olympic* (but was really *Titanic*) less than a fortnight before. With no previous experience of these giant liners Captain Haddock needed all of his experienced officers, not that his needs made any impression on the White Star Line. For what they had in mind they required experienced officers they knew to be loyal on the ship masquerading as *Titanic*. Haddock's senior officers were taken from him to serve on the sister ship. Olympic, as the class leader, was the flagship of the line and would remain so until well after the Great War. Nonetheless, although he was skipper of the flagship of the White Star fleet, he and his ship would just have to manage as best they could, and learn on the job.

A new black gang of men to serve the vessel's furnaces, boilers and engines was signed on at Southampton to replace those who had decided that they wanted nothing further to do with the ship after the short run down from Belfast. The new men, although many of them were experienced, did not have the same opportunity to spot the age of the ship as those who had previously toiled in the bowels of the vessel. Now, of course, after that voyage from the builder's yard the boilers could not be expected to look brand new, especially since the ship had been run hard and the furnaces had been fed tons of coal. Even so, not all of the new firemen and trimmers were fooled, as later conversations in the public houses of Southampton frequented by them showed. Rumours that the vessel lying in the Ocean Dock was not really the *Titanic* were rife. Just as had happened in Belfast, nobody in authority did anything to find out if there was any truth in the rumours and the newspapers were strangely silent on the subject. Then, as now, newspapers tended to print any sensational rumour they heard about, because sensational stories sold papers. Could it be that they had been told what to report just as it seems had been the case concerning the *Hawke* incident six months earlier?

As was usual at the time, not all of those members of the black gang who signed on for the maiden voyage joined the vessel straight away, as their services would not be required until the morning of the 10th when the ship prepared to leave port. Only then would the majority of the boilers be fired up and steam raised to feed the mighty engines. Until that time only a couple of boilers would be worked to provide power for the electrical generators and so forth, so a skeleton crew would suffice, and many of its members returned to their homes and visited their favourite public houses during their off-duty periods. This meant that the ship was short-handed when the time came to fill the bunkers, another reason to suspect that those bunkers were never properly filled. Under normal circumstances the firm of Thomas Rea would see to the loading of the coal, but these were anything but normal circumstances, and Rea's men could hardly be expected to transfer coal from one vessel to another. Usually all they had to do was pour the coal into the waiting bunkers through chutes, not to manhandle it up from deep within an assortment of other vessels, load it onto their own vessel and transfer it to the liner. Nevertheless, according to the received version of events, this is exactly what happened, despite all of the labour unrest that was crippling the rest of the country.

By the end of Monday 8 April 1912, most preparations as far as provisioning the ship were concerned had been all but completed. There were still civilian workmen aboard fitting carpets and finishing off the fitting-out of some staterooms, which would mean that those rooms could not be used. It should again be remembered that very few ships had recently been able to make an Atlantic crossing because of the shortage of coal. This meant that many would-be passengers had also been unable to make the crossing and were waiting for a ship, any ship. With this available pool of thousands of impatient passengers awaiting a ship to take them to America, there should have been no problem in finding enough eager travellers to fill every available space on the new White Star liner. She should have been filled to capacity. Curiously, instead of being fully booked, tickets for less than half of the available passenger berths had been sold. Supposedly in an effort to boost the numbers aboard for the maiden voyage, passengers who had already booked to sail aboard other, less prestigious, White Star vessels were transferred to *Titanic*. Many of the people transferred were not at all happy about what was going on as some of them had booked to travel first class on the ship of their choice, and now they were expected to occupy second-class accommodation for the voyage. While second class on *Titanic* was more ostentatious and comfortable than first on most lesser vessels, it did not carry the same cachet as first class. In fact, third-class accommodation on *Titanic* was better than first class on a lot of other liners. Even with the extra passengers pressed into sailing on the ship, still less than half of her cabins would be occupied.

To be fair, a lot of regular transatlantic passengers did not like to sail on ships making their maiden voyage but preferred to wait until any problems had been ironed out before booking passage. However, that does not explain the singular lack of people prepared to sail on *Titanic*, particularly when there were so few alternative vessels available. Perhaps they too had heard the rumours circulating in Southampton that all was not right with the ship. In any event, they stayed away in droves.

While *Titanic* was making her way to Southampton, then preparing for sea, other preparations were also under way. In New York the 13,603-ton second-rate Cunard liner *Carpathia* was undergoing a few minor alterations at the United States Navy's Brooklyn yard. Public rooms were being rearranged so that they could easily be used as emergency hospital wards and extra oil tanks were installed, even though the vessel was not oil-fired. While these alterations were still ongoing extra doctors were signed on. Normally only one doctor would be carried - sometimes, under exceptional circumstances, two. For the coming voyage, which was supposedly only a routine cruise from the US to the Mediterranean, no fewer than seven doctors would be aboard. These medical practitioners were Dr Frank Edward McGee, who would receive an illuminated certificate of thanks from the Liverpool Shipwreck & Humane Society for the part he would play in coming events; Dr Arpad Lengyer, who would also receive an illuminated certificate from the Liverpool Shipwreck & Humane Society; Dr Frank H. Blackmarr, from Chicago, who was supposedly travelling as a passenger but who somehow acquired a life jacket from a survivor of the *Titanic* disaster (marked Fosberry & Co, Rich Street, Limehouse, London, it was donated by Dr Blackmarr in 1935 to the Chicago Historical Society, which passed it on to the Smithsonian Institute in 1982); and Dr Vittoria Rosicto, an Italian physician whose identity was unknown until 2004. Little or nothing is known about the other three doctors aboard *Carpathia* except their names: Dr Henry F. Bauenthal, Dr Gottlieb Rencher and Dr J. E. Kemp. Quite clearly the owners and senior officers of the *Carpathia* were expecting trouble on this particular voyage.

Even though *Carpathia* herself was only a second-rate liner, she did have a few properties that would make her very useful in the event that she was obliged to take on large numbers of people in the middle of a voyage. The Cunard vessel was no midget, being 540 feet long and 64.5 feet wide. She was by no manner of means a fast ship, with a top speed of only 14 knots, but she was steady and reliable. More importantly, the vessel could carry more than 2,500 passengers, almost as many as the gigantic new White Star vessels. Granted, more than 2,000 of these passenger berths were in third class, but what would that matter in an emergency? Third-class sailing beats first-class drowning every time.

The captain of the *Carpathia* is also of interest. Arthur Henry Rostron was born at Bolton in Lancashire in 1869 and joined the Cunard line in 1895 after initially training as a cadet officer aboard HMS *Conway* and serving as a junior officer with other companies aboard both steamers and sailing ships. Captain Rostron was undoubtedly a first-class navigator and mariner who should have been in command of a far better vessel in the Cunard fleet. Unfortunately he had once displayed what the owners would have regarded as a serious flaw in his character; he had not kept his mouth shut when perhaps he should have done. While serving as Chief Officer on Cunard's *Campania* in 1906 he saw what he believed to be a sea serpent, off Queenstown in Southern Ireland (now Cobh). Excitedly he drew a sketch of what he had seen on the bridge scrap log, but was unable to draw the creature's features. Had the matter rested there, all would have been well, but the junior officers who were with Rostron on the bridge at the time reported the incident to the ship's master, Captain Hains RNR, who later asked his Chief Officer if he had seen anything. Unfortunately for himself, Rostron replied in the affirmative, prompting the captain to ask him if he had been drinking. Rostron then showed the captain his sketch in the log.

As soon as the vessel reached port the Chief Officer was packed off for a week's leave. On his return to the ship Captain Hains did his best to give Rostron another chance to deny seeing anything unusual. 'Did you see it?' he asked. Again Rostron said, 'Yes.' Shortly afterwards Arthur Rostron was dismissed from his post on *Campania*, Captain Hains writing 'unstable' on his record. Cunard then placed him aboard the brand new *Lusitania* as Chief Officer for the short run from Glasgow to Liverpool prior to the liner's maiden voyage. *Lusitania's* master thought this new Chief Officer unsuitable and he was discharged again before the new super-liner began her first transatlantic crossing.

Rostron had become something of an embarrassment to the Cunard Line, so the company promoted him sideways, away from the eyes of fare-paying passengers. He was given command of the small cargo vessel *Brescia* in 1907. He would not make the same mistake again, even though he did stand by his assertion that he had seen a sea serpent. In the future he would not say anything that might embarrass his owners, but he would not lie for them either. He would tell as much of the truth as he was able and beyond that he would say nothing at all. The strategy seems to have worked because over the next few years he steadily gained ground, being given command of ever larger ships in the Cunard cargo-passenger fleet. From *Brescia* he moved to *Veria*, then *Pavia* and *Panonia*. Then, in February 1912 he was given command of the eight-year-old passenger vessel *Carpathia*. The Cunard vessel was scheduled to leave New York exactly 24 hours after the ship we know as *Titanic* departed from Southampton on her maiden voyage. The two ships should pass one another somewhere south of the Grand Banks, a shallower area of sea south of Newfoundland that in those days abounded with fish.

Nor was *Carpathia* the only other vessel getting ready for sea under anything but her usual matter-of-fact routine. In the Port of London the Leyland Line passenger cargo ship *Californian*, under the command of

Captain Stanley Lord, was also hurriedly preparing to head out into the North Atlantic. Like *Carpathia*, *Californian* was an unremarkable vessel that would not under normal circumstances rate a second glance. She was not a large ship for the time, being just 447ft 6in long and 53ft 6in wide. The ten-year-old, 6,223grt ship had been designed with huge cargo holds for the transportation of cotton, but these, at a pinch, would hold a lot of people. While this may not have been the best accommodation afloat, as with *Carpathia's* dormitories it was infinitely preferable to swimming. As well as her cargo-carrying capacity, the vessel actually had passenger berths for 47 people, who would normally travel in considerable comfort, albeit relatively slowly. Again like *Carpathia*, the *Californian* had a top speed of around 12 knots, and, like so many other vessels, as a result of the coal shortage she had been laying idle for some time.

Captain Stanley Lord, *Californian's* fourth skipper, had taken command of the ship just the previous year. Although a strict disciplinarian, like almost every other captain in the mercantile marine, Captain Lord was liked and respected by the seamen who sailed with him. As a navigator he was the equal of both Captain Rostron of the *Carpathia* and Joseph Groves Boxhall, who was serving as navigating officer on the *Titanic*. Captain Lord also had another claim to fame. A few years earlier the British Government had carried out tests with a number of different ships and masters to find out who was any good at loading and unloading horses and men without benefit of proper docking facilities. Captain Lord had shown then that he was the best skipper in the merchant fleet at quickly taking aboard large numbers of people from small boats while the ship was at sea. It was this skill that almost certainly got Lord involved in what was to happen, and which came close to ruining his career.

While the *Californian* had been lying idle, some general cargo had been taken aboard, but nothing of any consequence. Leyland Line vessels were usually loaded to full capacity, and sometimes beyond, before they sailed, so much so that there was a joke going around regarding log entries from ships belonging to other lines that read, 'Passed two funnels going in opposite direction. Presumed Leyland vessel.' Like so many regular practices aboard vessels involved with the *Titanic* disaster, Leyland's habit of heavily loading its ships was suspended for *Californian's* next voyage.

Orders suddenly arrived for *Californian* to load with coal and take on a small cargo of blankets and warm woollen clothing, bound for Boston on America's west coast. Captain Lord was to take his ship to sea at the earliest possible moment and to make all possible speed on the journey. Under anything like normal circumstances *Californian* would not have received any

All photographs unless otherwise credited are from the Robert McDougall collection.

Above: The White Star Line's head offices in Liverpool.

Above right: J. P. Morgan. The ultimate owner of the *Titanic* and one of the few men in the world in 1912 who could sell large quantities of bullion without raising suspicion.

Below: Dominion Express vans leaving the quayside after making a delivery to a liner. Note the police and the shipping line officials in attendance.

Right: HMS *Hawke* dry-docked for repair after ramming Olympic in September 1911. At the Inquiry into the incident the Royal Navy claimed that *Hawke*'s armoured ram had been torn off in the collision and that they had recovered it from the sea bed, thus fixing the position of the collision. As can be clearly seen from the photograph the cruiser's ram survived the collision without any appreciable injury, proving conclusively that the Royal Navy lied. The *Hawke* incident was undoubtedly the single most important cause behind the *Titanic* disaster. *Author's collection*

Below: Captain Smith and his officers.

Above: The rescue ship *Carpathia* that made such extraordinary efforts to reach the stricken *Titanic* but then transmitted such confusing messages about how many persons had been saved.

Above right: Captain Rostron of the *Carpathia*.

Above: A *Titanic* lifebelt recovered from the sea at the site of the disaster by the *Carpathia*. Hundreds of these were found floating at the site but curiously the Captains of both ships that went to the rescue only saw one floating body.

Above: Californian, the ship meant to rendezvous with *Titanic* in the middle of the North Atlantic and take off passengers and crew.

Right: The ship that received *Titanic*'s last wireless transmission at 2.17am on that fateful Sunday. *Virginian*'s log entry of that signal establishes exactly when *Titanic*'s power failed and shows that the story told by Second Wireless Officer Bride cannot be the whole truth.

Above: The cable ship *Mackay Bennett* which recovered most of the bodies found after the disaster.

Right: Titanic's lifeboat davits which were specially designed so that each pair of davits could handle up to 10 lifeboats. No passenger liner has ever been equipped with 160 boats, which argues that *Titanic* was not built solely as a passenger liner.

Left: The forward end of *Olympic*'s bridge deck immediately after launch. The straight fronted wheelhouse framing can just be discerned. *Author's collection*

Below left: A curved-fronted wheelhouse being built aboard an Olympic-class ship, possibly *Britannic* but more probably on *Titanic*.

Below: The supposedly brand new *Titanic* departing the builders at Belfast.

Right: Olympic showing just how much alike the first two of this class of vessel really were.

Below right: Titanic detail from a photograph of the ship leaving Southampton showing daylight through the gaps between the top three rudder pintles.

Below: Titanic detail from photograph of ship leaving Queenstown in Ireland, her last port of call, showing daylight between only part of the gaps between the top three rudder pintles. The ship should have been riding higher in the water than she was when she left Southampton because tons of coal had already been consumed. This shows that the reverse is true and that the vessel was slowly settling by the stern.

Above: Detail from photograph of *Titanic* shortly before launch showing there to have been no joints in her port side hull plating immediately forward of the anchor.

Above: Detail from photograph of *Olympic* taken in 1911 clearly showing that there was an overlapped joint in her port side hull plating immediately forward of where her anchor would normally be secured.

Right: Detail from photograph supposedly of *Olympic* taken in late 1912 or early 1913 showing that by this time there was no longer any joint in her port side plating immediately forward of the anchor. The hull we are looking at here can only be that of *Titanic*, proving beyond all reasonable doubt that she and her sister ship *Olympic* had been switched.

Below: Titanic's crows-nest bell recovered from the wreck but bearing no identifying marks.

sort of priority treatment when it came to acquiring coal for her voyage, but somehow the fuel was found in very short order. Such was Captain Lord's hurry to leave London that a crew was rapidly signed on. He did not waste any time selling passenger tickets for the coming transatlantic crossing, even though there were hundreds of people waiting for just such a crossing. He despatched Harold Cottam, his wireless operator, to the Marconi office to pick up a wireless chart for the North Atlantic showing what ships would be where and when they would be within range of his own wireless equipment. Cottam, caught up by the sense of urgency in getting to sea, grabbed the first Atlantic chart he saw and hurried back to the ship with it. Unfortunately, when he got there he discovered that in his haste he had picked up the wrong chart. He had the one for the South Atlantic. He reported this to Captain Lord and requested permission to go ashore again and rectify the error. Captain Lord refused as there was no time before the *Californian* sailed. So it was that the *Californian* left London on 5 April 1912, heading for the North Atlantic, with no passengers aboard and with the wrong wireless chart, which meant that the operator would not know what ships he could contact at any point in the voyage.

What could possibly have been so urgent about a cargo of blankets and woollens that was so compelling that Captain Lord could not take the time to pick up the right wireless chart and take on a few eager fare-paying passengers? What could be so urgent that *Californian* should leave London and hurry out into the middle of the North Atlantic, burning coal that could much more profitably have been used transporting passengers, many of whom would have happily paid considerably more than the Leyland Line's usual charge of £10 just to get a berth aboard any ship? What could possibly have been so urgent on 5 April but had ceased to be of any great import just ten days later when the ship, in a position just to the east of the Grand Banks, stopped her engines and drifted upon first getting a glimpse of field ice?

The ice should have come as no surprise to Captain Lord. Many ships completing an eastbound transatlantic crossing had reported seeing a vast field of ice studded with huge icebergs. A chart showing the position of this icefield and the speed at which it was drifting southwards had been prepared and circulated for the attention of masters planning to cross the Atlantic and who might encounter it. Captain Lord, on filing his intended route to America, would automatically have been told about the ice he was bound to run into at some point in his voyage. Why then did Captain Lord choose to endanger his ship and crew by selecting a course that would inevitably take him into ice when he had little or no experience of dealing with that particular hazard?

Chapter 11

All aboard

Easter Monday and the following Tuesday came and went, and still *Titanic* was a hive of industry as beds were made up, cabins tidied and cleaned, and fresh provisions brought aboard. Down in No 5 hold Mr Morgan's people were carefully stowing and securing his crates. At the same time it seems probable that they were transferring the contents from Morgan's crates to those belonging to the British Treasury, and vice versa. Only after ample time for that task to be completed did word reach the liner that J. P. Morgan would not be making the voyage after all. His excuse, and excuse it definitely was, was that he was feeling unwell and was not up to the rigours of a transatlantic passage aboard the world's largest and most luxurious liner. Not only was Mr Morgan not sailing with the ship, but his cargo of valuable artefacts, without his presence to keep an eye on them, would not be going either. His crates were to be removed from the hold and put into secure storage until he was ready to accompany them to America. His instructions were carried out, but with one notable, and possibly intentional, oversight. One crate, containing a small ancient Egyptian statuette, was left on the quayside, unattended. It wasn't there for long before a dock worker spirited it away in the hopes that it might prove to be of worth. At that time ancient Egyptian artefacts had not acquired the tremendous value that they have today, but they were still expensive items to acquire. As it was, the small statuette, having suffered somewhat over the millennia it had spent beneath the desert sands, was not of any great value. It certainly had nothing like the value of the contents of Morgan's other crates. However, if it had been examined later it would have gone a long way towards establishing that Mr Morgan's cargo was exactly what it was claimed to be, should any questions be asked. Unfortunately, the dock worker, whoever he might have been, did not advertise the fact that he had made off with part of Morgan's shipment. To make matters worse, the liberator of the crate hadn't got the faintest idea of how or where to sell the statuette, so he packed it away out of sight, and there it remained for some years. Eventually the artefact was anonymously donated to the Southampton Maritime Museum, where it still resides.

So, on the morning of Wednesday 12 April 1912, as far as most of the passengers were concerned, all was well although some of them might have smelled a rat, or perhaps the smoke that must have been issuing from the forward coal chute. Whatever the reason, there were more than 50 last-minute cancellations.

Most of the ordinary crew members must have heard the rumours, that the ship had been switched with her sister, but they had no inkling that there was anything particularly dangerous about the coming voyage. Anyway, all they had were suspicions. Thomas Rea's employees might well have guessed that they had not put enough coal into the ship's bunkers to take her all the way to New York, but they could not know for sure just what the liner's requirements for the voyage actually were. Only Captain Smith and his senior watch officers, two or three of the highest officials of the White Star Line, Mr Morgan and a few trusted employees and associates, almost the entire workforce of Harland & Wolff, and the population of Belfast knew that there was anything seriously wrong! Nobody was about to listen to what anyone from Belfast had to say, not then or now. Stories about the *Titanic* and *Olympic* being switched still circulate in Belfast, as they have ever since 1912. Together with the rumours of the switch are the ones about the *Titanic* disaster being a massive insurance swindle. In fact, the insurance swindle is something rather more than a rumour inasmuch as it was still being taught as a part of the history of the event in schools in Southern Ireland as late as the 1960s, and may still be.

It was White Star Line practice to insure its vessels for only about two-thirds of their value. There were a couple of reasons for this seemingly cavalier attitude toward safeguarding the company's investments. The first reason was the belief that its ships, being probably the best-constructed vessels in the world, were exceptionally safe, even though White Star had lost one or two over the years. The second, and more important, reason was that, given the line's accident record, it had great difficulty in finding any insurers who were prepared to accept the risk. Nevertheless, with the ship we know as *Titanic* White Star persevered and managed to secure insurance cover to the tune of something like £4,000,000, almost three times what it had cost to build the ship (see Appendix 2 for details of the insurance). The major British underwriters were Commercial Union, which sold off the cover in small parcels to various other companies until they carried £1,000,000 worth. American insurance companies covered large sums. Even Lloyd's of London, the world's most famous maritime insurers, carried a large slice of *Titanic's* cover, although they later denied doing so even though they had paid out almost before the ship had reached the bottom of the sea. White Star did not have it all its own way. At least one major insurer refused to cover any part of the risk on the *Titanic*. Sir Edward Mountain, the supremo of the Eagle Star Company, took one look at the ship and pronounced that in his opinion she was sitting much too low in the water.

Those within the White Star company responsible for arranging the insurance cover for the ship were so intent on obtaining cover for the vessel itself that they clean forgot to arrange the third party insurance for the crew, passengers and baggage. This oversight would result in yet another insurance fraud and cost many other shipping lines a considerable amount of money, but we will come to that later (see Appendix 2).

To return to events immediately prior to the *Titanic* setting out on her maiden voyage, most of the crew had been signed on four days earlier, on Saturday 6 April, in union halls and the White Star Line's own signing office, so many of them had never set foot aboard the liner until that morning. Most of them lived in Southampton, but a few, driven by the necessity to obtain any sort of a berth because of the effect of the coal strike, made the trip from Liverpool, Belfast and London. On the Wednesday morning these men, totally unfamiliar with the ship they were about to take out onto the North Atlantic, began to make their way to the *Titanic*. Most of them had to be shown to their berths and to their places of employment. Their stay aboard the liner would turn out to be so short that they never would learn their way about the labyrinthine interior with any degree of certainty.

There was also considerable confusion among the officers, even though most of them had been with the ship ever since her trials more than a week before. At the last moment a new Chief Officer, Henry Tingle Wilde, was drafted aboard against his will. This meant that the existing Chief Officer, William McMaster Murdoch, would have to be demoted to First Officer. The existing First Officer, Charles Herbert Lightoller, would be demoted to Second, both with a commensurate decrease in pay. This would inevitably have caused a certain amount of bad feeling and also meant that the officers concerned would have no time to familiarise themselves with their new duties. Nor would they have time to become fully accustomed to their new cabins and surroundings. It is almost as if the White Star Line was intentionally trying to confuse the senior officers aboard the *Titanic* and make them less efficient than they might otherwise have been. Second Officer David 'Davy' Blair would have to leave the ship altogether, which from his viewpoint turned out to be no bad thing. However, Blair's leaving was to cause an unfortunate sequence of events that might well have had a considerable bearing on what was to come. Before leaving the ship he locked his company-issue binoculars, stamped 'Second Officer, *Titanic*' in what had been his cabin. These were the binoculars that would normally have been made available to the ship's lookout men stationed in the crow's-nest; indeed, they had used them during the short voyage down from Belfast. The new Second Officer seems to have been unaware that it was a part of his job to ensure that the binoculars were available for the lookouts, should they require them, so the glasses remained locked away in the cabin.

Sunrise on sailing day was at 5.18am, and shortly after that the first crewmen began to arrive in ones and twos. They came into the dock through Gate 4 and made their way to the ship. Over the next hour or so more and more of them arrived until by some time before 7.00am most of the crew were aboard, more than 800 of them.

Captain Smith came aboard at about 7.30am and went straight to his cabin, where he was met by Chief Officer Wilde, whose duty it was to inform the captain of any problems. All of the ship's officers with the exception of Captain Smith had spent the night on board. At about the same time that Smith had boarded the ship a Board of Trade immigration Officer, Captain Maurice Harvey Clarke, had also arrived. It was Clarke's job to inspect the ship under the Merchant Shipping Act to make sure that she was up to the standards required by the BoT for an immigrant ship. He had already visited the vessel on a number of occasions during the short time she had been lying in Southampton Docks, but nevertheless he would appear to make a thorough job of inspecting *Titanic* that morning. Clarke was famous among the officers of the various immigrant ships that used the port as being a pain in the neck. He always did everything by the book and inspected every nook and cranny of whatever vessel he happened to be aboard, and *Titanic* was to be no exception - or so we have been led to believe.

True to form, Captain Clarke toured the ship, poking his nose in everywhere. He had a couple of lifeboats lowered just to check that the gear worked properly and that the crew knew how to use it. For that particular exercise, of course, crew members who did know how to operate the lifeboat falls had been specially selected for the test; as later events would show, the majority of the crew didn't have a clue about how to lower the boats. Third-class accommodation was inspected, together with public rooms and life-saving equipment. Curiously, Captain Clarke, despite the nit-picking attention to detail for which he was so well known, failed to notice that the forward coal bunker was on fire. Heat and smoke must have been issuing from the bunker hatch and forward boiler room ventilators if there really was a fire. It is inconceivable the Clarke would have allowed the ship to put to sea with a coal bunker fire had he known about it. It is equally inconceivable that an inspector so well known for his thoroughness would have failed to notice such a fire. Nevertheless, the Board of Trade inspector did fail to report the fire and did issue the necessary paperwork allowing the *Titanic* to take on passengers and, when all was ready, to set sail. The last governmental safety check that might have averted the coming disaster had slipped away.

The crew were mustered by departments and inspected by a medical officer and Captain Clarke. Names were checked against those appearing on the sign-on list and the total number of crew aboard was ascertained. A master crew list was quickly put together and passed to Captain Clarke, a list we now know to have been horrifically inaccurate. Even if the list was somewhat less than authoritative it still showed that a number of crew members who had been signed on had failed to join the ship. There was nothing unusual in this and it was normal practice to sign up more men than were actually needed so that any shortfall could be corrected. However, the inspection by the medical officer and Captain Maurice Clarke should (and would) have shown up any crew member masquerading as another. Because of the inspections we can be fairly sure that all of those crewmen aboard were who they said they were, and more importantly who their documents showed them to be. Throughout much of his inspection the Board of Trade official was accompanied by White Star's own Southampton maritime superintendent, Captain Benjamin Steele, who might just have guided the inspector to carefully selected parts of the ship.

Joseph Bruce Ismay came aboard the ship at about 9.30 that morning with his wife, Florence, and their three young children, Tom, George and Evelyn. As supremo of the White Star Line, Ismay had the run of the ship but he only showed off the first class passenger areas of the vessel to his family, who would not be accompanying him on the voyage. Richard Fry, Ismay's manservant, had boarded the ship earlier to see that his master's suite, cabins B52, 54, 56 and the private promenade, were in order and to unpack his clothes. Fry had then retired to his own more spartan accommodation, cabin B102, across the hall from that of his master. Ismay's secretary, W. H. Harrison, would be travelling with his employer, apparently so as to be on hand when they reached America. Little or nothing seems to be known about either of Mr Ismay's two closest employees from that time onwards.

In the wireless cabin, just aft of the bridge on the starboard side, senior Marconi operator Jack Phillips and his mate, junior operator Harold Sidney Bride, were making sure that all was well with the ship's wireless equipment. Officially only Phillips would be on duty from 10 in the morning until 2 in the afternoon, when he would be relieved by Bride. However, as this was sailing day and there would be a lot to do, both men worked whatever hours were required to maintain a continuous service. Perhaps it should be mentioned here that Phillips and Bride, although subject to the ship's rules and discipline, were not employees of the White Star Line but worked for the Marconi company. They were not the only people aboard who appeared to be crew members but who in reality worked for another employer. All of the ship's Italian catering staff were actually employed by Mr Gatti, owner of the famous London restaurant, who was himself making the voyage with his secretary, Paul Mauge. Like the wireless operators, the caterers were effectively sub-contractors and, although subject to the ship's routine, do not appear to have reaped the benefits, such as they were, of being bona fide crew members, such as being allowed onto the boat deck in time to secure a place in a lifeboat should disaster strike.

The boat train carrying second- and third-class passengers left London's Waterloo station at about 7.30 that morning and arrived at the Ocean Dock a little under 2 hours later. A few minutes later second-class passengers began to board the ship through the entrance at the aft end of C Deck. They were met by their stewards and directed or taken to their respective cabins. Second-class passengers who had been allocated cabins right at the stern of the vessel also boarded through another entrance even further aft on C Deck. However, there was no lift handy by this entrance so passengers had to use the stairway to reach the decks where their cabins were situated. There was a lift at the main entrance for the use of the second-class passengers but many of those using that entrance preferred to walk down the relatively grand red-carpeted light oak staircase. Second-class passengers who made their own way to the ship could also board through the other entrance at the aft end, on the starboard side of E Deck. In any event, as soon as they passed through one of the entrances they were assembled into groups by the waiting stewards, then led to their cabins. From then onwards they were expected to find their own way about the huge vessel with the aid of somewhat inaccurate deck plans provided by the line for each ticket-holder. After all, there was little point in asking stewards or crew members for directions as most of them didn't know their way about the ship either. In fact, on more than one occasion members of the ship's crew had to ask the newly boarded passengers for directions as they had not been provided with even rough plans of the ship.

Third-class passengers were boarding at the same time as second class. They came into the ship through their entrance close to the stern on C Deck or via the gangway forward on D Deck. Like second class they were assembled into groups by the waiting stewards, but there were many more passengers per steward in third class than second, so the groups must have been larger and far more impersonal. As mentioned earlier, third class aboard a White Star liner was as good as or better than first class aboard vessels belonging to other less prestigious lines. The third-class areas of the ship must have seemed palatial, with their white-painted panelled walls and linoleum-covered floors. In groups the passengers were led to their cabins or dormitories. Single third-class male passengers were shown to accommodation at the forward end, deep within the ship on E, F and G Decks. Single female third-class passengers were taken aft to cabins on D, E, F and G Decks. There would be little fraternisation between unmarried members of the opposite sexes in third class if the White Star line had anything to do with it.

Married couples and families were spread between fore and aft accommodation, seemingly at random. Despite this attempt at segregation, all the third-class passengers could make use of their own public rooms. There was a smoking room and a large general room for drinking and making merry at the rear end of C Deck and the large dining saloon amidships on F Deck, as well as the promenade on the aft well deck and the large open space on D Deck beneath the forward well deck and crew galley. All in all, third class would be adequately provided for with regard to amusement throughout the first few days of the coming voyage. After that it wouldn't matter.

While second and third class were boarding, the Trinity House pilot, Captain George Bowyer, also arrived at the ship and made his way to Captain Smith's cabin. It was Bowyer's job to command the ship until she was clear of the shoal waters in the exit channels from Southampton. All ships over a certain size were obliged to employ a Trinity House pilot when entering or leaving the Hampshire port to minimise the chances of an accident. It will be recalled that George Bowyer had been with Captain Smith on the bridge of *Olympic* almost seven months earlier when that vessel had collided with HMS *Hawke*. Nor was that the only blemish on Captain Bowyer's accident record. He had been the pilot aboard the American liner *St Paul* when she had rammed HMS *Gladiator* of Great Yarmouth 3½ years earlier. A number of Royal Navy personnel had perished in that incident.

Captain E. J. Smith's accident record was easily as bad as Bowyer's, perhaps even worse. As well as the *Hawke* incident he had run the *Republic* aground off New York in 1889. Three crewmen were killed aboard that vessel shortly after she had been refloated when a boiler flue exploded. Almost two years later Smith ran the *Coptic* aground off Rio de Janeiro. In 1901 *Majestic*, while under Smith's command, caught fire, although the

Captain later denied knowing anything about this incident. In 1906, while still in Liverpool, his ship *Baltic* caught fire. The fire was extinguished with the aid of the port fire-fighting equipment but not before the ship and her cargo had sustained considerable damage. Then, in 1909, he managed to run another White Star liner, *Adriatic*, aground off New York. These were the men who would take the *Titanic* out of Southampton, and the accident-prone Captain Smith would take her on her one and only Atlantic voyage.

Just before 11.30am the first-class boat train arrived at the dockside and disgorged its passengers. In groups they wandered up the gangway leading to the first-class entrance on B Deck. They were arriving, so it is said, in sufficient numbers to make it difficult for Purser's Clerk Ernest King to keep his records in order. King's records are not the most reliable of documents, which leads one to wonder how he would have managed had there been a full complement of passengers boarding that morning. Once passengers had been identified their stewards conducted them to their respective cabins. This tells us that only passengers who could identify themselves and produce some sort of indication as to what cabins they had booked were taken aboard. Admission was a ticket-only affair. Nevertheless, there appears to have been a number of passengers aboard who were travelling under assumed names or who did not appear on any list at all.

With the Board of Trade inspection completed and all the passengers and crew aboard, *Titanic* was almost ready to depart. The last visitors were seen off the ship. The necessary tugboats were in attendance. A few minutes before midday the massive three-toned ship's whistles announced her imminent departure. Three blasts on the whistle is the traditional signal that a vessel is ready to leave port. The Blue Peter was run up the foremast. As a Royal Navy reserve officer, Captain Smith was entitled to fly that flag. The mooring lines were cast off and the tugboats took the strain as *Titanic's* massive engines began to turn. At noon on 10 April 1912, what must be the most famous voyage in history began. Within minutes the first serious hazard would be encountered and the ship would have to stop. Things were not going particularly well right from the very beginning.

Chapter 12

Cherbourg and Queenstown

Hardly had *Titanic* begun to move under her own power than things started to go badly wrong. When a vessel as large as *Titanic* moves it has to push a lot of water out of the way, and that water has to go somewhere.

As mentioned earlier, Southampton Docks were crowded with ships unable to leave because of coal shortages caused by the miner's strike. These ships were tied up two and three abreast. Somebody should have realised that the powerful currents created by the huge liner could cause some of these vessels to break free of their moorings. It should have come as no surprise when ship after ship strained at the ropes tying them to other vessels or to the quayside, but it appears that it did take everyone unawares. Nobody was prepared when the American liner *New York* snapped her moorings with a series of reports like pistol shots and began to swing toward the White Star behemoth. Fortunately nobody was hurt when the heavy mooring ropes parted and sprang back like enormous whips as the strain on them was released. Only the quick thinking of Captain Gale on the harbour tug *Vulcan* saved the day. Somebody had seen what was happening and shouted to Captain Gale to try and push the American ship back out of the way. Gale however, realised that getting in between the two much larger vessels would amount to suicide; the *Vulcan* would become the filling in a gigantic steel sandwich. Instead Captain Gale managed to get a line onto the *New York* and slowed her down slightly before that line parted. *Vulcan's* crew tried again and succeeded in getting a wire onto the American ship. This time the line held and *New York's* swing was first halted, then slowly reversed. There was no way that the little tug, powerful as she was, could manoeuvre the large American vessel back into her old mooring, so *Vulcan* towed her out of the way.

In the meantime Captains Smith and Bowyer, on the bridge of *Titanic*, had seen what was going on and had the liner's engines put full astern for a few moments, bringing *Titanic* to a standstill. The White Star liner waited for an hour while the *New York* was moved to another mooring before she slowly began to make her way towards the open sea. The prompt action of Captain Gale and the uncharacteristic efficiency of Captains Smith and Bowyer had averted what could have been a serious accident, but opened the way for an even more dramatic event. Even if a collision between the two liners had been relatively minor there would inevitably have been a considerable amount of damage done, which would at the least have delayed *Titanic's* departure, perhaps for a matter of days. Had that occurred, this and countless other books might never have been written. However, a collision was avoided and events would take their course. *Titanic* had come as close to '*New York*' as she ever would.

Titanic's journey from Southampton to her first port of call at Cherbourg was relatively uneventful except that the ship's lookouts, stationed in the crow's-nest, began to grumble about the fact that they had no binoculars. Captain Smith made no attempt to make up the hour lost in the *New York* incident. Although a deep-water port, Cherbourg harbour was simply not big enough to take a vessel of *Titanic's* dimensions, so the liner dropped anchor outside at about 6.30 that evening, just as it was growing dark. Passengers and mail were loaded and unloaded by two small tenders specially built for the job by Harland & Wolff. Class segregation was treated as a matter of course in those far-off days, just as it is now. First- and second-class passengers were brought out to the liner aboard the tender *Nomadic*, while third-class were carried by the slightly smaller *Traffic*. According to the White Star Line's records, 142 first, 30 second and 102 third-class passengers joined the ship at Cherbourg, while 13 first and seven second-class passengers left. Just over 90 minutes later, with her business at the French port concluded, *Titanic* weighed anchor and got under way towards her next port of call, Queenstown (now Cobh) in County Cork, southern Ireland.

Passengers of all classes were beginning to settle in and take stock of their surroundings. This would be their first night aboard the liner and for those in third class it must have been an eye-opener. Most of them had never previously seen anything as grand as this ship and had certainly never before been waited on by servants, and were thus a little overawed. The more jaded passengers in first class had seen it all before and not only accepted excellent service but expected it. However, for most in second class, while the experience was perhaps new, it wasn't in the least frightening, merely interesting. It was passengers in second class who noticed that the ship was listing to port. From the centre of their dining saloon on D Deck, when they looked out of the portholes on the right-hand side they could see the sky, but through those on the left side of the ship they could only see the sea. This clearly caused some interest as it was commented upon by those passengers who had noticed it. Lawrence Beesley, a school teacher who was travelling in second class, also noticed that the ship's engines were vibrating quite badly, so much so that the mattress on his bed was shaking about. If those second-class passengers had known more about the ship they might well have been a lot more concerned about the list and vibration. As it was they merely talked among themselves.

Deep within the bowels of the liner the engineers were running the engines at high speed and the stokers were pushed to feed enough coal into the boiler furnaces to keep pace. At breakfast time on 11 April second-class passengers noticed that the ship's list was still there although they still attached little importance to the observation. Had they been able to see the ship from outside, and if they had watched closely as she left Southampton, they might well have been a little more impressed, or even a little fearful. Photographs of the ship as she was leaving Southampton show her riding with two rudder pintles (hinges) exposed above water and a third almost completely exposed. A photograph taken at Queenstown shows the previously almost completely exposed pintle to be now more than half submerged. As these pintles are about 3 feet in height the rear end of the ship must have settled by somewhere between 1 and 2 feet in the time between her leaving Southampton and arriving at Queenstown. During that short voyage a considerable amount of coal must have been consumed by the ever-hungry furnaces, so the ship should have been riding slightly higher out of the water. Instead she appears to have been slowly sinking by the stern.

The port of Queenstown, like Cherbourg, was too small to take a vessel as large as the 'Olympics', so *Titanic* dropped anchor about 2 miles offshore. Then the liner waited for about half an hour as the two tenders, *Ireland* and *America*, brought 1,385 bags of mail, 113 third and seven second-class passengers out to her. Once the passengers heading for the New World were safely aboard, it was time for those travelling only as far as Queenstown to disembark. In all, 13 first-, 7 second- and possibly 2 third-class passengers left the ship at the Irish port. They were joined by a stoker, John Coffy, who, according to the official record, was deserting the ship. It is possible that Coffy, who worked deep within the bowels of the liner, had realised that she was not a brand new vessel at all. He might even have known that the ship was taking in water, in which case his eagerness to leave her would be entirely understandable. It has been said that Coffy might have only taken the position as a stoker in order to obtain free passage from Southampton to his home in Sherbourne Terrace, Queenstown. This seems a little unlikely as he actually lived at 12 Sherbourne Terrace, Southampton.

It seems much more likely that the stoker was leaving the ship quite legitimately and with Captain Smith's knowledge. It is inconceivable that he could have hidden himself away aboard a vessel as small as a tender, or that he managed to mingle unnoticed with the passengers, Customs officials, reporters and so on who were also leaving the liner at the time. Coffy had something of a record for leaving ships aboard which he was employed without completing the voyages he had supposedly signed on for, yet his papers showed no record of this tendency towards desertion. Nor was this the last time he apparently deserted. During the Great War he served as a rating in the Royal Navy. Desertion from the Army or Navy during wartime was a serious offence that would normally be punished by a term of imprisonment or even a death sentence. Peculiarly, Coffy was awarded a war medal, although this was taken away from him in 1922. Shortly after deserting *Titanic* he was taken on as a stoker aboard the pride of the Cunard fleet, *Mauretania*. A seaman's papers, upon completing a period of service aboard any ship, were endorsed by the Captain or Chief Officer to show whether or not he had performed satisfactorily. Obviously a deserter's papers would not show any such endorsement, merely that he had been signed on. Without his previous Captain's confirmation that a seaman knew his job he was virtually unemployable. He would certainly not be taken on as a skilled or semi-skilled sailor. Why then would the captain of the *Mauretania* allow a man with Coffy's lack of credentials to join his crew? The short answer is that he would not.

There is a possible explanation for John Coffy's departure from *Titanic* and the various other vessels he served aboard that would not involve his papers being incomplete or his needing to forge a Captain's signature. If he worked directly for the Liverpool Shipowner's Association, and therefore directly for the shipping lines themselves, to keep an eye on and report on any dissent among the various crews he served with, his papers would be in order. In that case his departure from the liner at Queenstown was probably prearranged. As we know, there was a lot of industrial unrest and even sabotage at the time, and Coffy could have been just one of many employed to infiltrate trade unions and the like.

Among the letters taken ashore from the liner during her stopover at Queenstown was one from her Chief Officer, Henry Tingle Wilde. The letter was to his sister and in it he wrote that he 'still' did not like this ship. According to the record Mr Wilde never saw or set foot on *Titanic* until the morning of 10 April, the day she sailed. How then could he have still disliked a vessel he had had nothing to do with until then? Mr Wilde had, however, served aboard *Olympic* before as Chief Officer, and it stands to reason that it was this ship he was referring to. If that was the case, Wilde must have known that the *Titanic* he was aboard was in fact really *Olympic*.

At about 1.30pm *Titanic* weighed anchor and got under way for New York. There was no particular hurry as she was not expected to arrive until after daylight on Wednesday 17 April, when the reception was arranged and the press would be ready. However, stokers later complained that the ship had been run at very high speed right from the very start of the voyage and that they had struggled to keep up with the demand for coal from the furnaces. This complaint by those in a position to know exactly how hard the boilers had been worked at first seems to make no sense. During her first day at sea, from 1.30pm on the Thursday when she departed Queenstown until noon on the Friday, the ship covered 386 miles. That is an average speed of just over 17 knots, which was nothing like her established top speed of 23.5 knots. Were the firemen grumbling for the sake of it or was there some hitherto unexplained reason why the ship needed so much steam to cruise so sedately. Could the water that had entered the after part of the ship be slowing her down, or might it be that the starboard engine was not producing anything like the amount of power it should have done for the amount of steam it was consuming? Vibration is wasted power and it takes a lot of power to continuously vibrate about 60,000-odd tons of steel ship, and we already know that the ship was vibrating badly. Evidently the firemen persevered because between noon on the Thursday until the same time on Saturday the vessel covered 519 miles, an average speed of about 21.5 knots.

Contrary to White Star Line standing orders, Captain Smith had elected to follow the 'Autumn Southern' route. Company orders forbade the use of this route after mid-March because of the danger of encountering icebergs. Instead the ship should have been on the 'Outward Southern' route, which would have kept her about 60 miles further south, and clear of the icebergs and masses of field ice that always came south from the Arctic at that time of year. The 'Autumn' route was the slightly shorter of the two, but even the parsimonious management of the White Star Line considered the extra expense in fuel a good investment if it meant not losing a ship. Obviously Captain Smith did not agree.

On that Saturday morning, then, *Titanic* was some considerable distance further north than perhaps she should have been. Some distance ahead and about 20 miles further north, the Leyland Line vessel *Californian* was making her best possible speed westwards, all 11 knots of it. *Titanic*, making almost twice *Californian*'s speed, was rapidly closing the gap between them. The White Star liner's captain and senior officers were all well aware that within 24 hours they would enter an area where masses of ice had already been reported. There was still plenty of time for Captain Smith to order a course change to the south, which would take his ship safely clear of the ice and still allow him to make *New York* on time if he wanted to. He obviously didn't want to because *Titanic* sped onwards toward the hazard ahead.

Patrolling the fishing grounds around the Newfoundland Grand Banks, an area of shallower sea that abounded in marine life, was the Royal Navy's cruiser HMS *Sirius*. It would have been a simple matter for *Titanic* to contact the *Sirius* by wireless to find out just how bad conditions ahead really were. Captain Smith chose not to take even this simple precaution.

As it happened, *Sirius* was not the only naval vessel abroad on the North Atlantic at the time. Both the British and American navies were ostensibly engaged on anti-submarine exercises in the area the liner was approaching. The naval presence was in fact quite substantial and included not only submarines and anti-submarine ships but heavier units as well, such as destroyers, cruisers and at least one new battleship. The majority of these warships would have been equipped with powerful wireless installations. They would also have been well aware that the liner was approaching them. Ships equipped with wireless were supplied with charts showing what ships should be where at any given time, so that they knew what vessels were in radio range. It would have been a simple matter to have sent a warning to *Titanic*, but it didn't happen.

The wireless apparatus aboard the American and British warships on the North Atlantic was strangely silent. There seems to be no record of any ship, civilian or military, picking up any radio traffic from the naval vessels, intended for them or not. However, it is certain that the warships were picking up the signals sent out from all the wireless-equipped merchant vessels within a couple of hundred miles of them. Wireless sets of the time were not the precision instruments they are today. Any transmission could, and probably would, be overheard by any receiving station within range. That is why all sensitive military traffic was sent in code. The curious radio silence observed by the warships argues that they were deliberately trying to conceal their presence. It wasn't wartime and the ships were supposedly engaged in a multi-national exercise. Wireless signals between the ships involved should have been almost constant. The anti-submarine exercise, which could have been carried out more conveniently much closer to home, could have been nothing more than an excuse for the naval vessels being in the area. It is not impossible that they were acting as distant escort for the liner and her cargo of gold. The distant escort principle has been used by navies to protect merchant ships for many years because large warships are not only very much faster than most of their civilian counterparts, but also require more sea room to manoeuvre.

Saturday was relatively uneventful aboard *Titanic*. Passengers wandered about their own areas of the ship, still blissfully unaware of the fire that supposedly raged in forward bunker No 10. Still nobody noticed the smoke and heat coming from the top of the coal chute for that bunker. Down in the forward boiler room some of the 12 firemen specially signed on to fight the fire apparently toiled to remove the coal from the bunker. The fire had apparently already done a significant amount of damage to the ship. The heat had caused the steel plating at the bottom of the watertight bulkhead to twist and buckle. It would also have burned any paint off the steel and caused it to go rusty. To disguise this damage it seems that the firemen had instructions to smear the bare, discoloured plating with old oil, or so they said. Hardly a satisfactory structural repair, but only what one would expect with this particular ship. The story is patently untrue. If the plating was hot enough to have buckled it was also hot enough to have vaporised any oil smeared on it. The smoke and vapour generated would have made the whole boiler room practically untenable, not to mention the fact that hot oil vapour is an explosive gas that is very easy to ignite, so it is not something anyone would want to see in a boiler room with a dozen furnaces. Getting volunteers for that job cannot have been easy.

As I have never believed that Captain Smith was demented, I have also never believed he put to sea with an uncontrolled bunker fire aboard. If I am right, there was some other reason why 12 men had been specially signed on to tend to that particular bunker. The most likely use for the bunker was as an extra trimming tank, probably filled with water, to balance that coming in further aft. This is of course mere speculation, as much of the space between the skins of the ship's double bottom was divided into sections that could be flooded to trim the ship. Those sections were not used as trimming tanks were filled with fresh water for the boilers. Drinking water was kept in special tanks along both sides of the electric generator room on the lowest deck of the ship, well aft.

First-class passengers stayed in their cabins, strolled on the promenade decks or enjoyed a cigar in their richly appointed, mahogany-panelled Georgian smoking room. Ladies talked or composed letters in the light and airy reading and writing room. Men and women gathered in the Louis Quinze Lounge. First and second class had access to the sycamore-panelled library, which was notionally a second class public room. Both upper classes had access to the restaurant and Café Parisien at the aft end of B Deck. Otherwise second-class passengers had their own oak-panelled smoke room and promenade decks. Too much fraternisation between first and second class was not encouraged, while fraternisation between third class and the upper two classes was actively discouraged, to say the least. Except when they were enjoying their own promenade areas on the aft well deck, and sometimes the forward one as well, third-class passengers were not even allowed to see those in first and second class, and even then they had to look up to them. Third class had their own areas on the ship and woe betide them if they strayed.

Much the same applied to the crew concerning the passengers in first and second class, and to a great extent to those travelling in third class. Only officers and stewards were allowed to meet first and second-class passengers. The ordinary working seamen aboard first-class liners had their own passageways throughout the ship, which took them well clear of the passengers. The firemen, for example, had their accommodation, messes and galleys on C, D, E, F and G Decks beneath the forecastle, right in the bows of the ship. To reach their workplaces in the vessel's boiler rooms they had to descend a couple of spiral stairways to the very lowest deck of the ship, the tank top. From there they would make their way through a specially constructed tunnel beneath the forward two holds and on into the forward No 6 boiler room. Then they would make their way aft to whatever boiler room they wanted through the watertight doors in the bottom of the bulkheads that divided the ship's hull into so-called watertight compartments.

The doors cut through these bulkheads were an obvious source of danger should the vessel's hull be holed. To minimise this risk watertight doors that could be closed by the flick of a switch on the bridge were provided. As an additional safeguard the watertight doors were also fitted with switches, operated by floats, that would detect any amount of water flooding the bottom of the ship and automatically close the doors - a fairly foolproof design, one might suppose, until one takes a closer look at the arrangement. In the first instance any opening in the watertight bulkheads is an undesirable feature and automatically means that they are not truly watertight. Before the automatic switches could operate a considerable amount of water would necessarily have entered the boiler rooms. The only true safeguard lay in the fact that these doors were closed by gravity (a law against which there is no appeal). They were held up in the open position by powerful electro-magnets. As soon as the electricity supply to those magnets failed, the doors would close under their own weight, provided that there was nothing beneath that could jam them open. In reality the watertight doors were a joke. Any piece of equipment or rubbish, a fireman's shovel or even a quantity of coal would suffice to prevent a door from closing properly. If the door was not fully closed then it might as well not have been there at all.

The previously mentioned tunnel used by the firemen to reach their workplaces was known to be vitally important to the safety of the ship in the event of a serious accident or collision. If the firemen could not reach the boiler furnaces there would be no steam to run the ship's engines, pumps or electrical systems. Because of the importance of this 'Firemen's Passageway' it was provided with its own watertight doors and pumps. The passageway ran along the lowest deck of the ship but it was, because of the way the hull was constructed, with a double skin at the bottom, at least 5ft 3in away from the outer hull and keel. The passageway ran along the centre line of the ship and at its closest point to the side of the hull was still more than 12 feet from the hull plating. The designers clearly believed that, barring a head-on collision with an immovable object, the firemen's passageway would survive intact, allowing firemen and engineers ready access to, and egress from, the engineering sections of the ship. In the event they were to be proved wrong.

Chapter 13

'Westbound steamers report bergs...'

Sunday 14 April 1912 on the North Atlantic dawned cold and clear. *Titanic* still headed westwards at better than 22 knots. Less than 200 miles further west and a little to the north the Leyland Line's *Californian* was also ploughing along westwards but at less than half *Titanic's* speed.

Even before *Titanic* had left Southampton Captain Smith had been informed that huge amounts of field ice and a great number of icebergs lay along the route he had chosen to follow. The winter of 1911/12 had been exceptionally mild in Greenland and many more than normal massive pieces of ice had broken away from the Disco glacier to become icebergs. The pack ice in those northern latitudes had not frozen anything like as hard as it usually did. As a consequence of this mild weather the Labrador ocean current, which flowed from the north, had begun to move massive quantities of this ice into the shipping lanes weeks before it would ordinarily have done so. However, a little ice did nothing to discourage Captain Smith; in fact, it appears to have had exactly the opposite effect on him.

All the time the ship had been at sea more and more indications that ice lay ahead had been received by wireless. Such messages, regarding the safety of the ship, were supposedly treated as a priority by Jack Phillips and Harold Bride, the Marconi operators, and were meant to be taken to the bridge immediately. In reality the wireless operators used their own discretion in deciding what was urgent and what could wait until a convenient time for them to deliver it to the Captain and his watch officers. This was only a natural attitude for the operators to adopt as many of the navigational signals were merely repeating information that those on the bridge had already received, and were mostly inexact in their nature anyway. On this Sunday, however, all that changed. At 9.00am the first of a series of specific ice warnings was received by *Titanic*. This message was from the Cunard liner Caronia eastbound from New York to Liverpool, via Queenstown:

'Captain, *Titanic*. Westbound steamers report bergs, growlers and field ice in 42° N, from 49° to 51° W. April 12. Compliments, Barr.'

This message, clearly indicating a concentration of dangerous ice in an area directly ahead of *Titanic*, was taken directly to the bridge and delivered into the hand of Captain Smith. The Captain appears to have had the position of the ice marked on the chart so that all of his officers would be aware of its presence.

A lifeboat drill for the passengers and crew had been scheduled for that Sunday morning, but it was Captain Smith's usual practice to hold a divine service every sabbath. The Captain, who also had to fit in a full tour of inspection of his ship that morning, decided that there was not the time available for all three, so the lifeboat drill went by the board. Clearly Smith considered the spiritual wellbeing of his passengers and crew to be of paramount importance. That the ships' boats were only capable of taking less than half of the people aboard the ship, and that the officers did not know how to effectively load and lower those lifeboats, probably had very little influence on the captain's decision. The service went off without a hitch and by about 11.15, with the singing of the hymn 'O God our help in ages past', it was all over, and with it went many of the passengers' and crew's chances of surviving the coming night.

At midday the ship's officers were assembled on the bridge with their sextants to take a sight on the sun and calculate the vessel's latitude. At the same time the massive ship's whistles were sounded and the engine room telegraphs were tested, in accordance with company rules. Captain Smith could adhere to company rules when it suited him.

In the wireless room shortly before 1.45pm another ice warning was received, this time from another White Star liner, *Baltic*, also eastbound from New York to Liverpool:

'Greek steamer *Athinai* reports passing icebergs and large quantities of field ice today in latitude 41°51'N, longitude 49°52'W. Wish you and *Titanic* all success. Commander.'

The second wireless operator, Bride, took this message directly to Captain Smith, who at the time was talking to J. Bruce Ismay, managing director of the White Star Line and Smith's employer. For some reason Smith handed the Marconi form to Ismay, who promptly put it into his pocket. After his conversation with Smith was concluded, Ismay showed the ice warning to several first class female passengers. He must have known that the contents of the message would be spread among the rest of the passengers by this 'jungle telegraph' more assuredly and quickly than if he had broadcast them through a loud hailer. He must also have known that the contents of the message would be distorted in the retelling and would inevitably cause a certain amount of consternation. From then onwards at least the first-class passengers would believe that anything unusual that occurred was occasioned by ice.

Captain Smith did not retrieve the message from *Baltic* until about 7.15 that evening and only then was the information it contained passed on to the rest of his officers and the position of the ice marked on the chart. Almost an hour and a half before Smith delivered the *Baltic* ice warning to the rest of his officers, Chief Officer Wilde, on the Captain's instructions, had the ship's course altered from 242 degrees to 265 degrees, directly towards where the ice mentioned would be later that night. At 6 o'clock, just 10 minutes after the course change, Wilde handed over control of the ship to Second Officer Lightoller and left the bridge.

At about 7.30pm, 15 minutes after the presence of icebergs directly ahead of the ship was made known to First Officer Murdoch, he ordered Lamp Trimmer Samuel Hemmings to secure the forward hatch covers. The light that usually escaped through the forward hatches would have seriously interfered with the crow's-nest lookouts' view forward through the darkness ahead of the ship. Clearly Mr Murdoch was fully aware that the ship was approaching an area where they could expect to meet a few icebergs. He was at least doing something to help the ship's lookouts see a berg in time for avoiding action to be taken. Murdoch also knew that he would be on the bridge himself from 10 o'clock and that then the safety of the ship and her passengers would be his responsibility. Knowing as he did that there was every chance of *Titanic* encountering an iceberg, Murdoch would have been fully justified in placing an extra lookout or two right in the bows of the ship where light pollution from the vessel would not adversely affect their view. Unfortunately he failed to do so. Placing extra lookouts in a ship's bows, the 'eyes of the ship', under the prevailing conditions would have been quite normal. Other vessels in the same area did take this simple precaution; all of them appear to have survived the night.

A quarter of an hour after Mr Murdoch had so completely demonstrated his knowledge that the ship was entering an area where ice was likely to be found, another wireless signal was received. This signal, the first as far as we know received from the Leyland Line's *Californian*, was not apparently directed at *Titanic* at all but was intended for another Leyland vessel, *Antillian*, Captain Lord's first command six years previously:

'To Captain *Antillian*. Six thirty pm, apparent ship's time. Latitude 42°3'N, Longitude 49°9'W. Three large bergs 5 miles to the southward of us. Regards. Lord.'

The watch officers on White Star vessels usually only spent 4 hours of their periods of duty actually on the bridge, effectively commanding the ship. Even during this time they would not usually make any alterations to the vessel's course or speed except in dire emergency, or on the direct orders of the captain. Just because an officer was not actually on watch duty did not mean that he was never on the bridge, just that he was not compelled to be there. The second wireless operator was later to claim that he took this message from *Californian* to the bridge and placed it in the hands of an officer there. The watch officer at the time was Mr Lightoller, but it seems that Mr Murdoch was also on the bridge. Neither of them recalled ever receiving this message. It seems probable that Harold Bride, instead of delivering the message, placed it on a spike for attention later. At the time the message was received Bride was busy with passenger traffic.

The message from *Californian* to *Antillian* is of some importance as it not only establishes the position of the *Californian* at 7.30pm on 14 April but also that of three icebergs. Allowing that Captain Lord's given position was fairly accurate, and he was noted as a good navigator, his ship was about 15 miles north of *Titanic* and about 85 miles ahead.

Despite Mr Bride's assurance that the message from *Californian* was delivered to the bridge, we can be sure that it was not immediately brought to the attention of Captain Smith. At 7.30pm the captain was in the a la Carte restaurant enjoying a dinner party given in his honour by the millionaire Mr George Widener and his wife. Also present at the dinner party were the Wideners' son Harry, US President Taft's advisor Major Archie Butt, the Carters and the Thayers. According to the received version of events, at this dinner party Captain Smith had nothing to drink of an alcoholic nature. While this might indeed be the case, it seems highly unlikely given the nature of such parties and Captain Smith's performance later that night. Wine would automatically have been served with the dinner, to be followed by port and brandy, accompanied by a good cigar to round things off. In any event Captain Smith did not leave the restaurant until about 5 minutes to 9 that evening.

There is some evidence to suggest that before the captain left the bridge to attend his dinner party he was visited by Joseph Bruce Ismay, Managing Director of the White Star Line, and Thomas Andrews, Managing Director of Harland & Wolff. The three men argued over the state of the starboard main engine, which was vibrating badly and in danger of shaking itself to pieces. The conversation was overheard by Second Officer Lightoller. If this really did happen it confirms that the starboard main engine was not operating efficiently and that Smith, Ismay and Andrews knew about it. As Ismay was later to deny that he had visited the bridge of the *Titanic* that evening, the story has to be viewed with a certain amount of caution, but it does fit in with what we already know about serious vibration affecting the ship.

In the meanwhile, at 7.30pm Second Officer Charles Lightoller took a stellar sight with his sextant. He then gave the readings to Fourth Officer Joseph Groves Boxhall, another noted navigator, to work out the ship's precise position. Boxhall did not actually mark the ship's position on the chart but left a note so that the Captain could do so when he next returned to the bridge, but that would not be for another hour and a half.

At about 8.30pm the Reverend E. C. Carter began a hymn-singing service in the second-class dining saloon. The event was well attended and more than 100 passengers sang along to the old favourites played on the piano. Later a couple of those passengers who had attended remembered one hymn in particular that they had sung that evening, 'Eternal Father strong to save'. Somewhat ironically the last line of the hymn is, 'O hear us when we cry to thee for those in peril on the sea'. Although those passengers did not know it, they were already in deadly peril, and it seems that God wasn't listening.

All evening the temperature had been falling steadily. Between 5.30 and 7.30pm the air temperature had fallen from 43° to 39°F (6° to 4°C) and it was still falling rapidly. The sea temperature was even more alarming and had already dropped to the freezing point of fresh water. Luckily seawater freezes at an even lower temperature than fresh water, but nevertheless ice crystals were beginning to form. By 8.40pm Lightoller was growing concerned that the fresh water in the ship's tanks and double bottom might be starting to freeze. The ship's carpenter, Mr J. Maxwell, was despatched to see to the fresh water tanks supplying drinking water and to instruct the ship's engineer, Mr Bell, to take steps to ensure that the supply of water for his boilers did not solidify. The ship's 29 boilers used only fresh water to make the steam that drove the engines and other machinery aboard. Once the steam had been used it was passed to the condensers where it was turned back into fresh water and returned to the tanks. Overall the system was very efficient, but fresh water was continuously being pumped into the boilers to replace that which had been converted into steam. If the boilers ever ran critically short of water they would explode, so it was important to keep a supply of water available at all times.

At about 8.55pm Captain Smith made his excuses and left the Wideners' party. He made his way to the bridge, where he found Second Officer Lightoller. The Captain and his watch officer found nothing better to talk about than the weather, which, as it was a perfectly still, flat calm, starlit night with no moon, somewhat limited the subject. Charles Lightoller later described the conversation.

'We commenced to speak about the weather. He [Captain Smith] said, 'There is not much wind.' I said, 'No, it is a flat calm.' As a matter of fact he repeated it, he said, 'A flat calm.' I said, 'Quite flat; there is no wind.' I said something about it was rather a pity the breeze had not kept up whilst we were going through the ice region. Of course my reason was obvious, he knew I meant the water ripples breaking on the base of the berg... We then discussed the indications of ice. I remember saying, 'In any case, there will be a certain amount of reflected light from the bergs.' He said, 'Oh yes, there will be a certain amount of reflected light.' I said or he said - it was said between us - that even though the blue side of the berg was towards us, probably the outline, the white outline, would give us sufficient warning, that we should be able to see it at a good distance and as far as we could see, we should be able to see it. Of course, it was just with regard to the possibility of the blue side being towards us, and if it did happen to be turned with the purely blue side towards us, there would still be white outline.'

If Mr Lightoller's description of the conversation between himself and Captain Smith is even vaguely accurate, one could be forgiven for believing that both men had been drinking heavily. There was no moon that night and no other light source in the vicinity apart from *Titanic* herself, so there could be no reflected light to betray the presence of an iceberg, no matter what side was turned towards them. The night was exceptionally clear and the sky was full of stars, so clear in fact that as stars set they appeared to be cut in two by the horizon. Unfortunately, although stars twinkle very prettily they do not give any appreciable illumination. Anyone who has ever been anywhere where there is no light pollution will know that in the complete darkness nothing at all is visible. You can literally hold your hand up in front of your eyes without seeing it.

The only chance those aboard *Titanic* had of seeing a berg, or anything else, in time to avoid it would have been when that object came between the watcher and a number of stars. They would never have actually seen an iceberg, but might have known there was one present because they could not see all of the stars. Even a couple of small clouds would have eliminated even that small possibility. Lookouts in the crow's-nest might spot a particularly dark patch of sky as a large berg first appeared above the horizon 10 or 12 miles from the ship. However, unless the berg was as high as the crow's-nest itself, as it came closer it would become invisible against the blackness of the sea as the lookouts looked down upon it. Only lookouts placed as low as possible in the ship would have a fair chance of seeing an iceberg under these conditions once it came within a few miles of the ship and, as we know, the officers on the *Titanic* had neglected to take any such precautions. Fortunately the passengers remained in ignorance of the conversation between Captain Smith and Second Officer Lightoller, and therefore in ignorance of the fact that their immediate fate lay in the hands of a pair of incompetents, and possibly drunken ones at that.

Captain Smith did not stay on the bridge for long and at about 9.20pm, after telling Lightoller to call him if things got at all 'doubtful', he decided to call it a day. Even though Smith had retired for the night he did not go to his cabin but instead decided to take a nap in the chartroom. That the captain felt the need for a lie down so early in the evening hints that he might have taken rather more to drink at the party than was perhaps good for him. What other explanation can there be? Unless he considered Mr Lightoller to be incapable of performing his duties as a watch officer, the captain had no possible reason to anticipate problems. All of the senior officers were master mariners in their own right and should have been equal to practically any emergency. In any event the captain was to prove almost useless, or worse, as the events of the night unfolded, and most of the responsibility for dealing with a series of disastrous events would indeed be dealt with by the senior officers. Unfortunately a couple of those officers would not handle their responsibilities at all well.

No sooner was Lightoller sure that the captain had really left than he decided to exercise his authority and showed for the first time some appreciation of the danger the ship was fast approaching. He ordered Sixth Officer Moody to convey a message to the crow's-nest, 'to keep a sharp lookout for ice; particularly small ice and growlers' until daylight (a growler is an iceberg that has partially melted to the point where it begins to roll over). Upon his return to the bridge Moody was questioned by Lightoller to ascertain whether or not he had passed on the message to the Second Officer's satisfaction. It seems he had failed to do so and was ordered by Lightoller to repeat the errand. This time Moody was not only to pass on the instructions to keep a sharp lookout, something the lookouts were employed to do anyway, but to pass the instruction on to the next pair of lookouts when they were relieved at 10 o'clock. Archie Jewell and George Symonds, the lookouts on duty at the time, probably thought their instructions were somewhat superfluous and perhaps even insulting. At the end of the day the ship's lookouts were professionals and were well aware that the safety of everyone aboard depended on them doing their job. That they took their responsibilities seriously is amply demonstrated by the fact that, for the vessel's short voyage from the builders to Southampton, the lookouts had been provided with binoculars, which was normal procedure, and that they had been asking for them ever since. As we know, it was usually the Second Officer's job to ensure that the lookouts had their binoculars, the same officer who issued the instructions for the lookouts to keep a special watch for ice on the evening of 14 April - the same Second Officer Lightoller who had neglected to issue binoculars to the lookouts when he had taken over Mr Blair's duties, despite continued requests. As the ship sped towards the waiting field of floating ice and bergs, the lookouts were still without their binoculars.

At 9.40pm another wireless message was received by the Marconi operators, Phillips and Bride:

'From *Mesaba* to *Titanic*. In latitude 42°N to 41°25', longitude 49°W to longitude 50°30'W, saw much heavy pack ice and great number large icebergs, also field ice, weather good, clear.'

According to later testimony from Second Wireless Operator Bride, he was asleep when this message was received. He added that Jack Phillips was extremely busy with passenger messages, although he never explained how he knew that when he was supposedly asleep. As we shall later see, Harold Sidney Bride was to testify to quite a lot of things that were obviously untrue, so much so that it is probably wise to view everything he said with suspicion. As Phillips did not survive to tell his own version of the story we are forced to rely on Bride's self-serving evidence. According to Bride, the senior operator, Phillips, instead of taking the ice warning to the bridge, simply stuck it on a metal spike and forgot about it. In any event the surviving officers all said that they never saw the *Mesaba* ice warning and that it never reached the bridge. The *Mesaba* warning clearly indicated the presence of a large amount of ice and a great many icebergs directly ahead of the ship, and not many miles away.

At 10 o'clock the watch changed. Mr Murdoch took over from Lightoller on the bridge. Up in the crow's-nest Jewell and Symonds were relieved by Frederick Fleet and Reginald Robertson Lee. Before leaving their post Jewell and Symonds passed on Mr Lightoller's instructions for Fleet and Lee to keep a special lookout for ice. The instructions had by this time become surplus to requirements as the lookouts had been able to smell icebergs for quite a while. As anyone who has ever come across icebergs that have travelled far enough south to have begun to melt will know, they smell of rotting vegetation and even animal matter. In the hundreds, possibly thousands, of years that the ice has formed part of a slowly moving glacier, all sorts of animal and vegetable matter has been picked up and frozen solid. As soon as the ice and what it contains begins to melt, all this organic matter starts to rot at an accelerated rate, creating a berg's unmistakable aroma. *Titanic's* lookouts had been close to icebergs before and consequently knew all too well what the smell meant.

Chapter 14

'Iceberg right ahead'

Up in the crow's-nest Fleet and Lee peered into the darkness ahead and to both sides of the ship for the icebergs they knew must be there. The 25mph icy wind caused by the ship's forward speed did nothing to help and made their eyes water continuously when they looked forward. Nevertheless they persisted, but they were sorely missing the binoculars that should have been available to them. Although binoculars were not much use for scanning large areas of sea and horizon they would at least have offered some eye protection from the wind. The almost total darkness did nothing to help either. The lookouts could see nothing at all except the thousands of stars above them.

Shortly before 10.30pm the lookouts spotted another ship, some little distance off, going in the opposite direction; it was the Furness Withy Line steamer *Rappahannock*. The lookouts rang the crow's-nest bell, then telephoned the bridge to report the presence of the other ship - there was a direct telephone link between the crow's-nest and the bridge. The lookouts on *Rappahannock* were also on the ball and had spotted *Titanic*, which would not have been difficult as the White Star liner was lit up like a floating Christmas tree. The acting master of the *Rappahannock*, Albert E. Smith (no relation of Captain E. J. Smith), had *Titanic* contacted by Morse lamp. 'Have just passed through heavy field ice and several icebergs.' Sea captains are still noted for their ironic wit. *Rappahannock's* master also explained that the steering gear of his vessel had been damaged by the passage through the ice. *Titanic* acknowledged the signal with one of her own: 'Message received. Thank you. Goodnight.' The two vessels carried on their respective courses. Those on the *Rappahannock* were to be the last to admit seeing the *Titanic* afloat, other than those actually aboard her. Yet even they were reluctant to do so. Just a couple of days after the loss of the liner the Furness Withy company sent a letter denying that they had any ships in the area close to *Titanic* when she sank.

One could be forgiven for thinking that the warning from *Rappahannock*, that there was field ice and icebergs very close by, might have resulted in a reduction in *Titanic's* speed, and perhaps the posting of a few extra lookouts. Instead, the liner seems to have accelerated. Passengers noticed that late on that Sunday night the ship's engines were running faster than at any other time in the voyage. Captain Smith's last words before leaving the bridge earlier that evening had been to the effect that he should be called if things became at all doubtful. The encounter with *Rappahannock* should have alerted Mr Murdoch to the fact that things had indeed become doubtful, and that the ship was about to enter a field of ice. Obviously Murdoch didn't attach too much importance to the *Rappahannock's* warning or that she had suffered damage, as he failed to act on the Captain's instructions.

Meanwhile, away to the north, the Leyland Line's *Californian* lay stopped. Although Captain Lord had left London for Boston in such a tearing hurry and had made his best possible speed for three-quarters of the trip to deliver his urgent cargo of pullovers and blankets, his sense of urgency seems to have evaporated. At about 10.15pm Captain Lord's lookouts reported 'ice blink' ahead. 'Ice blink', a sort of fluorescent glow, was an indication of field ice. Without waiting to see if there really was any ice about, Captain Lord had *Californian* stopped for the night, a reasonable precaution on the face of it, one might think. However, it was not normal practice for a ship to stop because of ice in the vicinity. In fact, it would be unusual for one to even slow down unless icebergs or growlers had been seen or reliably reported close by. Nobody on the *Californian* had actually seen any ice at all, merely the 'ice blink'. Nevertheless, it appears that Captain Lord was taking no chances. By stopping his vessel's engine and allowing the ship to drift, he had completely eliminated any chance of a serious collision. Ice and ship would all be moving in the same direction and at the same speed. Short of becoming the filling in an iceberg sandwich, a very unlikely occurrence, *Californian* was in no danger at all. That *Californian* had not even reached the ice before Captain Lord had taken his precautions to safeguard his ship was more than unusual when his cargo was supposedly so urgently required in Boston. By far the most likely reason for Captain Lord having stopped his ship is not the presence of ice at all, because there wasn't any where he was, but because he had reached the place towards which he had been hurrying.

Once his ship had stopped Captain Lord had his vessel's position ascertained. As previously mentioned it was a moonless clear night and the stars were clearly visible - perfect conditions for taking a star sight and working out exactly where they were. Captain Lord, it will be remembered, had a well-deserved reputation as a first-class navigator, so we can be fairly sure that the position he worked out was reasonably accurate. He knew exactly where he was and had done throughout the voyage, as had Captain Smith on the *Titanic*, thanks to Mr Boxhall.

Once he had ascertained his vessel's precise position Lord ordered his wireless operator, Cyril Evans, to alert other vessels in the vicinity that *Californian* was drifting and to give their position. Evans, as the ship's only wireless operator, had been on duty all day long and was looking forward to calling it a day at about 11.30pm. Nevertheless, although he would normally have switched off his equipment at about 11 o'clock, he set about carrying out the captain's instructions. At 10.55pm he called *Titanic* and, without waiting for a reply from the White Star liner, began to send his message. Harold Bride, *Titanic's* second operator, according to the evidence he gave later, was off duty despite the fact that earlier in the day the wireless equipment had broken down and consequently there was a large backlog of passenger traffic to deal with. Jack Phillips was dealing with the backlog on his own. As we know, Mr Bride's evidence is demonstrably inaccurate, so anything he said must be treated with suspicion. In this instance, judging by his later performance, it is entirely possible that the operator on duty aboard *Titanic* was none other that Bride himself.

In any event, Cyril Evans never managed to complete his message to *Titanic*. At the time the two ships were less than 30 miles apart, so *Californian's* signal came in so strongly that it almost deafened *Titanic's* operator, or so Bride said later. (How he would have known this unless it was him on the wireless at the time was not queried at either of the two major inquiries that came later.) Evans got as far as, 'We are stopped and surrounded by ice,' when *Titanic's* operator cut in with, 'Keep out! Shut up! You're jamming my signal. I'm working Cape Race.' Evans gave up and instead of passing on his warning he sat and listened to the signals being sent from *Titanic* to the powerful shore station at Cape Race. If anything, *Titanic's* wireless installation was more powerful than that on *Californian*, so how did Evans manage to listen in to the traffic without suffering the same sort of problems that had supposedly caused *Titanic's* operator to cut him off so abruptly? Evans listened in to *Titanic* until shortly before 11.30, when he decided to turn in for the night. He switched off his equipment and prepared for bed.

Although Evans had received no indication of it, events had been spiralling out of control aboard *Titanic* while he had been eavesdropping on the private passenger traffic coming from the liner. Describing conditions later, Fred Fleet said, 'It was the beautifullest night I ever seen. The stars were like lamps.' Lee also described conditions, saying it was a 'clear, starry night with haze extending more or less round the horizon, very cold.' At the inquiries to come, in an attempt to discredit the lookouts, Second Officer Charles Lightoller was adamant that there was no mist or haze that night, although he never explained how he knew that. He had left the bridge very shortly after 10 o'clock and had spent the better part of the time since then in the warmth of his cabin.

At about 11.15pm the senior lookout in *Titanic's* crow's-nest spotted an iceberg on the horizon, more than 10 miles ahead of the ship. Fred Fleet rang the crow's-nest bell to alert the officers on the bridge, then tried to telephone them, to tell what he had seen. Although the telephone appeared to be working normally, there was no reply from the bridge. Over the next few minutes he tried repeatedly to raise some sort of response from the officers on the bridge, without success. The lookouts tried to peer round the foremast and attract the officers' attention, but they could not see anyone on the bridge. Fleet began to suspect that there were no officers on the bridge at all and that the ship was charging blindly towards the berg. Realising that he had to get a message through somehow, and that if the ship struck a berg head-on the mast supporting the crow's-nest would in all probability go over the side of the ship into the sea, he made a decision. Although it was against orders, he instructed the junior lookout, Reginald Lee, to leave the crow's-nest and make his way to the bridge and report the ice in person. Lee had descended the mast before he realised that Fleet had sent him down as much for his own safety as anything else. Without further ado, and without carrying his message to the bridge, Lee went back to the crow's-nest. While this had been going on Fleet had continued trying to alert the bridge by ringing the crow's-nest bell and trying the telephone. In the forecastle crew-quarters fireman John Podesta was lying in his bunk. He heard the repeated ringing of the crow's-nest bell and several cries from the lookouts, 'Ice ahead, sir.' Only after Lee had returned to the crow's-nest did Fred Fleet have any luck. He rang the bell again and gave the telephone another try. This time Sixth Officer Moody answered the phone: 'Yes. What did you see?'

'Iceberg right ahead,' reported Fleet.

'Thank you,' replied the Sixth Officer and hung up.

Even as he was talking to Moody, Fleet noticed the ship's bows starting to swing to port, which made him believe that the berg had been seen from the bridge before his warning had got there. This would make perfect sense as by that time the berg, which had first been sighted more than 10 miles ahead of the ship, was now less than half a mile away.

On the bridge Mr Murdoch had supposedly been spending his time out on the open wing where he could see ahead more clearly than from inside. Perhaps that is why he never heard the telephone ring, but it does not explain why he failed to respond to the repeated ringing of the crow's-nest bell. If Podesta, inside the forecastle of the ship, could hear the bell and the lookouts' warning cries, then so should have Mr Murdoch on the open bridge wing. By far the most likely explanation for Fleet's inability to contact the bridge must be that he was right and that there was nobody there. It was a very cold night and it is quite possible that the officers had retired to the warmth of the chartroom for a spell. If that was indeed the case, then what happened immediately after their return makes sense as well. Had Murdoch really been on the open wing of the bridge he should have seen the berg, silhouetted against the stars, in plenty of time to take avoiding action. Instead, immediately on his return to the bridge and seeing the berg ahead, Murdoch ordered the helm, 'Hard a-starboard' and the engines put full astern.

A more lethal combination of orders is difficult to imagine. However, Murdoch's orders would not have taken effect immediately. Down in the engine room the steam to the engines would first have to be shut off. The engines would have to be stopped and the changeover valves operated to send the exhaust steam directly to the condensers instead of the turbine engine. Then the main engines could be restarted in reverse. This would all have taken only a matter of seconds rather that minutes, but they were seconds that the ship did not have. With her engines at full ahead, *Titanic*, running at 20 knots, could turn through 90 degrees in about 800 feet. Mr Murdoch had at least three times that distance, even at this late stage, to avoid a collision. However, with the ship's engines either stopped or going astern the thrust from the central propeller was no longer magnifying the effect of the rudder, and the vessel's manoeuvrability was drastically reduced. Clearly Mr Murdoch did not have time to think and had issued his orders in panic.

Even so, the ship almost managed to miss the ice as she swung away to the south and, if later evidence is to be believed, might actually have done so. In any event the White Star liner was not badly damaged and was still quite capable of manoeuvring under her own power. At the very worst a couple of seams in the hull plating had been sprung open to create what amounted to a 300-foot-long slit, just half an inch wide, along the vessel's starboard side. In effect, *Titanic* had a 12-square-foot hole in her hull below the waterline. In the *Hawke* incident a hole at last five times that size had been torn in the side of *Olympic* without even threatening to sink her. The 'Olympic' class ships were fitted with no fewer than 83 high-pressure pumps for clearing water from within the hull, but above the double bottom, ranging in size from 3 to 18 inches in diameter. With the 215lb per square inch of steam pressure at which the ship's boilers operated to drive them, the pumps should have been easily able to deal with a 12-square-foot hole in the outer plating - that is providing that the majority of the pumps could have been brought into play.

The supposed slit in the ship's side was something in the order of at least 300 feet long, so it must have extended through at least five compartments, more likely six. With six compartments open to the sea, the vessel could not remain afloat without relying on the pumps. Under those circumstances the watertight doors would be left open to allow the incoming water to spread throughout the full length of the ship, allowing all of the pumps to be used. Allowing the water to flood the whole of the ship rather than remain trapped in just the forward five or six compartments would also mean that the bows of the vessel did not fill so quickly and drag the ship down. In the received version of events the watertight doors were not opened and the ships bows were dragged under by the weight of the water trapped in them. Mr Murdoch, the senior officer on the bridge at the time of the encounter with the iceberg, closed the watertight doors throughout the ship immediately after giving his disastrous 'Hard a-starboard' order. Now we must assume that Mr Murdoch, as a professional seaman holding all of the necessary qualifications to act as commander, and having previously served aboard another of the 'Olympic' class ships, would be familiar with their specifications and capabilities. As we already know, the manager of Harland & Wolff, Thomas Andrews, was also aboard the ship. Andrews had overseen the design of the vessel and would certainly have known what to do to increase the time that the ship could stay afloat, no matter how seriously she was damaged. Closing the watertight doors immediately before or after a collision is the natural thing to do, even though in this case it was the wrong action. The question is, why were the watertight doors not opened again as soon as it was discovered that so many compartments had been opened to the sea, even though the hole in the ship's hull was not large enough to admit massive quantities of water immediately, particularly when Andrews was made aware of the extent and nature of the damage sustained? No matter how seriously damaged the ship was, as long as the damage extended over more than four or five compartments, it could always survive for longer with all of the pumps operating than without them. This is simple common sense. It therefore follows that the ship, if more than four or five compartments (depending on where they were located) were open to the sea, could remain afloat longer with her watertight doors open than if they were closed.

There is, and has long been, a standard procedure for carrying out the planned scuttling of a ship. Simply opening the sea cocks does not guarantee that a vessel will founder, and if it does then the sinking will be uncontrolled after the sea cocks are submerged. The accepted method is usually to open the sea cocks but to also reverse the non-return valves in the ship's pumps so that instead of pumping water out they pump it in. This was the method used by the captured German High Seas fleet when its crews scuttled their ships in Scapa Flow after the Great War. Using this method the sinking is at least under some sort of control and can be accelerated or slowed by turning the pumps off or on. If some of *Titanic's* pumps had been set to scuttle the ship, that might account for Captain Smith's reluctance to have them started when a real catastrophe overtook his vessel, as we shall see.

To return to events immediately after the collision - if there really was a collision - for a few moments the engines seem to have been stopped, but then they were run forwards and backwards for some little time, at low and relatively high speed. The engines were first put astern by Murdoch in his attempt to avoid the iceberg. This on its own is quite enough to have created the illusion of a collision as the ship was moving forward at high speed at the time. It would have caused the propellers to lose their grip on the water and to 'cavitate', as it is known, setting up an enormous vibration felt throughout the vessel. This massive vibration is exactly what was reported by nearly all of those aboard who later gave evidence. They did not mention any sort of crash or massive shock running through the ship. In fact, the collision was hardly felt by most of the people on the liner; all they felt was the vibration that would automatically have occurred when the engines were suddenly put full astern. We will examine the so-called collision and its effects in some detail in the next chapter.

Immediately after the alarm and Mr Murdoch's avoiding action, Captain Smith seems to have reappeared on the bridge. He asked Murdoch what was going on and the First Officer told him that they had struck an iceberg. There is no eye-witness evidence as to what orders Captain Smith gave at this juncture, although the helmsman, Quartermaster Robert Hitchens, and Quartermaster Alfred Olliver, who were on hand to take over the wheel or act as messenger should either be required, both survived. However, we do know that a series of orders from the bridge reached the engine room via the engine room telegraph, hardly something that could have happened without everyone on the bridge knowing about it.

After the ship had been stationary for a few minutes the engine room telegraph rang for 'Half Ahead'. Then, a short while later the engines were stopped again. Next came the order for 'Slow Astern', which lasted for about 2 minutes before the vessel was again halted. According to Greaser Frederick Scott, who was on duty in the engine room, this was really the time that the watertight doors were closed, about 3 minutes after the seemingly insignificant collision. About a quarter of an hour later the engines were put 'Slow Ahead' yet again for a while before stopping, then going astern for another 5 minutes. Eventually the engines were finally stopped according to Trimmer Robert Patrick (Paddy) Dillon, who was also on duty in the engine room. However, there is some evidence to show that after Dillon's departure from the engine room the vessel was again run 'Slow Ahead' for some time. There has never been a satisfactory reason given for this running of the main engines to and fro following the accident, but we should remember that there was absolutely nothing wrong with the ship's propulsion system. If another vessel was to be seen, there was nothing to stop the liner from moving towards it. Obviously, if the *Titanic* was seriously damaged, another vessel close by would reassure passengers and offer sanctuary should the worst happen. Perhaps those controlling the liner's movements in the period immediately after the accident believed they were doing just that.

Chapter 15

'A slight jar'

In the received version of events surrounding the loss of the *Titanic* it is usually believed that in a freak accident the vessel struck an iceberg and sank 2 hours and 40 minutes later with the loss of more than 1,500 lives. Unfortunately that scenario does not fit in with the known facts or the eye-witness evidence of the disaster.

As *Titanic* swung to port in answer to Mr Murdoch's order she supposedly scraped along a ledge of ice protruding from the berg, below the waterline, springing rivets and opening seams along something like 500 feet of her hull. Although *Titanic* was a big ship, even by modern standards, she was nothing like the size and weight of a large iceberg.

The iceberg seen by the ship's lookouts, Fred Fleet and Reginald Lee, was large enough to tower over the foredeck of the ship. As that deck was about 50 feet above the water, we can safely assume that the iceberg was considerably taller than that, say 60 to 65 feet high at least. One witness, Colonel Archibald Gracie, described the iceberg as towering more than 100 feet above *Titanic's* A Deck, which would make the berg more than 160 feet high. Quartermaster Rowe, on duty on the liner's poop deck, also saw the iceberg and described it as being 100 feet tall. The iceberg was later described as looking something like the Rock of Gibraltar, so even the most conservative of estimates must put its weight at somewhere around half a million tons or more, ten times the weight of the ship. Even at better than 20 knots *Titanic* was not going to push this iceberg out of the way. She would just bounce off it, like a tennis ball off a wall. The change in direction of the ship's travel would necessarily have been violent and practically instant.

Any almost instantaneous change in the ship's course would have been noticed by all aboard. Most of those in the forward part of the ship, closest to the point of impact and therefore closest to the point of greatest deflection, would have felt a severe shock to the extent that they would have been thrown off their feet. Articles on tables would have fallen off as they tried to continue along the vessel's previous heading. Newton's first law of motion states:

'A body resists changes in its state of motion - a body at rest tends to remain at rest unless acted upon by an external force, and a body in motion tends to remain in motion at the same velocity unless acted upon by an external force. This property is known as INERTIA.'

Newton's laws do not change to suit the *Titanic* or anything else; they are constant throughout the universe. Practically all so-called studies of the disaster that befell the vessel we know as the *Titanic* ignore these immutable laws of nature because they do not happen to fit in with the theories being put forward. As the very much larger body in motion, the iceberg would automatically have been less disturbed by the collision, if it really happened, than the smaller ship. The iceberg was moving in a roughly southerly direction at something like 2 knots, under the influence of the Labrador current. *Titanic* was heading roughly westwards at about 22 knots, so one would expect any collision to be more than just noticeable to anybody on the ship.

Fred Fleet and Reginald Lee, the lookouts in the crow's-nest who had seen and tried so desperately to warn the officers on the bridge of the presence of the iceberg, watched closely as the ship reached it. They thought that the ship had just missed the ice. Fred Fleet noticed no impact at all, just a slight grinding noise lasting 'a matter of a few seconds'. The lookout said later, 'I thought it was a narrow shave.' The lookouts, the two witnesses in the best position to see what was going on, were so unimpressed by the event that they settled down to continue their watch. They continued to peer into the darkness around the ship but could see nothing at all. The iceberg had passed astern and was no longer visible. Even though we now know that there were other ships in the immediate vicinity, they could not be seen from *Titanic*. So intent had they been on watching the iceberg as the ship passed close alongside it that they didn't notice tons of ice cascade from it onto the liner's forward well deck, which is what the received version of the collision would have us believe. The lookouts didn't see the ice fall from the berg onto the ship for the simple reason that it did not happen.

For ice to have fallen onto *Titanic's* well deck, the berg would have had to have hung over it. In that case, as the ship passed close alongside it, the overhanging ice must have struck the ship's starboard bridge wing, which protruded a few feet from the superstructure. The iceberg must also have crushed the forward starboard boat, which was kept swung out when the ship was at sea. There is no evidence to suggest that the bridge suffered any damage in the incident, and the forward starboard boat was certainly all right because it was used later that night. By far the most likely source of the ice that found its way onto the well deck is the ship's own rigging and wireless aerial. The vibration set up by the engines suddenly going full astern could easily have shaken ice from the rigging. It will be remembered that it was an extremely cold night, so ice might well have formed on the wireless antennae. This formation of ice on a ship's rigging and superstructure has long been a problem for vessels operating in both northern and southern latitudes. Any number of ships have been capsized by the weight of ice that has built up on them in the colder reaches of the North and South seas, and even occasionally in harbour. A similar problem besets aircraft at high altitude, and a number have been lost simply because the accumulated ice became to great a burden for them to carry.

To return to the curious lack of any noticeable impact when *Titanic* supposedly struck the iceberg, in the wireless cabin, just behind the bridge, Second Wireless Operator Harold Bride didn't notice any impact at all and was hardly aware that anything had happened. First-class passenger Jack Thayer said, 'If I had a brimful glass of water in my hand not a drop would have been spilled.' Another first-class passenger, the wife of John Jacob Astor, the wealthiest man aboard, was so unimpressed that she thought there had merely been some sort of accident in the kitchen. Joseph Bruce Ismay thought the ship had lost a propeller blade (something that White Star ships seem to have been prone to). In the first class smoking room on A Deck US presidential advisor Archie Butt, Hokan Bjornston Steffanson, Spencer V. Silverthorne, Lucien P. Smith, Hugh Woolner and Clarence Moore hardly noticed anything. Woolner described '...a sort of stopping, a sort of - not exactly shock, but a sort of slowing down. [The ship's engines had just gone full astern.] Then we sort of felt a rip that gave a sort of slight twist to the whole room.'

First-class passengers William T. Stead and Father Byles were strolling on deck at the time but didn't think anything serious had happened. Mrs Dickinson Bishop, in first class, slept through the whole thing. Steward Alfred Crawford, on duty at the forward end of B Deck, where any impact might have been felt, heard a slight 'crunch' on the starboard side. Quartermaster George Rowe, right at the rear end of the ship, noticed a 'slight jar'. He looked towards the starboard side of the ship and saw a large berg, arguing that either the stern of the ship was still in contact with the ice or that only the stern had struck.

Seamen Brice, Buley and Osman were in the mess on the port side of the forecastle on C Deck. Buley noticed '...a slight jar. It seemed as though something was rubbing alongside of her at the time.' Brice described something that 'was like a heavy vibration'. Fireman Jack Podesta described the noise of the collision as 'like tearing a strip of calico, nothing more'. First class passenger Mrs E. D. Appleton used exactly the same words as Podesta to describe her experience of the accident. Able Seaman Joseph

Scarrott merely felt a kind of tremor as if the ship's engines had been put astern, which of course they had. He didn't think the ship had struck anything. Most of the seamen mentioned were right in the bows of the ship when the accident occurred and should have felt strongly anything that happened; they obviously felt nothing to alarm them. The vast majority of the people aboard who later had anything to say about the event told similar stories. The crash, if they noticed a crash at all, was so slight as to be negligible. All that most of them reported feeling was the vibration caused by the engines going astern.

However, there were a few people who described something more serious. In the firemen's quarters in D Deck some of the men were preparing to go on duty at midnight. John Thompson described how he '...felt the crash with all its force up there in the eyes of the ship, and my mates and I were all thrown sprawling from our bunks. It was a harsh grinding sound.'

Curiously, on the deck immediately below the firemen's quarters 24 coal trimmers had their cabin space. The collision was felt here but nothing like as violently as it appeared to have been on the deck above. The trimmers knew that the ship had struck something but they didn't know what. Lamp Trimmer Samuel Hemmings did notice a peculiar hissing sound very shortly after the accident. He investigated and discovered the noise was air escaping from the forepeak water tank as it filled from below. The forepeak water tank was situated low down in the bow of the ship and had been seemingly opened to the sea by the collision. This tells us that the ship had struck whatever had been in her way practically head-on and had not caught it a glancing blow at all. The forepeak tank was about 100 feet further forward than the point of impact suggested by Fred Fleet.

Aft of the trimmers' quarters the ordinary seamen were housed. Lookout Archie Jewell and Seaman Fred Clench were both awakened by the collision. Clench described his experience, '...by the crunching and jarring, as if it was hitting up against something...' Jewell, it appears, leapt out of bed and rushed up on deck without taking time to even put on his shoes. Once there he saw the ice that had fallen onto the forward well deck, but he did not see an iceberg.

In cabin 50 on E Deck Mr and Mrs George A. Harder noticed a scraping noise as the ship struck. They also felt the vessel vibrate, but that was probably just the effect of the engines going astern. James R. McGough also heard the scraping noise, and as he already had his porthole open he took a look out; he saw what he took to be an iceberg passing alongside the ship. Luigi Gatti's secretary, Paul Mauge, slept through the entire event, as did

John Edward Hart. In the stewards' quarters Samuel Rule, a bathroom steward, also slept through the collision but was woken up by the engines stopping. Steward Frederick Dent Ray was woken by the accident but thought something had gone wrong in the engine room. Alfred Pierce, Third Class Pantryman, was standing outside the pantry on F Deck when the ship struck. He thought the collision was nothing to speak of.

The great majority of the evidence regarding the severity of the collision from those who were present seems to point towards a very minor sort of a bump, certainly not a large ship striking an effectively immovable object such as a massive iceberg. This impression of a minor accident is reinforced by an examination of the ship's structure in the areas that supposedly came into contact with the ice.

In spite of the so-called evidence uncovered in recent years, the 'Olympic' class ships were quite sturdily constructed. The frames supporting the 1-inch-thick hull plating were made out of 10-inch steel channel. Forward, where the point of impact is assumed to have been, these frames were spaced at regular intervals, only 2 feet apart. The plating was doubled to reinforce the bow so that small ice would simply be pushed aside. Throughout the centre section of the vessel the space between the frames was extended to 3 feet but reduced to 2ft 3in towards the stern. All joints in the framing, including those where the deck beams joined them, were reinforced with steel plates known as 'knees'. All joints in the hull plating were double, triple or even quadruple riveted, about 3,000,000 rivets (the largest being 1¼ inches in diameter) going into the construction of each vessel; the rivets alone weighed more than 265 tons. The 6-foot-wide hull plates overlapped one another by at least 6 inches along all of the horizontal joints. The ships were immensely strong.

Fireman John Thompson, who you will remember was sent sprawling from his bunk and heard a harsh grinding sound when the accident occurred, got dressed. Shortly afterwards Leading Fireman William Small came into the cabin and ordered, 'All hands below.' Thompson and his colleagues would normally have gone down the forward spiral staircase and through the firemen's tunnel beneath the forward holds to reach the boiler rooms, but that wasn't possible on this occasion because the bottom of the stairwell and the firemen's passageway were flooded. It will be recalled that this stairwell and passageway were considered to be vitally important to the safety of the ship by her designers and were therefore fitted with their own watertight doors and pumps. If they were flooding, it is certain that the damage inflicted on the vessel extended inboard to a depth of no less than 15 feet, something we will return to later when we attempt to analyse what we know. Instead of using their stairs and passageway, the firemen went up on to the main deck to use an alternative route to the boiler rooms. No sooner were they there than their Leading Fireman ordered them back to their quarters to collect their life jackets and proceed to the boat deck. Following orders, they eventually arrived on the boat deck where they were stopped by the Chief Officer, Mr Wilde. Wilde asked them 'What the hell' they were doing and ordered them below. All of this toing and froing must have taken 10 minutes at least, so these men would not have reached the boiler rooms before about 11.55pm. According to the received version of events aboard the liner, the order to draw (extinguish) the boiler fires was given immediately after the collision, but this, given the obvious confusion aboard, seems unlikely. It is even more unlikely that the order was carried out immediately, as it seems that half the firemen who would have done the job were running about on deck and therefore not at their posts.

We do have an eye-witness to at least some of the damage done to the ship during the collision. Down in No 6 boiler room (the most forward), Fireman Fred Barrett had been working. He had just stopped for a break and a chat to Second Engineer James Hesketh when all at once the alarm bell rang and the red warning light came on, he later testified. This evidence must give pause for thought as there was no alarm bell fitted in the boiler room. Hesketh and Barrett supposedly both shouted 'Shut the doors!', meaning the doors on the furnaces. Then came the crash and a jet of water burst in through the side of the ship about 2 feet above the boiler room floor. As already mentioned, Fred Barrett's evidence needs to be treated with caution. His version of events so far was contradicted by another witness, Fireman George Beauchamp. Beauchamp testified that water did not enter the stokehold through the side of the ship but came in through the coal bunker door, meaning that the bunker was flooding and the stokehold was otherwise intact. Beauchamp's exact words were, 'Water entered No 10 stokehold through the bunker door.' This leaves us with a minor problem, as No 10 stokehold was at the after end of the forward boiler room - No 11 stokehold was closer to the bow. The half-inch slit in the side of the ship obviously was not there.

As the watertight doors began to close Barrett and Hesketh did the sensible thing and rushed through into the next boiler room aft, No 5. According to Barrett, the damage he saw extended the full length of the forward boiler room and about 2 feet into the bunker at the forward end of boiler room No 5. In reality it would appear that the hull plating of the ship was breached somewhere about the junction of the two forward boiler rooms, a single hole at that point. Already we see evidence that the damage to the liner was not a long slit or a seam between hull plates forced open by continuous contact with the ice but a series of punctures. In any event, Barrett didn't hang about to find out but hurried up the emergency escape ladder to the deck above. He then, he said, went to the hatch above No 6 boiler room and looked down to see how much water was in there. He estimated there to be about 8 feet of water in the forward boiler room by this time. He said, 'I went to No 5 fire room when the lights went out. I was sent to find lamps, as the lights were out, and when we got the lamps we looked at the boilers and there was no water in them. [Boilers that run out of water while the furnaces are still alight explode.] I ran to the engineer and he told me to get some firemen down to draw the fires. I got 15 men down below.' As usual there is evidence to contradict what Barrett had to say. Coal Trimmer George Cavell, who was working in the starboard bunker in No 4 boiler room, testified that the lights went out almost immediately after the collision.

Again according to Fred Barrett, the forward bunker in No 5 boiler room contained the water coming in through the ship's side for some while. Eventually the bunker, which had never been intended to hold water in the first place, gave way. Barrett 'saw a wave of green foam come tearing through the boilers.' True to form, Barrett quickly made his escape up the emergency ladder. By this time more than an hour had elapsed since the collision. Again Barrett's evidence needs to be treated with caution. It appears that water had been coming into No 5 boiler room for some time and that Junior Second Engineers Jonathan Shepherd and Herbert Harvey had managed to start the pumps there. The engineers had already ordered most of the firemen out of the boiler room as, once the fires were drawn, there was nothing further they could do. They were keeping pace with the incoming water and the boiler room was relatively dry up until the time the bunker collapsed. Shepherd had broken a leg and was laid in a pump house at the after end of the boiler room. Barrett said that Harvey ordered him out of the boiler room when the bunker failed, although we only have his word for that - but he can hardly be blamed for having a well-developed instinct for self-preservation. Unlike some of the so-called heroes of the *Titanic*, Fred Barrett never made himself out to be a hero at the expense of those who really were. He told how Harvey, as soon as the water came pouring into the boiler room, made straight for the fallen Shepherd in a valiant attempt to save him. He failed and both engineers died. Had Barrett stayed to help then it is all but certain that he would have merely added his own name to those of the lost.

From what we already know it is apparent that, whatever the vessel had struck, there was no continuous damage along her side and that what damage there was extended at least 15 feet into the interior of the ship, and that most of the people aboard were practically unaware that the liner had struck anything at all. Are we looking at iceberg damage? It doesn't seem so. We will look at the discrepancies in the next chapter and perhaps come up with an explanation that comes closer to fitting in with what the eye-witnesses reported.

Chapter 16

What had *Titanic* hit?

From what we already know it is apparent that whatever the liner had run into she had first struck it with the knife edge of the bow, or somewhere very close to it, or the forepeak tank could not have been damaged. The 10-inch-thick frames of the ship at the very front of the vessel were set just 2 feet apart and covered with 1-inch steel plating, much of it doubled in thickness. The detailed description of the ship appearing in the Report produced by the official British Inquiry into the disaster states quite clearly that the framing and plating at the forward part of the ship was specially reinforced to prevent damage when meeting thin ice. The watertight bulkheads were also specially stiffened and strengthened to stop them buckling in the event of a collision, thus reinforcing the side frames and plating of the ship. It would obviously have taken a considerable impact, a great deal of force, to have breached the hull anywhere close to the bow. There seems to be little or nothing in the eye-witness accounts to suggest that any such impact ever took place.

If we move slightly further aft to where the lookouts thought that the ship might have gently bumped the iceberg, we find that something penetrated the hull to a depth of at least 15 feet and breached the vitally important firemen's passageway beneath the two forward holds. This, it will be recalled, was flooded and impassable very shortly after the collision took place. While an iceberg might be quite tough, it is nothing like as hard as steel. An iceberg is essentially a 'blunt instrument', a club rather than a knife. These floating mountains of ice do have projecting spurs and ledges, but any one of these coming into contact with a liner's heavy steel hull plating and massive frames would be quickly snapped or ground away. Only a solid piece of ice could have penetrated so deeply into the interior of *Titanic*. At its very best such a solid projection on the berg could not have had a cutting edge of anything less than 90 degrees, a right-angle, or it simply would not have been strong enough to survive the initial impact. If anything even remotely that shape had in fact penetrated the hull to a depth of 15 feet or more, it must have quickly torn a hole at least 30 feet across in the hull plating and destroyed no fewer than ten of the ship's massive steel frames. Obviously anything smashing its way through about 250 square feet of hull plating, at least ten of the frames and tearing aside at least 900 square feet of steel deck, would have been quite noticeable. Once again we have little or no evidence to support any sort of collision that could have caused this kind of extensive structural damage.

We move further aft, to the forward boiler room where Fred Barrett said he saw a 'jet' of water enter the ship about 2 feet above the floor. He did not describe a wall of water suddenly flooding the boiler room, which is what we would expect had the steel plating and the frames along the side of the ship been crushed by a huge piece of ice. The reverse appears to have been the case, as Barrett and the junior engineer he was talking to at the time, Hesketh, had time to escape from the boiler room through the door in the watertight bulkhead. Nor did Barrett mention any pulverised ice entering the vessel, which must have happened as pieces broke away from the iceberg and were carried inside the ship by the inrushing water. The only indication we have of any great amount of water entering the forward boiler rooms was when the bunker between boiler rooms Nos 5 and 6 collapsed, when engineers Shepherd and Harvey were engulfed. The engineers had managed to start the pumps in that boiler room and were keeping ahead of the incoming water until the bunker collapsed, which tells us that the boiler room itself was almost undamaged, and that some considerable time had elapsed before the bunker failed. It is therefore reasonable to assume that the bunker itself was not extensively damaged in the collision. Had a large hole been torn in it to admit the sea, it would have filled and collapsed quite quickly. If it had filled with water without failing straight away there is no apparent reason why it should fail later. No 5 boiler room is supposedly as far aft as the damage extended. At no point in our brief examination of the eyewitness reports have we seen any indication of the catastrophic damage we would expect had the vessel collided with a large iceberg.

The United States Hydrographic Office calculated the amount of force required to have inflicted the damage to the ship as described at the time. To have opened a half-inch slit over a length of some 350 to 500 feet in the vessel's side, about 1,173,200 foot tons of energy would have been required, enough to physically throw the whole ship 20 feet sideways. This amount of energy is comparable to the liner being struck by a full broadside from a contemporary battleship. *Yet hardly anybody noticed!*

Either the eye-witnesses were all mistaken, in which case we have to believe that nothing else they had to say was reliable, and that there is then no way to discover what really happened to the ship, or the collision with an iceberg that has long been the accepted version of events never really took place. It seems unlikely that hundreds of people who witnessed the same event and who told substantially the same story were all inaccurate, and as they continued to tell the same tale throughout their lives it is equally unlikely that they were all lying. Is it then possible that the lookout, Fred Fleet, was right when he thought that the ship had just missed the iceberg?

Quite clearly the ship struck something, but if not an iceberg what might it have been? A small piece of ice would have been pushed aside by the liner's reinforced bow. A growler, an iceberg that has partially melted to the point where it begins to roll over, is without doubt a possibility. Growlers can be quite substantial and are as dangerous as the icebergs themselves, if not more so. A growler that has rolled relatively recently has mostly waterlogged ice showing above the surface of the sea, ice that does not reflect light and appears black at first glance. However, if the ship had struck a large growler the effect aboard, felt by the passengers and crew, would have been similar to her striking an iceberg. The same applies to the damage forward where the firemen's passageway was opened to the sea. A large hole would have been torn in the ship's side. As we know, there is no evidence of such a hole apparent on the wreck so the indications are still that the vessel struck something else.

There was very little in the way of an impact felt by those aboard *Titanic*, so whatever she struck was relatively small and easily pushed away or under the ship. It must have been pretty hard to have punched a hole though the liner's hull to a depth of at least 15 feet to breach the firemen's passageway without breaking off prematurely. The odds are stacked against it having been a finger of ice that had punctured the firemen's passageway, for two reasons. The first reason is that a finger of ice would have been snapped off the main body of the iceberg before it ever penetrated as far as the passageway, or it would have been strong enough to have torn a huge hole in the liner's hull as she slid past the iceberg at more than 25mph. There is no evidence to suggest that any such hole was ripped in the hull plating of the ship there, or anywhere else. Nor is there any evidence of ice within the hull of the vessel in the compartment at the forward end of the passageway, as there must have been if a finger of ice had punched its way into the ship and broken off. In fact, there is not a single piece of evidence from any survivor to suggest that there was any ice at all anywhere in the interior of the liner. As previously mentioned, had the vessel's hull been seriously damaged below the waterline by ice, particles of that ice would inevitably have been carried into the ship by the incoming water. So where was this ice? Clearly, nobody saw any evidence of it whatsoever. The only evidence of ice aboard *Titanic* is that found on the forward well deck shortly after the engines had been suddenly put full astern from full ahead at the time of the accident. This ice, in all probability, came from the liner's own rigging and wireless antennae, shaken free by the heavy vibration caused by the vessel's engines going into reverse. After any examination of the evidence it should be apparent that the ship did not strike an iceberg at all, but something much smaller, lighter and harder. By far the most likely candidate must be another ship, perhaps even a submerged wreck.

As it turns out there is evidence to suggest that the *Titanic* struck another ship, although that evidence was not brought out in any detail at either the British or American Inquiries. Able Seaman Edward Buley, making his first voyage as a merchant seaman after serving for 13 years in the Royal Navy, said that he saw another ship close by at the time of the collision.

'There was a ship of some description there when she struck [when the liner supposedly hit the iceberg] and she passed right by us... You could see she was a steamer. She had her steamer lights burning. She was off our port bow when we struck...'

Soon after the collision first class passenger Mrs Marion Thayer made her way up onto the boat deck. She described what she saw:

'While still on the boat deck I saw what appeared to be the hull of a ship, heading in the opposite direction to our ship, and quite near us, from which rockets were being sent up. The vessel (about a mile off by this time) was half the size of the *Cedric* and higher out of the water at her bow than the *Carpathia*.'

Cedric was another White Star vessel of 21,000grt that had entered service nine years earlier. *Carpathia* was the 13,603grt vessel that picked up the vast majority of the survivors from the stricken liner the following morning. Mrs Thayer also said:

'Upon looking over the side of the vessel [*Titanic*] I saw what looked like a number of long black ribs, apparently floating nearly level with the surface of the water. Parallel with each other but separated from each other by a few feet of water. These long black objects were parallel with the side of the ship.'

It was a moonless night, so whatever Mrs Thayer saw was very close alongside *Titanic*, within the area illuminated by the liner's own lights. She had seen a ship with its bows high out of the water and therefore down by the stern, firing rockets. Edward Buley had seen a ship close by. Mrs Thayer had also seen what appears to have been wreckage floating alongside the liner, wreckage that according to all the available evidence did not come from the *Titanic* herself. The conclusion is inescapable. *Titanic* had struck another ship. Unfortunately we do not know just what other vessel was involved in the accident, but the area around the Newfoundland Grand Banks, where the incident occurred, was regularly frequented by ships illegally hunting for seals. These seal poachers did not advertise their presence for fear of encountering the British and American warships policing the area. If such a vessel had seen a ship approaching at high speed, as *Titanic* was doing, it is not beyond the bounds of possibility that she would have put out all of her lights and attempted to hide behind a large iceberg. There would have been no way that *Titanic's* lookouts, Fleet and Lee, could have seen such a ship in time to avoid a collision. It would have been doubtful that they would have seen such a vessel at all, even when the liner ran it down, if their attention had been distracted by a huge iceberg close alongside.

Is it possible that a relatively small hull breach reaching more than 15 feet into the interior of the liner could have been caused by her brushing alongside the rear end of another ship? The answer has to be yes. *Titanic* herself had more than 80 feet of propeller shaft, driving each of her two wing propellers, outside her main hull, so it must have been possible for even a much shorter exposed shaft on a smaller vessel to have been driven into the liner's vitals, like a stiletto. Such a scenario has one massive advantage over the received version of the accident that sank the *Titanic* inasmuch as it is not utterly impossible. Neither does it contradict any survivor testimony or other evidence. Another ship scraping along the side of the *Titanic* would have had a very similar effect on the liner's hull plating as an iceberg except that no ice would have been carried into the liner by the inrushing water. It is even possible that this other vessel survived the encounter, although somewhat battered. Curiously, the steamer *Rappahannock* did pass close to *Titanic* on the evening of 14 April, and did suffer from damage to her rear end, although her owners later denied having any vessels in the vicinity when the liner foundered. Not that *Rappahannock* was in any way involved in the sinking of the *Titanic*, but her presence in the immediate vicinity, and her owner's denial, does illustrate the difficulties encountered in trying to identify a mystery ship.

According to the received version of events aboard the stricken liner, Captain Smith ordered the fires in the forward boiler rooms to be extinguished within a very few minutes of the collision, which was a usual and sensible precaution. Cold water reaching hot boilers could easily cause a major explosion. Passengers on deck, however, recalled a tremendous roaring sound as the ship's boilers vented steam through the funnels. This noise, which made conversation on deck difficult if not impossible, continued for some considerable time. The senior wireless operator, Jack Phillips, asked the captain if the noise of the venting steam could be reduced as he could not hear what was coming through his headphones because of it. As the Captain did not visit the wireless cabin until about 12.15am, we can be fairly sure that the steam was still being vented then, indicating that the fires were still alight and the boilers producing steam.

Captain Smith did not order his ship's pumps to be started until about 12.25am, about 43 minutes after the damage to the ship had occurred and much too late for them to have any real expectation of prolonging the vessel's life. By that time most of the forward pumps were completely submerged and unreachable, so that they could not be started in any case. This delay in starting the pumps begs the question, 'Why?' The pumps should obviously have been started the instant the Captain or his officers knew that water was entering the ship. About 3 minutes after the collision Captain Smith had sent for Mr Maxwell, the ship's carpenter, and had ordered him to sound the ship (find out how much water had entered the vessel). It would not have taken the carpenter long to check the forward compartments; all he needed to do was take a quick look or speak to anyone who had been in them. Before long he was back on the bridge to report that No 6 stokehold was dry. If he meant the position usually occupied by the stokers feeding the furnaces at the aft end of No 4 boiler room, this information tells us nothing. If, however, he was referring to No 6 boiler room, which seems more likely, it tells us a great deal. If No 6 boiler room was still dry when the carpenter looked at it, we can safely assume that the damage to the skin of the ship did not extend that far back. In that case, why would the boiler room begin to fill with water shortly afterwards? There is a frighteningly simple possible explanation.

We already know that the junior engineers in at least one of the forward boiler rooms started the pumps there without waiting for orders from the bridge. If both boiler rooms Nos 5 and 6 were only slightly damaged, it would be reasonable to believe that the engineers in the very forward room were as efficient as those in the next compartment aft. In that case they too would have started the pumps very shortly after the collision. Under normal circumstances the engineers would have been doing the right thing by starting the pumps the instant they thought their ship's hull had been breached, and their actions would have been commended. But what if these were not normal circumstances and the non-return valves in the pumps had been reversed so that instead of pumping water out of the ship the opposite occurred? Reversal of these non-return valves in the pumps would also provide an explanation for Captain Smith's delay in ordering them to be brought into play. He knew exactly what to expect and would have been able to control the amount of time it took his vessel to sink by judicious use of those pumps had his vessel been undamaged. Unfortunately the ship was not undamaged and at least the forward two or three compartments were filling with water. In that case the Captain was doing the right thing, actually extending the life of the ship by not starting the pumps. By waiting for 45 minutes before ordering the pumps to be started, Smith would have believed that those in the forward boiler rooms were already under water and inoperable. But even 45 minutes after the supposed collision he was still unaware that his junior engineers had already done what they thought was the right thing, and had already started the pumps in those two forward boiler rooms. With the ship's hull breached in the first three compartments and the pumps sucking water into the two forward boiler rooms, the ship, although relatively undamaged, was doomed.

Thomas Andrews, who had a hand in designing the ship and was aboard for the maiden voyage, could not have known that the forward pumps were filling the ship with water and would naturally assume that the damage to the hull extended as far back as No 5 boiler room, and said as much to Captain Smith. Even if he had known about the reversal of the valves in the pumps and guessed what had happened, there was little that could be done to rectify the situation. Even if the watertight doors were reopened to allow the incoming water to flow further into the ship and help prevent the bows from being dragged under, there was still no way of getting rid of it unless at least some of the pumps further aft had not been tampered with. It is a curious fact that when the ship's lifeboats were lowered only one of them encountered a jet of water being pumped overboard from the liner. This jet of water was not coming from the ship's pumps but from her condensers where exhaust steam from the engines was turned back into fresh water to be used again. There is nothing else at all in the eye-witness statements to suggest that water was actually being pumped out of the ship.

From the time water began to flow into the five forward compartments the situation was disastrous, but had Mr Murdoch not given the order to turn the ship towards the south immediately upon hearing of an iceberg right ahead, then all might not have been lost. Had he ordered hard a-port, the ship would have turned towards the north, toward where the SS *Californian* lay waiting. Instead, the turn towards the south opened the gap between the two ships until they were the better part of 20 miles apart, too far apart for distress signals fired from one to be visible from the other. By the time *Titanic* stopped she was on her own in an otherwise empty sea, with the exception of a great number of icebergs and possibly a couple of mystery ships, of course.

Preparations began to get as many people off the ship as was thought possible. The officers of the *Titanic* knew only too well that the ship's lifeboats were only meant to accommodate about 1,200 people at best and that there was almost double that number aboard. They would have to be a little selective about who was allowed access to the boat deck. The steel mesh doors leading to the forward third-class accommodation were closed and locked, sealing in most of those berthed there with no chance of escape. Those doors are still locked. The all-Italian catering staff, who after all were not White Star employees at all but worked for Mr Luigi Gatti, owner of a famous London restaurant, were rounded up and locked in the second-class dining saloon. They were only Italians who would clog up the boat deck and prevent more deserving American and British passengers getting into the few available boats.

While these preparations were going on Captain Smith went along to the wireless cabin and instructed the operators to send out a distress call. Clearly the captain was losing his grip on reality even at this early stage in the proceedings, as he gave the Marconi men the wrong position to send. The first distress call sent out at 12.15am from *Titanic* gave her position as 41°46'N, 50°24'W, about 20 miles from where she actually was. This erroneous position was transmitted for about 10 minutes before it was corrected to 41°46'N, 50°14'W. The mistake was possibly nothing more than a simple error in writing down the position, but it immediately reduced any chance of a rescue.

Twenty miles away, to the north, the Leyland Line's *Californian* lay with her engines stopped, drifting with the field ice. Her wireless operator had switched off his equipment at 11.30 that evening after contacting *Titanic* and being told off by Phillips or Bride for interfering with their commercial communications with the shore station at Cape Race.

Chapter 17

The view from the *Californian*

While the events described in the last chapter were going on aboard the *Titanic* a very different scenario was being played out aboard the Leyland Line's *Californian*, about 20 miles away to the north. Although his wireless operator and about two-thirds of his crew had turned in for the night or were off duty, Captain Lord was neither of these things. In fact, Captain Lord would not go to bed at all that night.

The *Californian* was by no manner of means a small vessel herself. Launched at Dundee on 26 November 1901, she was 447ft 6in long and weighed in at 6,223grt. She was predominantly a cargo vessel but did have 19 staterooms that could comfortably accommodate up to 47 passengers. Captain Lord had taken over command of the ship in 1911. Born in Bolton on 13 September 1877, he had joined the West Indian & Pacific Steam Navigation Company in 1897 after first going to sea as a cadet in 1891. The WI&PSN Co was taken over by the Leyland Line in 1900, shortly before Leyland was itself taken over by J. P. Morgan's IMM company. Lord obtained his Master's Certificate in February 1902 and his Extra Master's three months later, on 3 May. He served, mainly as Chief Officer, on the *Antillian* from August 1904 until 1906, when he took over as captain for a further five months. He then captained a series of Leyland vessels, including *Louisiana* and *William Cliff* before taking command of the *Californian* in March 1911. He was paid the princely sum of £240 a month as captain of the *Californian*, less than half the £500 per month paid to Captain E. J. Smith of the *Titanic*, even though, judging from the record, he was at least his equal as a seaman.

As we already know, *Californian* had left London on 5 April in so much of a hurry that her wireless operator, Cyril Furmston Evans, did not have the time to pick up the correct Marconi chart for the coming voyage. Without that chart Evans could not know what ships were within range of his wireless equipment until he either contacted them, or they him.

It should be remembered that at the time a national coal strike was just coming to an end, a strike that had caused such a shortage of fuel that most ships, including first-class liners, had been unable to gather enough to put to sea. As described earlier, despite this fuel shortage enough coal had been found for *Californian's* obviously urgent mission. A passenger ticket aboard

Californian cost £10, one way. As there were so many transatlantic vessels confined to port because of the fuel shortage, there must have been thousands of people willing to pay that or more to gain passage. Despite having practically cornered the market in transatlantic voyaging, *Californian* sailed without a single passenger aboard.

Californian made her best speed for the first nine days of her journey and had reached a position 42°5'N, 47°25'W. During the afternoon of 14 April she changed course so that longitude 51°W would be crossed at latitude 42°N. At about 6.30pm *Californian* passed three distinctive flat-topped icebergs, about 5 miles to the south of the ship. Lord had been previously warned of the presence of these icebergs and their position in a wireless message from the *Parisien*. Being in no doubt whatsoever as to whether or not his ship was in an area inhabited by large icebergs, Captain Lord ordered the lookouts to be doubled and had a man placed right in the bows of the *Californian* as an extra precaution. His attitude toward icebergs, it seems, was somewhat different from that of *Titanic's* Captain Smith.

Californian hurried onward until, at about 10.15pm, a strange brightness was spotted along the western horizon. Captain Lord guessed that the glow, known as 'ice blink', was caused by field ice. The vessel continued towards that ice for a further 5 or 6 minutes before Lord decided that discretion was the better part of valour and ordered the helm hard a-port and the engines full astern. *Californian* swung toward the east-north-east as she slowed to a stop. Captain Lord then ordered the engines stopped but steam to be kept up throughout the night in case the engines were required urgently. He never explained why he thought the engines might be urgently needed during that night. His ship, drifting slowly and safely in the same direction and at the same speed as the field ice and icebergs, could be in no conceivable danger from them. The captain was obviously aware that the ice presented no threat to his ship because he had the extra lookouts dismissed and sent below. After taking these simple precautions Captain Lord should have felt himself able to put his trust in his senior watch officers and look forward to a good night's sleep, but sleep seems to have been the last thing on his mind.

Once the *Californian* had stopped for the night Captain Lord calculated the ship's position. To do this he used the vessel's course, S89°W (true), the 120 miles she had travelled since the noon position had been established, and a stellar observation taken at 7.30pm. He and his officers had managed to get perfectly good sights all day. *Californian's* position, worked out by Lord, was 42°5'N, 50°7'W, and his calculations would be reinforced by sightings taken the following day.

Captain Lord was about to leave the bridge when he spotted the masthead light of another ship, to the east of *Californian*, on her starboard quarter. He pointed out the light to his Third Officer, Charles Victor Groves. Groves initially thought the light was nothing more than a star and said as much to Captain Lord but, as he later testified at the official inquiries into the sinking of the *Titanic*, he changed his opinion as the night wore on. Before another hour had passed, at about 11.25pm, Mr Groves was convinced that what he had first believed to be a star was in fact two masthead lights belonging to a passenger liner. (*Titanic*, although the largest vessel in existence at the time, only ever displayed one masthead light. Two lights were usually displayed by vessels with four or more masts, whereas *Titanic* had only two masts.) The Third Officer also believed that he saw the mystery vessel's port-side red light. At no time did Mr Groves mention seeing any of the myriad lights coming from portholes, public rooms and promenade areas invariably shown by a passenger liner.

Captain Lord, still convinced that the lights he had seen were coming from nothing more than a small cargo ship, left the bridge and made his way down to the saloon Deck. Once there he sent for his Chief Engineer, W. S. A. Mahan. When the Engineer arrived Captain Lord confirmed his instructions that steam should be kept up and the engines ready for instant use in an emergency throughout the night. He also pointed out to the engineer the lights of the mystery ship to which he had so recently drawn Mr Groves's attention. It was a perfectly clear, flat calm night with no moon but with thousands of stars twinkling down. Under these conditions it was not at all easy to discern the horizon and Captain Lord had already been fooled into thinking that stars, low down on the horizon, had been the masthead lights of ships. He wanted the Engineer's opinion as to whether the lights they could see were a ship or merely stars. Mahan's opinion was the same as that of his captain, that the lights were those of a small cargo vessel. It was some time around 10.45pm when the Chief Engineer left to continue with his duties.

A few minutes later Lord met his wireless operator, Cyril Evans, on deck. The captain asked Evans if he knew of any other ships in the immediate area. As far as Evans knew the only vessel equipped with wireless close by was *Titanic*. If only Evans had possessed the correct wireless chart for the North Atlantic he would not have had to guess what ships were close by from the strength of the signals he received from them. Pointing out the approaching steamer, Lord said, 'That's not the *Titanic* - she's a vessel close to us in size. You'd better contact *Titanic*, however, and let her know we're stopped in ice.' Evans left immediately to carry out his instructions and began his transmission to the White Star liner at 10.55pm.

Evans managed to get through the first part of his message to *Titanic* before he was interrupted by one of the liner's operators. 'We are stopped and surrounded by ice' was as far as Evans got. 'Keep out! Shut up! You're jamming my signal. I'm working Cape Race.' Evans gave up the attempt and merely listened to *Titanic's* signals for a while. Even at that time the wireless operator aboard *Titanic*, whoever it was, should have recognised the message from *Californian* as an ice warning, or at least as an important navigational signal. He should have taken the message down and immediately conveyed it to the senior officer on the liner's bridge, which is clearly what Captain Lord intended. The wording of the message would have been dictated by Captain Lord when he told Evans to contact *Titanic* and advise her of his situation. Why else then did Evans send a message saying that *Californian* was stopped and surrounded by ice when in fact she was on the edge of the ice field where there was only field ice and no icebergs in sight at all?

Evans listened to *Titanic's* wireless traffic up until about 11.30, then, as usual at that time of night, switched off his radio and began to prepare for bed. He had been on duty since 7 that morning and, having put in a 16½-hour day, he was feeling a little tired. It was quite normal for Marconi operators aboard ships that only carried one operator to work a ridiculously long week. For this they were paid the princely sum of £4 a month but, as Senator Smith at the American Inquiry was to sarcastically point out to Cyril Evans, 'You have your board on the ship, and a room. Four pounds a month and all this for a 105-hour week!'

At about the time Evans switched off his wireless the mystery ship, which was still approaching *Californian* from the southeast, had come close enough for Captain Lord to see not only her masthead lights but what appeared to be deck lights and her green starboard light as well. Lord estimated that the stranger was only about 5 miles away from him at this point. The captain ordered his Third Officer, Groves, to try and contact the mystery ship with the Morse lamp, but they could get no response. By 11.40pm Captain Lord must have left the bridge again, for whatever reason, because it was then that Groves saw the stranger put her lights out and come to a stop. He did not tell Captain Lord what he had seen. (*Titanic*, as we know, did not come to a halt until well after 11.40pm when she supposedly struck something, and her lights did not go out until about 2.15 the following morning. It is therefore safe to assume that the ship visible from *Californian* was not the *Titanic*, despite continued attempts by some to make us believe that it was.)

There is a very simple rule for working out the distance to the horizon from any vantage point at sea: V (distance in miles) = the square root of the height in feet of the observer's eyes above the waterline, multiplied by 1.14. Using this simple formula we can work out that from *Californian's* bridge, about 49 feet above the water, the visible horizon (had there been one that night) would have been about 8 miles away. From *Titanic's* crow's-nest the horizon would have been about 12 miles off. Had *Titanic* and *Californian* come within 5 miles of one another they would have been clearly visible to each other.

Although it is painfully apparent that *Titanic* and *Californian* never came within sight of one another that night, one person's incredible evidence was given entirely unwarranted credence by both the British and American Inquiries to the point where it has clouded the story of what happened that night for the better part of a century. According to his own account, at about 11.55pm (12.05am *Titanic*) Donkeyman Gill made his way up onto *Californian's* deck to smoke a cigarette. There was no smoking allowed between decks because of the combustible nature of the urgent cargo of blankets and pullovers the vessel was carrying, according to Gill. Looking over the starboard rail Gill saw a 'very large steamer about 10 miles away'. The donkeyman never explained quite how he managed to see a ship 3 or 4 miles beyond the horizon. Gill watched this steamer, he said, for a full minute. Going back below, he told a mate, William Thomas, who was in bed, that he had seen a steamer 'going full steam'. Thomas later denied that Gill had mentioned a steamer or rockets, but said that they had only talked about the ice. Gill was very specific about the time, so the ship he saw was hardly likely to have been the *Titanic*, which had been in some sort of collision 20 minutes earlier. Unable to sleep, Gill was back on deck at 12.30am. He had been there for about 10 minutes when he noticed a white rocket 'about 10 miles away on our starboard side. I thought it must be a shooting star.' There had been a meteorite shower that night. 'In 7 or 8 minutes I saw distinctly a second rocket in the same place.' Gill clearly did not think that the rockets were of any great importance, and said as much: 'I do not know if anyone did who saw them, but I did not. It was not my business to notify the bridge or the lookouts…' Obviously seeing the rockets set Gill's mind at rest because shortly after seeing the second he turned in for the remainder of the night.

Gill's statement has more holes in it than a colander and it seems more than likely that he made up his entire story simply to squeeze a few dollars out of American newspapers. At 12.05am (*Titanic*) the White Star liner was not 'going full steam', if she was moving at all. Third Officer Groves said that he saw the stranger's lights go out at 11.40pm, yet Gill claims that the ship he saw was ablaze with lights. Gill saw only white rockets when we now know that *Titanic* fired a selection of red, white and blue ones. Whatever ship Mr Gill was watching, it certainly was not *Titanic*.

The confusion over the mystery vessel seen from *Californian* was further compounded by a newspaper article, based on a statement from *Californian's* Carpenter, McGregor, which appeared in the Clinton Daily Item:

'…that the *Californian* was within 10 miles of the *Titanic* when she sank. At the time the *Californian* was sailing just ahead of the *Titanic* but had seen a big field of ice but in order to avoid it had turned south and went round the big mass. It was also said that the wireless operator on board the *Californian* notified the *Titanic* and all other vessels in the vicinity of the presence of the big ice field.

It was shortly after the *Californian* had gone past the ice field that the watch saw the rockets that were sent up by the *Titanic* as signals of distress. The officer on watch, it is said, reported this to the boat (sic) [Captain] but he failed to pay any attention to the signals excepting to tell the watch to keep his eye on the boat. At this time the two boats were about 10 miles apart. It being in the night the wireless operator on board the *Californian* was asleep at the time.

It is said that those on board the *Californian* could see the lights of the *Titanic* very plainly, and it is also reported that the *Titanic* saw the *Californian*. Finally the first mate on the *Californian*, who with several of the officers had been watching the *Titanic*, decided he would take a hand in the situation and so roused the wireless operator and an attempt was made to communicate with the *Titanic*. It was then too late, as the apparatus on the *Titanic* was out of commission. The operator did, however, catch the word '*Titanic*', which was probably being sent from the *Carpathia* or some other boat, and this information was given to the Captain. He immediately ordered the boat to stop and was very much concerned as to the fate of the *Titanic* after that, but it was far too late. The *Californian* had during this time continued ahead under full steam and by the time the name of the boat was ascertained it is believed to have been about 20 miles away.

The *Californian* turned back and started for the scene but it is a very slow boat as compared with the *Carpathia* and several others, and although the *Carpathia* was about 50 miles away when it first learned of the accident it was able to get there much sooner than the *Californian*. The next morning the *Californian* learned from the *Carpathia* that it had reached the scene and that the *Titanic* had gone down and that all the survivors had been picked up.

According to McGregor, the Captain of the *Californian* had the appearance of being 20 years older after the news reached him. It is the belief of McGregor that the Captain will never be in command of the *Californian* again and he told Mr Frazer [his cousin] that he would positively refuse to sail under him again and that all of the officers had the same feeling. Mr Frazer says that according to the story as told him, that had the Captain of the *Californian* turned back when the rockets were first seen, hundreds of the *Titanic's* passengers could have been taken off on that boat.'

Like so many newspaper articles, television documentaries and books since, the article shows little regard for the facts of the matter and is completely misleading. It shows Captain Lord as derelict in his duty and unfit for command. As we already know, *Californian* was not ahead of *Titanic* by this time, she did not turn to the south to avoid the icefield, the Leyland Line vessel was not steaming at all but drifting with the field ice, Chief Officer Stewart did not send for Evans (the wireless operator) and order him to contact *Titanic* while the mystery ship was in view, and *Californian* did not turn back in order to go to the rescue.

Far from showing Captain Lord as incompetent, the ascertainable facts of the incident point in the opposite direction. They argue that Captain Lord was aware that something was going to happen that night, possibly that the *Titanic* would be involved in some sort of accident. Could it be that he was torn between going to the rescue of what he believed to have been a small cargo ship or doing what he had been told to do and go to collect the thousands more people who would need rescuing from the liner? In that case Lord did the only thing he could do in deciding to sacrifice the few in order to save the many. So just what did Captain Lord do as that fateful night wore on?

When Second Officer Herbert Stone came on duty at about midnight he found Captain Lord at the wheelhouse door. Lord pointed out to him the steamer, which was a little astern of the *Californian's* beam by then. Lord also pointed out the field of dense ice to their south. Captain Lord then told Stone that he would not be going to bed that night but that he intended to rest, fully clothed, on the chartroom settee (where he would be easily available if needed). Lord was a little over 6 feet tall and the chartroom settee was only 5ft 6in long. Anyone who has spent a night on a bed that is too short to stretch out on will know that Captain Lord was not anticipating a good night's rest. The best he could hope for was a night's fitful dozing in the steam-heated chartroom. Clearly Captain Lord, well aware that his own ship was in no conceivable danger, was expecting something to happen during the night. He left the bridge at 12.15am.

All times from the bridge of the *Californian* are imprecise because there was no clock on the ship's upper bridge, so times are taken from individual officers' watches or is estimated.

Second Officer Stone took over the watch from Third Officer Groves at about 12.10am. Groves had only very recently checked the ship's heading against the compass and informed Stone that she was swinging around to starboard. He also drew Stone's attention to the mystery ship and told him that they had already tried to contact her by Morse lamp, without any success. The Third Officer had already noted that the stranger was constantly changing her bearing from *Californian* and was moving away towards the west. (It will be recalled that by this time *Titanic* was either stopped or heading slowly away towards the south.)

Stone studied the mystery vessel for a while and determined that she was only showing one masthead light and her red port-side light, so she was heading towards the east. There does seem to have been some confusion among *Californian's* watch officers with regard to the stranger. Stone could also see some indistinct lights that he thought were just portholes, deck lights, or open doors. He did not see a brilliantly lit liner. The Second Officer thought the ship they had in view was nothing more than a small tramp steamer, about 5 miles away. Stone tried the Morse lamp for himself, but even though *Californian's* light was visible at a range of about 10 miles, double the estimated distance to the mystery vessel, he too could get no response.

Californian's apprentice officer, James Gibson, joined Groves and Stone on the bridge at about 12.15am. He too tried to attract the stranger's attention with the Morse lamp, again without result. Then he saw a flash of light on the deck of the mystery ship as she fired a rocket, but, even though they were only 5 miles away, the watchers on *Californian's* bridge did not hear any explosion as the rocket burst to release a shower of white stars. (*Titanic* did not fire ordinary rockets but used socket signals, a sort of mortar that fired a shell 800 feet into the air from the bridge, not from the deck. These shells exploded with an ear-splitting report that should have been clearly audible on a still, clear night at a distance of 5 miles.) Gibson studied the mystery ship through his binoculars and thought that she had only the one masthead light. He also saw both her red and green lights, which were on opposite sides of the ship, and thought that the red (port side) light was higher out of the water than the green, indicating that the vessel had a pronounced list to starboard. Like Stone, Gibson thought they were watching a cargo ship, not a liner.

At about 12.35am Captain Lord, resting in the chart room, blew up the voice-pipe connected to the bridge, sounding the whistle. When Stone answered Lord asked whether the mystery ship had moved. Stone told him that it had not and that, despite repeated attempts with the Morse lamp, they had not been able to make contact. Ten minutes later Stone saw a flash of light in the sky in the direction of the mysterious steamer, which might have been another rocket, or might have been just another shooting star. As we already know, there had been a number of shooting stars visible in the heavens that night. Shortly afterwards he saw another flash of light directly above the stranger. However, Mr Stone did not think that this was a rocket from the mystery ship but that the light came from a good distance beyond. Between then and about 1.15am Stone saw another three flashes in the sky, which might have been rockets although he didn't think that they were. He was sure that they were all white in colour. As we shall shortly see, *Titanic* fired an assortment of red, white and blue rockets, not just white ones. This is an important point to bear in mind when we come to what Captain Lord had to say when, still half asleep, he was informed that the officers on the bridge had seen rockets at all.

The Second Officer thought he saw five rockets in all, the last at about 1.10am. Gibson obviously didn't see the earlier rockets because he said that Mr Stone told him about them, and that the last one he saw was at 12.55am. Stone was still of the opinion that the rockets, if they were rockets, had not come from the ship they had in view but from a much greater distance away. The signals only rose to half the stranger's masthead height, so if they did come from that vessel then they could not be rockets, only Roman candles. Roman candles were regularly used for signalling between ships at night and usually only to establish the identity of the vessels involved. These small pyrotechnic devices fired a succession of coloured fireballs to a height not exceeding 50 feet. They could never be mistaken for distress rockets.

Soon after 1.00am the stranger began to move away towards the southwest. The Second Officer whistled down the speaking tube to the Captain's cabin. Lord, dozing in the chartroom next door, must have heard the whistle and went into his cabin to answer. Stone told the captain about the signals they had seen. Captain Lord asked if they were private signals, meaning Roman candles. Stone replied, 'I don't know, but they are all white.' Lord then ordered Stone to keep trying to signal the stranger with the Morse lamp, saying '…when you get an answer let me know by Gibson.' Stone continued, without success, to attempt to contact the mysterious ship while the captain returned to the chartroom settee. Clearly Lord was making an effort to stay awake by resting on the relatively uncomfortable settee even though he would have been more easily reached by voice-pipe if he had gone to his own cabin. However, he would have been well aware that to have stretched out on his bed in the warmth of his cabin after spending any length of time out in the bitterly cold conditions of the bridge would have invited sleep. Anyone who spends time out of doors in winter will know exactly what happens when they later sit down in a warm room. They are asleep within minutes.

By 2.00am the mystery ship was still heading away from them. Since they had first seen her the stranger had moved between 5 and 8 miles, so she was only making a couple of knots. Nevertheless she had moved sufficiently far that her side lights could no longer be seen - only her stern light remained visible. Only then did the Second Officer remember his instructions about keeping the Captain informed.

'I told Gibson to go down to the master and be sure and wake him up and tell him that altogether we had seen eight of these white lights, like white rockets, in the direction of this other steamer; that this steamer was disappearing in the south-west, that we had called her up repeatedly on the Morse lamp and received no information whatsoever.'

Captain Lord was dozing on the chartroom settee when Gibson put his head around the door. The apprentice must have thought the master was wider awake than he actually was when he delivered his message, as instructed by the Second Officer. He later said that the Captain acknowledged his report by saying, 'All right. Are you sure there were no colours in them?' The master then asked the time. Gibson then returned to the bridge and reported the conversation to Stone.

The fact that Captain Lord had not gone to bed that night and had ordered the ship's engineer to maintain steam pressure so that the engines were ready for instant use tells us that he was expecting something to happen. He was expecting to have to get under way at short notice. Also, the Captain's repeated questions about the signals seen from his ship, as to whether they had any colour in them or were private signals (also usually coloured), tells us that he was expecting to see coloured signals that night. All of these facts point towards a carefully planned event taking place, an event in which Captain Lord was supposed to play an active part. Lord was doing his level best to be ready when he was needed. As we know, there was an event that night in which Captain Lord and his vessel might well have played an important part, an event in which coloured rockets were indeed sent up. Unfortunately that event took place almost 20 miles from where *Californian* lay drifting with the ice, too far away for pyrotechnic signals to be seen.

Both *Titanic* and *Californian* were equipped with wireless and it would normally have been a simple matter for them to contact one another at a distance of only about 20 miles. Unluckily for those aboard the White Star liner, Captain Lord considered wireless an insecure means of communication, so *Californian's* wireless operator was not privy to that night's plans. Even so, all might have been well but for an unlucky sequence of events that was nobody's fault. Cyril Evans had turned in for the night at shortly after 11.30pm and, as is to be expected after working a 16½-hour day, had no difficulty in falling asleep. Third Officer Groves had finished his stint on duty at midnight but had not left the bridge until at least 10 minutes after that time. Instead of going straight to his own cabin and turning in for the night, Groves stopped off at the wireless room. Evans was in bed and half asleep when the Third Officer entered the room. We must assume that his knocking on the cabin door had at least partly woken Evans. Groves had more than a passing interest in the new electronic marvel, wireless, and took whatever opportunity presented itself to learn as much as he could about it. He had even gone to the trouble of teaching himself the Morse code, although he was not up to the standards required by the Marconi company. Nevertheless, the Third Officer could understand the code well enough to get the gist of whatever he heard and had spent a considerable amount of time in the wireless room listening to the traffic. Evans was used to these nocturnal visits.

Groves asked the operator what ships he had made contact with. 'Only the *Titanic*,' replied Evans, and went on to say that judging by her signal strength the liner was about 100 miles away from them at 11 o'clock. If Evans had been wider awake he might have reminded Groves to wind up the mechanical signal detector, but he didn't. Groves put on the headphones and switched on the receiver, but because of the disabled signal detector he heard nothing. He listened for a few minutes, then switched off the set and left Evans in peace. If only Groves had wound up the signal detector it is almost certain that he would have heard *Titanic's* distress call and alerted Captain Lord.

Cargo ships at that time usually only carried a single wireless operator, so not a lot of traffic passed between them after about midnight. At the British Inquiry, Captain Lord was asked why he didn't have the wireless operator wakened when rockets were first reported to him. 'When? At 1 o'clock in the morning?' Lord clearly knew that it was all but useless to wake the wireless operator in order to make contact with another relatively small cargo ship at that time of night. Even Marconi operators had to sleep sometimes.

Stone and Gibson remained on the bridge watching the stranger. They had already noticed that she had a list to starboard. (After the collision *Titanic* developed a list to port.) They watched as the mystery vessel moved away, its stern light slowly fading. Stone did not believe that the way the light disappeared resembled in any way a vessel sinking. Then, at exactly 3.40am, Gibson saw another white rocket a long way off to their south. He was sure of the time because it was just before dawn, and anyway he was due to go off duty at 4am. However, despite his certainty as to timing, Gibson may have been mistaken. According to Second Officer Stone the apprentice told him that he had just seen a white light in the sky at 3.20am. Stone watched through his binoculars for a little while where the light had been seen, and after a short while he too saw a white light in the sky, quickly followed by two more. He did not think that the lights were rockets and therefore did not report them to Captain Lord. (It has been suggested that the rockets, if they were rockets, were those fired by *Carpathia* as she came to the rescue. Unfortunately that cannot be true, as the Cunard liner came up from the south and was therefore even further from *Californian* than was *Titanic*, too far away for rockets to have been seen, but we will look at *Carpathia* a little later.)

First Officer Stewart came onto the bridge at about 4.00am to begin his watch. Stone and Gibson told him about what they had seen during the night. In his opinion the vessel the other two officers had been watching had been firing rockets in reply to yet another vessel even further away. Stewart looked towards the southwest and saw a four-masted steamer.

'There she is,' he said, believing that he was looking at the same ship that had been visible earlier and had moved off. 'There is that steamer. She looks all right.' Stone said, 'That's not the same steamer. She has two masthead lights.'

As it began to grow light, at about 4.30am, the Chief Officer left the bridge to wake up Captain Lord, who was still dozing in the chartroom. As soon as the Captain seemed to be fully awake, Stewart told him that the vessel that had been firing rockets was still in view to the south of them. Three senior ships' officers, including the Captain, and Gibson the apprentice, had been aware of the rockets but had attached no importance to them, believing them to have been nothing more than company signals. Given that weight of expert opinion, it is fairly safe to assume that the lights seen were indeed nothing more than company signals (Roman candles) being exchanged between the ship seen from *Californian* and another vessel beyond their horizon.

Events on the bridge of the *Californian* on the night of 14/15 April are important for two reasons. First, they establish the presence of at least one steamer, possibly two, between the Leyland Line vessel and the *Titanic*. Second, they establish that Captain Lord was expecting something to happen that night, something involving coloured rockets and the necessity for him to move his ship at short notice. As far as we are aware only one event that night fits these conditions, and that was happening almost 20 miles to the south and out of sight of the *Californian*.

Chapter 18

The view from the *Carpathia*

Aboard *Titanic* things were going from bad to worse. It seems that preparations to stage a controlled sinking had come back to bite them. The senior officers involved in the original scheme to scuttle the ship were so blinkered by what they had planned to do that they could not react rationally now that things had gone horribly wrong. The mere fact that there was a plan already in place to scuttle the ship condemned many of those aboard the liner to death.

If a good percentage of the forward pumps were useless, and they may well have been, there was relatively little that could be done to extend the life of the ship. Sails - all ships then carried sails for use in an emergency - could have been dropped overboard in the vicinity of the hull breach where the inrushing water would carry them into the hole and help block it up, but it would appear that nobody thought of trying that. This emergency measure was as close to a standard response as there could be in what were, after all, exceptional circumstances. It had been tried just three years earlier when the White Star Line's 15,378-ton *Republic* had been rammed by the 5,118-ton Lloyd Italiano liner *Florida*, just a little south of the Nantucket lightship. About 30 feet of *Florida's* bow was crushed in the collision, killing three crewmen asleep in the forecastle. A huge hole reaching from the promenade deck to well below the waterline and more than 20 feet wide had been torn in the *Republic's* side. (This gives us some indication of the sort of damage that even the unarmoured bow of a ship of that size could do to another ordinary commercial vessel. *Florida* was roughly the same size as HMS *Hawke*, so imagine the sort of damage we could expect to see on *Olympic* when the armoured ram bow of the warship crashed into her side.)

A canvas sheet was soon stretched across the crumpled bow of the Italian ship as she stood by to take off the passengers and crew of the *Republic*. The White Star liner was severely damaged and clearly sinking, but even so, in an attempt to extend the life of his vessel, Captain William Inman Sealby had a sail stretched over the yawning hole in his ship's side. It worked and the flow of water into the stricken liner was reduced to the point where it was thought possible to tow her to shore and beach her. The attempt failed and *Republic* foundered while under tow, almost 15 hours after the collision.

Had a similar effort been made with the *Titanic* it is certainly possible that she might have remained afloat long enough for help to reach her.

Instead of trying even this simple emergency measure to keep his ship afloat for a little longer, Captain Smith elected to do nothing except signal for assistance and try to get some of those aboard into the lifeboats. Even with many of the people who had been berthed in the forward third-class accommodation locked securely below and under armed guard, and with all but one of Mr Gatti's Italian restaurant employees confined to the second-class dining room, there was still nowhere near enough lifeboat space for those supposedly remaining. Of course, if there were not as many people aboard the liner as were shown on the passenger lists, the problem would automatically be somewhat reduced. Allowing that there was already a plan in place to dispose of the liner on this voyage, it would have made good sense to reduce the numbers aboard to manageable proportions. It is much easier to take a thousand people off a ship at sea than to rescue two thousand. There is some quite compelling evidence to suggest that there were nowhere near the numbers aboard the ship as is usually believed, as we shall see.

Titanic carried no life rafts, but some of these useful articles could have been easily improvised by lashing together anything that could be found which would float, such as deckchairs, tables and other furniture. Even if these failed to save any lives, the construction of them would help keep both passengers and crew members occupied and stave off the onset of panic. It is curious that at least one surviving experienced seaman did describe in detail seeing a purpose-built life raft after the liner had sunk. In fact, he described how the lifeboat he was in stopped to pick up the people on the raft. As we know that *Titanic* did not carry life rafts, we must assume that this one came from another ship - but we are getting ahead of ourselves.

About 25 minutes after the accident Captain Smith ordered his officers to prepare the boats. Chief Officer Wilde was to uncover them while Sixth Officer James Moody fetched the list of boat assignments. Like today, people had lifeboat accommodation assigned to them so that they were supposed to know where to go in an emergency, another measure designed to help minimise panic; unfortunately the passengers had not been told what these arrangements were. There had been no lifeboat drill aboard *Titanic* even though this simple precaution was usual practice aboard White Star liners. First Officer Murdoch was to begin mustering passengers ready for loading the boats. While waiting for Moody to reappear with the list of lifeboat assignments, Murdoch assisted, with the help of some crew members, in uncovering the boats. Second Officer Lightoller, Fourth

Officer Boxhall and Third Officer Pitman had been off duty but were summoned to help with the boats. As it was to turn out, those awaiting an escape from the doomed ship might have been better off if one of those officers had remained in his cabin. It is a curious circumstance with the *Titanic* that those officers who showed little efficiency in saving the lives of others somehow managed to save themselves.

At 12.15am the first wireless distress calls were sent out from the liner, but gave the wrong position for the sinking ship. Ten minutes later, after the Navigating Officer, Mr Boxhall, had calculated the true position of the ship, this error was rectified and from then onwards the correct coordinates were transmitted. The signal was received by the lone wireless operator aboard the Cunard liner *Carpathia*, who was just getting ready for bed and had, luckily for *Titanic*, not got around to switching off his equipment. At the British Inquiry into the sinking the wireless operator from the Canadian Pacific liner *Mount Temple* testified that he heard *Titanic* and *Carpathia* exchanging signals earlier that evening, at 11.35pm. Either *Carpathia's* operator, Harold Cottam, had fortunately left his wireless tuned to the same frequency, or the earlier exchange had forewarned him to expect another call. *Carpathia* was supposedly almost 60 miles away from *Titanic* when the distress call was received, a long way for a ship with an advertised top speed of only 14 knots.

On receiving the distress call, Mr Cottam, only half dressed, went directly to the bridge of the *Carpathia* and reported to the senior officer there, First Officer H. V. Dean. At first Dean did not believe the wireless man and made him repeat the message. Finally convinced, Dean propelled Cottam before him all the way below to the Captain's cabin. Without knocking, Dean and Cottam barged into the room where Captain Rostron slept. Initially the Captain was less than pleased by the conduct of his First Officer and wireless operator in bursting in unannounced. Regardless of the master's obvious displeasure at being disturbed, Cottam and Dean proceeded to tell him about the distress signal and the White Star liner's given position. Captain Rostron's attitude changed completely as soon as he took in what the wireless operator was telling him. From that moment onwards Rostron did not make a single mistake. It was almost as if he had been waiting for just this situation to arise and had been practising exactly what he should do.

First he ordered his wireless operator to check *Titanic's* position, then he started for *Carpathia's* chartroom. Captain Rostron quickly worked out that his ship was about 58 miles from the sinking liner and immediately ordered a new course. *Carpathia's* head swung northward onto North 52° West (308 degrees). All 18 of the lifeboats were swung out ready for immediate launching. Off-duty crew members were woken and all of the crew were given hot drinks, ready to stave off the chill night air. Orders were given that the crew were to prepare the ship to receive survivors. Barrels of machine oil were to be taken to the lavatories so that it could easily be flushed overboard to calm the sea, if necessary. Then Captain Rostron sent for his Chief Engineer, Johnson, and ordered him to squeeze every ounce of power possible out of the reciprocating engines. All unnecessary steam-powered systems, including the heating to passenger cabins and public rooms, was to be shut down so that all available steam pressure could go to the engines. It appears that Johnson's crew of engineers and stokers did all that was asked of them, and more, performing a minor miracle. *Carpathia* headed to the rescue at an incredible 17½ knots, about 25% faster than her design speed. The whole ship shuddered as she raced to the rescue, so much so that passengers were awakened by the massive amount of vibration coming from the overworked engines, and possibly by the bitter cold that began to creep into their cabins. While some of the crew collected blankets and prepared hot drinks for the survivors, others prepared public rooms as makeshift dormitories and hospitals. Passengers, although under strict instructions to keep out of the way, gave up their accommodation so that the survivors would have somewhere to sleep after they were brought aboard. Still Captain Rostron was issuing orders: extra lookouts were posted on the bridge, in the crow's-nest, and two in the eyes of the ship, right in the bows. All obstructions on deck were cleared and gangway doors in the sides of the ship were opened and hooked back. Nets and rope ladders were prepared to help the fittest of the survivors scramble aboard *Carpathia*. Sacks were tied to ropes so that children could be hoisted aboard and bosun's chairs were improvised to lift those that could not manage the nets and rope ladders. Lights were prepared to hang over the ship's sides. Captain Rostron thought of everything, with the possible exception of his own passengers.

It was a dark moonless night where even something as large as an iceberg could not necessarily be seen in time to avoid it, as Captain Rostron must have been all too aware from the messages relayed to him by his wireless operator. Nevertheless he took his ship into an area he knew abounded with icebergs, at better than her highest possible speed. The captain must have believed from what Cottam had told him that there were no other vessels close enough to come to his assistance should he strike a berg, so he was taking a tremendous risk with the lives of his passengers and crew. On the other hand he also doubtless thought that his was the only ship with any chance of reaching the stricken White Star giant in time to do any good. Rostron had made his decision. The lives of those aboard *Titanic*, which were certainly in danger, outweighed the risks to his own people, who might shortly be facing the same perils, or so we have been led to believe.

There was also the fact that by saving the lives of those on the *Titanic* Captain Rostron would also save his own flagging career; he had a lot to gain and little to lose. As mentioned in Chapter 10, a few years earlier he had seen what he believed to have been a sea monster. Instead of keeping quiet about the sighting he had the incident put in the ship's log, from where it became public knowledge. In just the same way that modern-day airline pilots are discouraged from reporting strange aerial phenomena, ships' officers were discouraged from reporting marine monsters. The incident came close to ending Rostron's career and played a large part in why he had only risen to command a second-rate liner like *Carpathia*. Although he was a first-rate master mariner, Captain Rostron was clearly seen as unreliable by his superiors. His career desperately needed a shot in the arm, which begs another question or two.

Could Captain Rostron and the *Carpathia* really have been as far from *Titanic* when the distress call was received as the usually accepted 58 miles? Could the *Carpathia* really have exceeded her design speed by as much as 25%? Could the Captain have picked his way through an area studded with hundreds of giant icebergs at high speed and in total darkness? Is it likely that Captain Rostron could have issued the string of concise and incisive orders detailed above if he had only recently been awoken and was unprepared for what he had to do? The answer to any one of these questions is more likely to be no rather than yes. What are the chances of being able to answer yes to them all?

Carpathia had a top speed of about 14 knots, and as she reached the site of the sinking in a little less than 3½ hours she was probably no more than 46 miles from *Titanic*, if she could actually steam at her top speed. However, Captain Rostron knew that the area he was steaming through was thick with icebergs, growlers and floating field ice, so it would have made good sense to have moved his ship at a speed that would allow his lookouts to see a berg in time to avoid it. It was a very dark, moonless night and the area around the Newfoundland Grand Banks is notorious for fog; even a slight mist would further hamper the lookouts. Captain Rostron was taking a terrible chance by entering the area at all, and unless he was totally irresponsible it seems unlikely that *Carpathia* would have steamed at anything more than 7 or 8 knots. If this is what did happen, *Carpathia* can have been no more than about 25 miles from *Titanic* when the distress signals were first received. (As we shall see, even in daylight Captain Lord of the *Californian* could not negotiate the icefield at anything better than an average speed of less than 8 knots without putting his ship and passengers at risk, and for at least some of the time *Californian* was in open water and able to move at top speed.)

Captain Rostron's string of seemingly efficient orders gives the impression that he had rehearsed them. At first glance it appears that he did not make a single mistake and, in my experience, nobody is that good. In fact, Captain Rostron seems to have prepared for all eventualities, even one in particular that was not likely to occur that night. He had barrels of machine oil standing by to pour overboard to calm rough seas. It was a flat calm night with no wind; there was no chance whatsoever that *Carpathia* would encounter rough seas. The presence of so many large icebergs, all acting as floating breakwaters, would have also tended to keep the waters smooth. Captain Rostron had his list of things to do and he stuck rigidly to it. It apparently had come as no surprise to the Cunard master that he would have to take people aboard from small boats at some time on that voyage.

As described earlier, before setting out from New York on this voyage *Carpathia* had spent some time in Brooklyn Navy Yard having her public rooms prepared so that they could easily be converted for use as hospital wards and dormitories. She had taken on board extra blankets, and no fewer than seven doctors. It would seem that as the Cunard liner left New York only one day after *Titanic* left Southampton, Captain Rostron and his superiors were either clairvoyant or had been forewarned. *Carpathia* was, with her ability to accommodate more than 2,000 passengers and with her master's pre-eminence as a navigator, in many respects the ideal choice of rescue ship.

As *Carpathia* hurried to the rescue Captain Rostron ordered rockets to be fired so that those either still aboard *Titanic* or in her lifeboats would be reassured that deliverance was on the way. Indeed, these rockets were seen from survivors in *Titanic's* lifeboats. It has also been suggested that they were seen from the bridge of the *Californian* as she lay drifting with the ice, far to the north. This is of course nonsense. If the distress signals from *Titanic* could not have been seen from *Californian*, it stands to reason that rockets fired from a ship even further away could not have been seen either. However, rockets were seen from *Californian* at about this time, but if they did not come from *Carpathia* they must have been sent up by some other vessel. As it happens, as *Titanic* was slowly sinking, another ship, possibly two other ships, was seen from her bridge. One of these was seen so clearly that the liner's Morse lamp was used in an attempt to attract her attention, without success. *Titanic's* Second Officer, Charles Lightoller, had been so annoyed by the stranger's lack of response that he said at the time how he wished he had a 6-inch gun so that he could put a shot into the mystery vessel and wake her up. Others on the liner had seen what they believed was the masthead lights of yet another mystery ship, which was also studiously ignoring their distress signals.

There can be absolutely no doubt that there was another steamer within 5 miles of *Titanic* as she was sinking. Captain Smith even went so far as to instruct a couple of lifeboat crews to row to the ship they had in sight, offload the passengers, and come back to collect another load. As the Captain had already been informed by Thomas Andrews, who had played a major part in designing the ship, that the liner could only remain afloat for a couple of hours, he must have believed that the mystery ship was very close indeed. Four men rowing a 30-foot lifeboat with 30 or 40 people in it could not have been expected to move at much more then a couple of miles an hour. Allowing half an hour to get the people from the lifeboat on to the mysterious steamer, we are left with little more than an hour for a lifeboat to complete the round trip. Smith must have thought that the ship he had instructed his crewmen to go to was no more than a mile or so away, or he believed that this vessel would come closer. Knowing, as he must have done, that the unidentified vessel had not seen or was ignoring their signals, Captain Smith could only have expected her to approach if there was already some arrangement for her to do so. In that case Captain Smith must have thought that the stranger was one of the rescue ships put in place to take off his passengers and crew when the plan to scuttle the liner was put into practice. He was expecting there to be a vessel close by. Once again we see the possible plan to dispose of the ship getting in the way of Captain Smith and his officers putting into practice any new plan to ensure the safety of those aboard. If Smith and his officers believed that the mystery ship was there to rescue them all, it would make sense of their allowing the few lifeboats available to leave *Titanic* only partly full of people. They would be easier to manage by the few crew members aboard who knew how to row, and much faster in making the round trip to the stranger and back. In the event the mysterious stranger, instead of coming closer, moved away from the sinking liner.

An affidavit was sent to the American Inquiry into the sinking of the *Titanic* by a Dr Quitzrau, a passenger on the Canadian Pacific liner *Mount Temple*, which details events aboard that vessel at about the relevant time (see Appendix 4). In that affidavit Dr Quitzrau tells how *Mount Temple* approached the site of the sinking, with her lights out. She came close enough for Quitzrau to look down into some of *Titanic's* lifeboats before moving off without making any attempt to pick up survivors. Dr Quitzrau does not mention actually seeing *Titanic*, and it is therefore possible that

Mount Temple did not reach the scene until after the White Star vessel had foundered, but his story does have more than a passing similarity to that told by survivors. The affidavit was not presented in evidence although it does remain on file. No matter what ship it was, there was certainly a vessel close enough to *Titanic* as she was sinking to have helped. There was no apparent reason for her failing to do so. It is inconceivable that the mystery ship's lookouts could have failed to see the liner or her distress signals. *Titanic's* mortar-type signals could have been seen and heard by any vessel close enough to have been in sight from the liner's bridge, especially on such a calm, clear night.

There has to be some very compelling reason why this mysterious vessel did nothing. All sailors have a built-in predisposition to help others in peril on the sea. Even in wartime, seamen go to extraordinary lengths to rescue people from enemy vessels with which they have shortly before been doing battle. Usually, the only time this rule of the sea is waived is when to go to the assistance of others would seriously endanger the lives of those aboard the would-be rescuer. In the case of the *Titanic* there was no apparent physical danger to a would-be rescuer if it was already close by, so perhaps the danger was not physical. If the captain of the mystery ship was already party to the plan to scuttle the *Titanic* but could see for himself that the plan had gone awry, he might well have considered it prudent to keep away. If he became involved and the original scheme came to light he would have found himself in hot water, but if he kept out of the way he could later deny all knowledge of the affair, in the unlikely event that his ship was identified. He might even have moved his ship out of the way for a while, then, prompted by conscience or the fact that he could then say that he had not previously been close by, returned to affect a rescue.

Chapter 19

Boats away

Even as *Carpathia* hurried towards her, conditions aboard *Titanic* descended into chaos. The officers overseeing the loading of the lifeboats seem to have had no idea that they could be fully loaded before they were lowered. The first boats away from the liner were ridiculously underfilled. The excuse given later for this incompetence was that the officers were afraid that the boats would buckle in the middle if they attempted to lower them properly filled. That this was an excuse is demonstrated by the fact that the last boats lowered were filled to capacity and survived lowering without any serious problems.

The wooden lifeboats were carried on the boat deck and arranged in two batches of eight, one batch at the forward end of the deck and the other at the aft end, with four boats on each side. In total the ship carried 16 wooden lifeboats, two of them at the very forward end, which were kept swung out ready for instant use all the time the ship was at sea; they were 25 feet long and capable of carrying 40 persons each, and were known as emergency boats. Aft from the emergency boats were 14 full-sized lifeboats, 30 feet long and capable of carrying 65 people each. In addition to the wooden boats the vessel carried four Engelhardt collapsible lifeboats, each just over 27 feet long and able to carry 47 persons. If the boats were fully loaded they could carry between them a grand total of 1,178 people. However, while two of the collapsible boats were stored on the boat deck just inboard of the emergency boats, the other two were stowed upside down on top of the officers' quarters. As the rigging wires for the forward funnel came over the top of these collapsibles, it would be extremely difficult to remove them from the roof where they were stowed and get them under any of the forward lifeboat davits in a hurry.

Once the order came to begin loading and lowering *Titanic's* boats, First Officer Murdoch took charge of those on the starboard side and Second Officer Lightoller those to port. Although they were not to know it at the time, male passengers stood a far greater chance of survival if they stayed on the starboard side of the boat deck.

The first boat into the water at 12.45am was No 7 on the starboard side, with just 28 people in it. Starboard No 5 and port No 6 both went into the water just 10 minutes later; No 5 had 41 people and No 6 just 28. Boat 3 went in at 1.00am with 50 aboard, followed by No 8 about 10 minutes later, with a mere 28 persons. At the same time as boat 8, No 1 was lowered with just a dozen people in it, seven of them crew members. Murdoch had been assisted in the loading of No 1 by Fifth Officer Lowe, who would distinguish himself later that night. Why these two experienced officers allowed a boat designed to take 40 people to leave the ship with just 12 was never satisfactorily explained, although at the inquiries following the disaster it did come out that Sir Cosmo Duff Gordon presented each of the seven crewmen with a cheque for £5. The passengers in No 1 were Sir Cosmo, his wife and her secretary, and two of their friends. The survivors from boat 1 later claimed that they were ordered into the lifeboat by First Officer Murdoch himself.

Because the ship was sinking by the bow it made sense to get the forward boats away first, but Mr Lightoller had encountered some problems with No 4 inasmuch as there was a wooden spar projecting from the ship's hull directly below it, which had to be cut away before the boat could be lowered. Rather than wait for the spar to be removed, Lightoller moved to the batch of boats further aft, leaving No 4 and emergency boat 2 hanging from their davits. Meanwhile Mr Murdoch had sent all of the forward starboard-side wooden lifeboats away from the ship.

As he had moved on to the aft boats before Murdoch, one would have expected Mr Lightoller to have been first to get one of them away, No 10 at 1.20am, with 55 persons in it, but no. Murdoch lowered No 9 at exactly the same time with 56 people aboard. It is already apparent that Murdoch was very much more efficient than Lightoller when it came to loading and lowering lifeboats, not that either of them would have won any prizes. Boats 11 and 12 were lowered simultaneously at 1.25am. Murdoch had slightly overloaded 11 and had squeezed 70 people in, while Lightoller had settled for just 43 in boat 12. Curiously, according to eyewitness testimony, a Frenchman leapt into this boat from B Deck as it was being lowered. B Deck, at this point, should have been completely enclosed, not a promenade, lined with locked cabins - yet another indication that the B Deck layout was not as it should have been. Port-side boat 14 was next away at 1.30am, almost fully loaded with 60 people in it. Fifth Officer Lowe assisted in the loading of No 14 and intended to take command of it when it was lowered. He obviously thought that 60 was as many people as the boat could handle as, in order to make room for himself, he ordered a 14-year-old boy to get out of the boat at gunpoint. Boats 13, 15 and 16 were next, all at 1.35am. Sixth Officer Moody appears to have dealt with boats 13 and

15. No 13 left the ship almost fully laden with 64 persons, and No 15 had 70 aboard. Again according to eyewitness evidence, boat 13 was loaded from A Deck where potential passengers had to climb over the ship's rail to get into it. No 16 also appears to have been dealt with by Mr Moody, but with Mr Lightoller in attendance; it left *Titanic* with 56 people in it.

Mr Murdoch now moved back to the forward end of the boat deck to see what could be done with the collapsible boats still there. He managed to get collapsible C away at 1.40am with 39 people before turning his attentions to boat A. He had some problems in getting A off the roof of the officers' quarters, so much so that it was, according to the received version of events that night, still there when the ship sank, when it floated free. However, Steward E. Brown testified that there were no real problems encountered in getting A off the roof and under the davits vacated by one of the forward lifeboats. August Wennerstrom, a third-class passenger, later said that boat A went into the water the right way up, which argues that it was launched in the usual way, and that it was only capsized after the liner had foundered by people in the water trying to climb aboard. Both Brown and Wennerstrom survived by making use of the waterlogged collapsible as a makeshift life raft along with about 13 others.

With the last of the aft boats gone, Mr Lightoller came forward again to deal with the remaining port-side boats. He found boat 2, which for some unaccountable reason he had failed to load and lower earlier, even though it was one of the emergency boats that was always kept swung out and ready for instant use, full of what he described as 'Dagoes'. He cleared these interlopers out of the boat at gunpoint and began embarking a few more deserving individuals, almost all first-class passengers or crewmen. No 2 was launched at 1.45am with 25 people. Boat 4, which had been delayed because of the projecting spar below it, was next and went into the water at 1.55am with just 40 aboard, almost all either first-class passengers or crew members. Lightoller next turned his attentions to collapsible boat D. He had some problems getting the boat under the davits, so it wasn't until about 2.05am that the boat got away with 44 people in it. By this time it was obvious to all aboard the ship that she could not remain afloat for many more minutes. Lightoller started to prepare boat B and tried to get it down from the roof of the officers' quarters, but there was no more time.

Even as the boats were being prepared and lowered there were other things going on aboard the stricken liner. Armed junior officers were sent below to lock the steel mesh doors leading to the forward third-class accommodation, cutting it off from the rest of the ship. This part of the vessel, it will be recalled, housed mostly single male third-class passengers who didn't take being locked in at all well. Some of these passengers tried to open the doors and force their way out, but the ship's officers were prepared for this and opened fire. On the wreck the area around those doors, which are still locked, shows evidence of scarring where it appears some of the bullets struck. With a high proportion of the third-class male passengers effectively prevented from occupying valuable lifeboat spaces, the crew turned their attentions to the Italian restaurant staff. These, it seems, were also deemed unworthy of lifeboat space and had been rounded up and locked in the second-class dining saloon. After all, there were a lot of first-class passengers and crew members who could make use of the all too few lifeboat places. It seems that at least some of the third-class passengers from the forward part of the ship were later released, but they did not reach the boat deck until after the last boats had gone. The unfortunate Italians don't seem to have escaped from the dining saloon at all.

According to the received version of events, in the wireless room Jack Phillips and Harold Bride continued to send out distress calls and exchange signals with various vessels. They stayed at their posts until told by Captain Smith that they had done their duty and were free to attempt to save themselves, or so Harold Bride was to say at both later Inquiries. Bride also said that shortly before they were relieved by Captain Smith a stoker had come into the wireless room. The stoker, half crazed with fear, had attempted to remove Phillips's life jacket while the wireless man was engrossed in sending out distress calls. Phillips was so intent on what he was doing that he didn't even notice the stoker's presence. Harold Bride promptly struck the stoker over the head with a convenient spanner, rendering him unconscious at the very least. When the wireless operators were released from duty, Bride testified that they vacated the wireless room, leaving the comatose stoker on the floor, still without a life jacket. Once outside, the operators parted company; Bride made his way forward towards where the last remaining boats were still aboard, while Jack Phillips headed aft.

However, there is compelling evidence to show that Bride's story was something less than the whole truth. The last wireless signals from the sinking liner were received by the *Virginian* at 2.17am. The signals were blurred and weak, as if the transmitter was running on reduced power, and ended abruptly as if the power had suddenly and completely failed, which indeed it had. By that time *Titanic's* bow, and the wireless cabin, were under water and the liner's stern was high in the air. Survivors in the boats saw the ship's lights flicker and go out at precisely that time, 2.17am. If Harold Bride had been telling the truth about Phillips and himself having left the wireless room about 10 minutes before that last signal was sent out, whose hand could it have been on the Morse key? There seems to have been nobody else aboard the ship who could have sent that signal except Jack Phillips, and if he had left the cabin and gone aft he could not have returned as the cabin was submerged. There can only be one believable explanation - that Bride had deserted his post, leaving his fellow operator to his fate before anyone had officially told him it was time to leave. While such action might have been reprehensible, it is also understandable. Bride was a young man, just 22 years old, two years younger than Phillips. What is inexcusable is what Bride had to say about Phillips later.

As the bows of the ship went under and water swept back across the decks, Second Officer Charles Lightoller was washed overboard, he said. After swimming about for a little while he came across collapsible boat B, which was floating upside down and acting as a life raft for between 25 and 30 people. According to Lightoller there was nobody actually on the boat when he reached it but there were a lot of people in the water around it. He promptly boarded the upturned boat and took command.

When boat B had been washed overboard wireless operator Bride had gone with it and finished up underneath the collapsible lifeboat where he remained for between a half and three-quarters of an hour. He then swam away from the already heavily laden boat for the best part of an hour before returning and being taken aboard. By that time Bride thought that there were between 30 and 40 people on the boat, Jack Phillips among them. According to Bride, Phillips died later that night from cold and fear. (We already know that Phillips could not have made it to boat B, being still in the wireless cabin when the ship foundered. Water rushing into the vessel would have carried him deeper inside if he had attempted to leave the cabin after it was submerged. There a number of eye-witness accounts of the sinking that tell of people being sucked into the ship through open doors, windows and portholes as she filled with water, which is exactly what one would expect.)

Colonel Archibald Gracie was another who made good his escape from the sinking ship on boat B. His story is even more unbelievable than most. According to Gracie he was on the opposite side of the ship from B when he was dragged under as the bow sank. Swimming furiously he swam underwater for a period of minutes before breaking surface and spotting the upturned lifeboat. He reached the boat but was unable to climb completely aboard and had to remain partly in the water.

Baker Charles Joughin also made an extraordinary escape. As the aft part of the ship reared up until it was almost perpendicular he climbed up the outside of the hull until he was standing on the very stern. Here he patiently waited until the ship sank beneath him, when he casually stepped off and began swimming. According to Joughin he didn't even get his hair wet. He swam about for 2 hours, or so he thought, before coming across boat B and clambering to safety.

In all about 15 people survived the disaster by escaping aboard boat B. At one point there may have been as many as 40 persons clustered on the upturned lifeboat and probably many more in the water close by it. Not one of those that survived could have been telling the truth about how they swam to the boat, climbed aboard, and got through the night by standing huddled together on the bottom planking, as we shall shortly see.

The nine or ten people who survived the disaster aboard collapsible boat A are in the main as mendacious as those from boat B. If we are to believe the official version of events that night, collapsible A, like B, was washed overboard as the ship sank. The boat floated the right way up but the people who managed to clamber into it could not get the canvas sides up or bale out the water in it. They were obliged to sit in the partly submerged craft, in freezing cold water up to their waists, in saturated clothes.

There was nobody in the boat when it first went into the water and we do not know who reached it first. P. D. Daly, O. Abelseth and Rosa Abbott, all passengers, were pulled into the boat from the sea, Abelseth after he had been swimming about for 20 minutes or so. In fact, all of the people in boat A had supposedly been in the sea for varying lengths of time, just like those on boat B.

It will be recalled that it was a very cold night, with both sea and air temperatures well below freezing. It is impossible for anyone to have survived for more than a couple of minutes in sea that cold, and being wet through they would have been no better off aboard either boat A or B. Therefore all of these people who supposedly survived the night on or in these two collapsible boats must have been lying. The question is, why?

By far the most likely explanation is that boats A and B were launched in the usual way and that they were capsized or otherwise disabled once they were in the water. There is some evidence to suggest that this might have indeed been the case. August Wennerstrom, the third-class passenger, said that boat A was overturned by people in the water after the ship had sunk. Steward Edward Brown said that they had no difficulty in getting boat A down off the roof of the officers' quarters, where it was usually stowed. When boat B was found a few days after the sinking it was surrounded by floating corpses, buoyed up by their life jackets. Many of these corpses were clearly not people who had been prepared to swim far in an effort to survive. Some of them were quite heavily dressed in pyjamas, a couple of shirts, two pairs of trousers, two vests, two jackets and an overcoat. Some pockets were stuffed with meat and biscuits. Quite clearly these people had been given ample time to prepare to leave the stricken liner in a lifeboat. One of the bodies recovered was later identified as that of John Jacob Astor, the wealthiest of the many millionaires aboard the ship. Crew members' bodies found there had pockets full of tobacco and matches. We are all aware that wet matches are useless and that waterlogged tobacco doesn't make much of a smoke. These crew members obviously had not intended to go into the water. The only reasonable explanation for these bodies being discovered in close proximity to boat B is that they were originally its crew and passengers, which argues that the boat was lowered in the usual manner and only upset later. It is quite possible that boat B went into the mass of people struggling in the water after the ship sank and was overturned there. Perhaps the millionaire passengers on B forfeited their lives in an attempt to save others. Or perhaps those struggling in the water, unimpressed by the occupants' first class status, overturned the boat in an attempt to save themselves.

Whatever happened, it should be clear that the evacuation of the sinking ship was not the orderly affair usually described but the horrific panic-stricken scramble that one would have expected. Of course those that survived in boats A and B kept quiet about how they managed to do so if they were responsible for the deaths of many others who had previously occupied those boats. As it was, many of the men who survived the disaster were later ostracised for saving themselves while women and children died.

During her final moments, as her bow sank ever deeper, *Titanic's* stern lifted out of the water until the aft part of the hull was standing almost vertically. The ship's lights, which had continued working throughout the time the vessel was slowly settling in the water, remained on until just before the hull reached the perpendicular, when they flickered and went out, only to flash on again briefly before failing completely. As mentioned earlier, we know exactly what the time was because the last wireless signal to come from the ship at 2.17am was cut off as the power failed. As soon as the lights failed those on the boats and in the water were left in total darkness, unable to see anything at all. Nobody actually saw the ship sink.

Fifth Officer Lowe, in boat 14, determined to go to the assistance of the people he could hear struggling in the water, but he was not such a fool as to do so straight away. He knew that the mass of people would try to board his lifeboat if he went too close too soon and would almost certainly overturn it. He waited until the cries of those in the water had all but died away as the cold killed them before heading back towards where the liner had sunk. He had waited too long, and found only four people still alive. Nevertheless it was the best effort to save people from the water that night, with the possible exceptions of boats A and B.

Next Mr Lowe turned his attention to rounding up as many of the lifeboats as possible and collecting survivors from the two half-sunken collapsible boats. His own boat was almost loaded to capacity so he transferred most of his passengers to other lifeboats. Most of the other boats already had barely enough crewmen aboard to row and steer them, but Mr Lowe took as many competent seamen from them as possible to make his own, now relatively lightly loaded, more manageable. He then set off towards collapsible boats A and B, and collected the people that were still alive from them. Somewhere along the way Lowe encountered what seaman Joseph Scarrott described as a life raft, which seemed to be constructed of 'air boxes'. 'It was not a collapsible,' Scarrott was positive. As *Titanic* did not carry any life rafts we are left wondering where this one had come from.

By the time Lowe had picked up everyone from the two damaged collapsibles and had distributed the people in the other boats he had collected as evenly as he was able, there was nobody left alive in the water. For some little while passengers in the boats had been seeing lights in the sky, away to the southeast. Most of them were aware that *Carpathia* would be coming to their rescue from that direction and were heartened to see what they correctly believed to be rockets fired from that ship. However, it does seem a little odd that people sitting in small boats only just above sea level could see any indication at all of the approaching rescuer. It was a pitch-black night and they were surrounded by huge icebergs like floating mountains. From as low down as the survivors were, even growlers would have looked pretty impressive and would have interfered with their line of sight. This is a recurring problem with *Titanic's* survivors: either they could see in total darkness and through icebergs or there were many fewer bergs than there should have been according to other accounts.

As dawn approached *Carpathia* arrived on the scene and prepared to pick up survivors. For the people from *Titanic* the first, and worst, part of their ordeal was over.

Chapter 20

Too many survivors

Captain Rostron continued to navigate *Carpathia* at high speed all the way to the position given to him by his wireless operator, as indicated in *Titanic's* distress signals. He arrived at that position at just before 4.00am. Several times during his mad dash to the rescue Rostron had to take violent evasive action to avoid running into icebergs and growlers that had loomed up out of the darkness. The Captain never explained how his lookouts managed to spot these hazards on a pitch dark night in time for his vessel, moving at something like 17½ knots, to avoid them. However, avoid them they did, and at 4 o'clock *Carpathia* stopped engines. About 300 yards ahead could be seen a green light - they had the first lifeboat in sight.

Slowly Captain Rostron eased his ship closer to the lifeboat, intending to bring it alongside on his port side where it would be sheltered from what little wind there was. Suddenly a large iceberg loomed up out of the darkness, directly ahead of *Carpathia*. Captain Rostron was obliged to make an emergency alteration to his course and had to bring the small boat in on his starboard side. Had *Carpathia* not been manoeuvring very slowly this berg alone would have ended the rescue attempt. Rostron was no fool and fully appreciated the risks he had been taking with his ship and the lives of all aboard her. He later said he was 'devoutly thankful' that the race to the boats was over. 'Every moment had brought its risk - a risk that only keen eyes and quick decisions could meet.' We already know that there was nothing indecisive about Captain Rostron.

A former shipmate of Captain Rostron, who had served with him aboard several vessels, wrote, 'The great thing about Rostron was, he was a great navigator. There was nothing slapdash about Rostron and the navigators around that night, and I would certainly place Rostron and his team at the top of the list.' We already know that Captain Rostron had steered for the position of the sinking as worked out by *Titanic's* navigating officer, Joseph Boxhall. That he found the lifeboats at that position tells us that Mr Boxhall had got his sums right and that this was indeed the position where at least the first of the boats had been launched. (Curiously, when the wreck was discovered it turned out to be several miles from Boxhall's position, suggesting that the ship steamed for some considerable distance after many of the lifeboats went into the water.)

This first boat turned out to be No 2 with none other than Fifth Officer Boxhall in command, which had been launched at about 1.45am after all *Titanic's* aft boats were away from the ship and only about half an hour before the liner finally sank. Rostron noticed that one of *Titanic's* officers was in the boat and had him brought to the bridge to report on what had happened. Boxhall told Rostron that *Titanic* had sunk at about 2.30 that morning, a mere hour and a half before *Carpathia* arrived on the scene.

It was just about dawn and the growing light revealed a terrifying vista to those aboard *Carpathia* and in the *Titanic's* lifeboats close by. Everywhere they looked they saw huge icebergs, dozens of them. A junior officer on *Carpathia* counted 25 that were around 200 feet tall, and dozens more ranging in height from 150 feet down to 50 feet, all within a couple of miles of *Carpathia*. Less than half a mile away was the monster that had almost caught them out at the last moment, and only 100 feet or so off the port quarter was a growler. Captain Rostron had been extraordinarily lucky, it seems. Floating pathetically among the bergs and growlers were *Titanic's* lifeboats. Captain Rostron was actually impressed by this awesome display of nature, which is more than can be said of *Titanic's* Second Officer, Charles Lightoller. By this time Lightoller had been picked up from capsized collapsible boat B by Mr Lowe in No 14. As it grew light he looked around but couldn't see any icebergs at all. As we have already seen, quite a lot of Mr Lightoller's evidence flies in the face of that given by the vast majority of the other witnesses. Either Mr Lightoller wasn't there at all, or he had his own reasons for concealing the truth.

Captain Rostron continued to seek out the remainder of the lifeboats and bring what survivors he found aboard *Carpathia*. As these people came aboard their names were taken and a list of survivors was compiled so that the authorities ashore could be informed at the earliest possible moment, by wireless, just who had survived the sinking. According to second-class survivor Lawrence Beesley, only 17 of *Titanic's* small boats were brought alongside *Carpathia* instead of the 18 that we know were supposedly launched from the liner without any serious problems. Where then was the other one? Just 13 of *Titanic's* small boats were hoisted aboard the Cunard vessel, the others, having discharged their survivors, were cast adrift with the bodies of those who had died from the cold during the night.

Having taken the people from all of the small boats he could find, Rostron ordered the whole area to be searched in the hope that more survivors might be discovered. As his vessel moved slowly through the area where *Titanic* had presumably foundered he noticed that there was not much wreckage floating about, just a deckchair or two, a few lifebelts, a good deal of cork, and just one floating body. 'No more flotsam than one can often see on a seashore, drifted in by the tide,' is how Captain Rostron described what he saw. However, he did note one anomaly, although he didn't attach any importance to it at the time, or intentionally play it down later. He found too many proper wooden lifeboats at the scene. When asked, at the British Inquiry into the *Titanic* disaster, 'Altogether, how many boats did you pick up?' Captain Rostron replied:

'We got 13 lifeboats alongside, and we picked up 13 lifeboats, two emergency boats, and two Berthon [collapsible] boats. One lifeboat we saw capsized, and one of the Berthon boats was not launched from the ship. There was also a Berthon boat we saw capsized. This made a total of 20.'

We already know that none of *Titanic's* proper lifeboats were capsized and that all of them transported their survivors to *Carpathia*. Captain Rostron also described seeing collapsible boat B drifting at the site, so the upturned full-sized lifeboat cannot have been that. Rostron is quite clear in his distinctions between full-sized (30-foot-long) lifeboats, emergency (25-foot-long) boats and collapsibles. He obviously saw an upturned full-sized ship's lifeboat, but it cannot have been from *Titanic*, so where did it come from? Captain Rostron's sighting of this extra boat was confirmed by the captain of the only other ship to reach the scene of the sinking in a rescue attempt, Captain Stanley Lord of the *Californian*.

Aboard *Californian* Captain Lord had spent the greater part of the night dozing, fully dressed, on the chartroom settee. As we know, Lord was obviously expecting something to happen during the night, which was why he had not responded to the sighting of white rockets by his watch officers but had asked if there was any colour in them. We also know that the only ship in the area that night that fired coloured rockets was the *Titanic*. Unfortunately the liner's coloured signals had not been seen from *Californian*, or had at least not been reported to Captain Lord, so his ship had remained inactive, waiting. At about 4.00am *Californian's* Chief Officer, G. V. Stewart, came onto the bridge to begin his watch. The officers already there, Stone and Gibson, reported the rockets they had seen during the night. Steward looked towards the south-southwest and saw a four-masted steamer. 'There she is!' he said, believing he was looking at the same ship that had been seen earlier, and that it had steamed away, then come back again. Stone quickly told the Chief Officer that the ship he was looking at was not the same vessel that had been in sight earlier. The ship that Stone and Gibson had seen earlier had two masthead lights whereas the steamer they could see now had but a single one. (A four-masted ship should normally have displayed two masthead lights.)

It began to get light at about 4.30, so Stewart left the bridge to wake Captain Lord, who was still dozing in the chartroom. When Stewart woke Lord he told him that the ship from which rockets had been seen during the night was still to the south of them. With no apparent reason to suspect that there was anything wrong, Captain Lord took a few minutes to make his way to the bridge. Once there he waited until full daylight, when he could see the best way through the ice, before ordering the engine room to stand by. At about 5.15am *Californian* got under way, but not seemingly towards *Titanic* or *Carpathia*. It was only now that Chief Officer Stewart told Captain Lord that he was concerned about the steamer to the south of them. Stewart thought that she might have been damaged by the ice and have been firing distress rockets during the night. Captain Lord ordered Stewart to wake the wireless operator and tell him to contact this other vessel and find out if anything was amiss. Shortly afterwards *Californian's* wireless operator, Cyril Evans, sent out his first 'CQ' of the day. Almost immediately the *Frankfurt* replied with the information that *Titanic* had sunk during the night. The *Virginian* confirmed the news about *Titanic*. Evans made a note of what he had heard and took it straight to Captain Lord.

As soon as he received the information about *Titanic* Lord ordered Evans to get confirmation of the position in which she had foundered. Immediately on receiving this confirmed position Lord worked out the best course towards it. *Californian* would have to steer S16°W for a distance of 19½ miles to reach the site of the sinking. Perhaps even more coldly efficient than Captain Rostron, only when Lord was sure of his facts did he start towards *Titanic's* last given position. Because of the ice it would take *Californian* about 2½ hours to cover slightly less than 20 miles in broad daylight. *Californian's* performance at least has the merit of being believable, which is more than can be said of *Carpathia's* mad dash through the darkness for almost 60 miles in just 1 hour more.

By the time *Californian* reached the site of the sinking, *Carpathia* had finished picking up the people from the boats and was preparing to get under way towards New York. Before she left, Captain Rostron requested that Lord make a search of the area in case he had missed anyone. *Californian* scoured the area, steaming slowly, but did not find a living soul. However, Captain Lord did see the small boats Rostron had left behind. 'There were about six of them, the remainder having been picked up by the *Carpathia*,' he said. 'One was capsized, and there were two smaller boats with collapsible canvas sides.' Captain Lord's description is characteristically clear and concise. He only saw two collapsible boats and made a clear distinction between them and proper wooden lifeboats. He did see a capsized wooden lifeboat exactly as described by Captain Rostron, a lifeboat that had no business being there when all of those from *Titanic* have been accounted for. As the collapsible boats are very different in appearance from real lifeboats there is little or no chance that Lord and Rostron were confusing them. Captain Lord also said that they saw about six boats at the scene, so if we add the two damaged collapsibles, which he clearly did not see, to the 13 boats recovered by *Carpathia*, we have a total of 21 small boats there. *Titanic* only carried 20, so we have at least one boat that must have come from another vessel.

There is one other piece of evidence to show that there was another vessel involved in the *Titanic* disaster. As we know, Captain Rostron had a list of survivors from the liner compiled so that he could notify people ashore of exactly who had survived. *Carpathia's* wireless operator, Cottam, duly transmitted that list. There were 803 names on it, 135 of which do not appear on *Titanic's* passenger or crew lists. It is entirely possible that a good many of those whose names do not appear on the liner's lists simply had their names misspelled on one or other of the records. However, we now know that 705 people actually survived the sinking of the *Titanic*; 98 fewer than appear on the list sent out by *Carpathia*. Captain Rostron was certain that his vessel had picked up 705 survivors from *Titanic*, and said so quite forcibly. He was careful to include the qualifying 'from *Titanic*' wording in his statements, hinting that any extras came from somewhere else. Nevertheless we are left with 98 people who were picked up by *Carpathia* but who did not come from the White Star liner. *Titanic's* lifeboats saved an average of about 40 people each that night, but we know that their loading was very badly managed. Allowing that the crew of another vessel present might have been more efficient than their counterparts on *Titanic*, perhaps they managed an average of 50 persons per lifeboat. That would account for there being too many lifeboats in the area when *Carpathia* arrived to take on survivors. There would have had to have been 22 boats there in all, which in the light of the available evidence is not unlikely.

It is now abundantly clear that the orderly and even heroic evacuation of the sinking *Titanic* after an accidental collision with an iceberg simply did not happen. That there was an accidental collision seems almost incontrovertible, but the iceberg appears an unlikely participant. The most likely scenario must be that another ship substituted for the berg and that this unnamed vessel was seriously damaged to the extent that her crew began putting passengers off in lifeboats. The evacuation of the *Titanic* was anything but orderly as is evidenced by the haphazard loading and lowering of the lifeboats, which were not even launched in any logical order. That there was panic aboard is shown by there being no serious attempt to prolong the life of the ship once she was damaged, and by the fact that a number of survivors testified to either hearing gunfire or actually seeing people trying to get into the boats shot down by the ship's officers. At least one of those officers did admit to firing his gun, but not at anyone in particular. It is also clear that at least some of those who survived the sinking did not do so in the manner they later claimed.

Remember that anyone who went into the sea for any more than a few seconds that night would have had almost no chance of surviving; the cold would have killed them. It is a fact that sudden immersion in very cold water causes the human body to immediately react by immobilising the limbs and sending all warm blood toward the heart and lungs. This reaction actually gives the best chance of survival, whereas attempting to swim accelerates cooling. Even without attempting to swim, survival time for a human being in water at sub-zero temperatures is only a matter of a couple of minutes. Nobody from *Titanic* could have swum more than a couple of yards before being fished out of the water that night. Possibly those who escaped on or in collapsible boats A and B were already in them when they were upset by people in the water as the ship went down. They would then have been close enough under those circumstances for some of them to have scrambled back aboard before the cold immobilised them. Of course that would mean that officers who should have remained at their posts had in fact left the ship before the last of the boats was lowered and while there were still many passengers aboard, men, women and children. It would also mean that these people who had saved their own skins without regard to the duty they owed to those in their care would have to come up with some sort of story to hide the fact. Once aboard *Carpathia* they began to do just that.

Titanic's surviving officers, aware that there was bound to be an inquiry into the disaster, met to decide what story they should tell. It would definitely be better for them if all the crew's stories matched up. It would be even better if the tales told by the surviving passengers were similar as well.

Shortly before *Carpathia* reached New York a note was circulated among *Titanic's* survivors requesting that they make no statement, in any detail, when they arrived. As a result, not one survivor in ten would submit to questioning; clear evidence that the cover-up had already begun aboard *Carpathia* well before she reached New York.

More evidence of the cover-up beginning in earnest aboard *Carpathia* can be gathered from other decrees issued by the survivor committee led by Samuel Goldenberg aboard the *Cunarder*, which display technical knowledge of shipping in general and *Titanic* in particular of which ordinary passengers would have been ignorant. Obviously these decrees were the work of Ismay, Lightoller and Lowe. It is interesting to note that the majority of these so-called decrees were not supported by the great majority of the survivors, being signed solely by the 25 members of the committee. The statement stated:

'We the undersigned surviving passengers from the steamship *Titanic*, in order to forestall any sensational or exaggerated statements, deem it our duty to give to the press a statement of facts which have come to our knowledge and which we believe to be true.

On Sunday, April 14, 1912, at about twenty minutes to twelve PM on a cold, starlit night, in a smooth sea and no moon, the ship struck an iceberg which had been reported to the bridge by lookouts, but not early enough to avoid collision. Steps were taken to ascertain the damage and save passengers and ship. Orders were given to put on lifebelts and the boats were lowered.

The ship sank at twenty minutes past two AM Monday, and the usual distress signals were sent out by wireless and rockets fired at intervals from the ship. Fortunately the wireless message was received by the Cunard steamship *Carpathia* at about twelve o'clock midnight, and she arrived on the scene of the disaster at about four AM Monday.

The officers and crew of the steamship *Carpathia* had been preparing all night for the rescue and comfort of the survivors, and the last mentioned were received on board with the most touching care and kindness, every attention being given to all, irrespective of class. The passengers, officers and crew gave up gladly their staterooms, clothing and comforts for our benefit, all honour to them.

The English Board of Trade passengers' certificate aboard the *Titanic* allowed for a total of approximately 8,500. The same certificate called for lifeboat accommodation for approximately 950 in the following boats: Fourteen large lifeboats, two smaller boats and two collapsible boats. Life preservers were accessible and apparently in sufficient numbers for all on board.

The approximate number of passengers carried at the time of the collision was:

First class, 330; second class, 320; third class, 750; total, 1,400; officers and crew, 940; Total, 2,340

Of the foregoing about the following were rescued by the steamship *Carpathia*:

First class, 210; second class, 125; third class, 200; officers, 4; seamen, 39; stewards, 96; firemen, 71; Total, 210 of the crew. The total saved, about 745, was about eighty percent of the maximum capacity of the lifeboats.

We feel it our duty to call the attention of the public to what we consider the inadequate supply of lifesaving appliances provided for a modern passenger steamship, and recommend that immediate steps be taken to compel passenger steamers to carry sufficient boats to accommodate the maximum number of persons carried on board. The following facts were observed and should be considered in this connection:

The insufficiency of lifeboats, rafts, &c; lack of trained seamen to man the same (stoker, stewards, &c, are not efficient boat handlers); not enough officers to carry out emergency orders on the bridge and superintend the launching and control of lifeboats; absence of searchlights. The Board of Trade rules allow for entirely too many persons in each boat to permit the same to be properly handled. On the *Titanic* the boat deck was about seventy-five feet above the water, and consequently the passengers were required to embark before lowering boats, thus endangering the operation and preventing the taking on of the maximum number the boats would hold. Boats at all times to be properly equipped with provisions, water, lamps, compasses, lights, &c. Life saving boat drills should be more frequent and thoroughly carried out, and officers should be armed at boat drills.

Greater reduction in speed in fog and ice, as damage, if collision actually occurs, is less. In conclusion, we suggest that an international conference be called to recommend the passage of identical laws providing for the safety of all at sea, and we urge the United States government to take the initiative as soon as possible.'

The statement was signed by Samuel Goldenberg, chairman, and a committee of 25. (*New York Herald*, 19 April 1912, p7)

This statement shifts all blame for the loss of life onto the Board of Trade and its regulations while hardly mentioning the disaster itself, and is a somewhat transparent attempt to clear the owners, officers and crew of *Titanic* of any charge of negligence. It does, however, reinforce the belief that *Carpathia* picked up more people than there were *Titanic* survivors brought into New York.

Probably to give *Titanic's* surviving officers and crew time to get their stories straight, Captain Rostron forbade his wireless operator to give out any details about the disaster except the names of survivors. Even though US President Taft sent out two cruisers to meet *Carpathia* and collect all possible information, the blackout continued. Rostron ignored the

President's plea for information, even though Taft was primarily interested in what had become of his aide, Major Archibald Butt.

At about 6.00pm on Thursday 18 April, *Carpathia* stopped at the entrance to the Ambrose Channel to pick up a New York harbour pilot. She and her cargo of *Titanic* survivors had finally reached New York and real inquiries could begin. Instead, the cover-up continued.

Chapter 21

The Inquiries

When *Carpathia* entered New York Harbour she did not immediately proceed to her own berth to unload her own passengers and *Titanic's* survivors. Captain Rostron took his ship to the White Star pier and offloaded the 13 lifeboats he had collected from where *Titanic* had foundered. Only then did *Carpathia* head for her own berth and disgorge her passengers. There was a huge crowd of spectators on the quayside, including quite a few newspaper reporters, who had come to see the survivors from the sunken liner. However, the New York authorities had anticipated this curiosity on the part of the general population and had taken steps to ensure that only those people they approved of could get anywhere near the survivors. Although the usual Customs formalities had been suspended for the people from *Titanic*, the police were there in force to control the crowds. No fewer than 150 patrolmen, 12 mounted policemen and 25 detectives were on hand to man the barricades that blocked the streets leading to the quayside. Only close relatives were supposed to be allowed onto the pier to greet survivors, and all applications were vetted by 40 inspectors who had instructions not to let any newspapermen through. Even that was not enough to satisfy the authorities in New York, and the pier itself was roped off for 75 feet on either side of *Carpathia's* gangplanks. This blanket ban on newsmen and anyone who was not related to a survivor didn't apply to Mr Marconi and *New York Times* reporter Jim Spears, who were not only allowed through the police cordon onto the pier but onto the rescue ship itself. Clearly someone didn't want the survivors questioned by anybody who did not know what questions were allowed.

Eventually *Titanic's* first- and second-class passengers began to appear. Singly, or in small groups, first and second-class passengers came down the gangways and were greeted by their relatives. Some of them didn't look like first- or second- class any more because they had lost everything except the clothing they were wearing when they left *Titanic* and were now dressed in whatever had been donated to them by the passengers on *Carpathia*. Of the 327 in first class, 198 had survived. From the 258 who had set out in second class, 112 survived. Those that were up to it were taken away by their relatives, while those suffering from the effects of a night in the small boats or other injuries were whisked away to hospital in ambulances. Very few were questioned about their experiences that first night ashore.

Then, at about 11.00pm, *Titanic's* third-class passengers began to appear. Of the 709 who had sailed on the liner, just 175 made it to New York. Most of these had lost everything they owned when the ship sank and were destitute. Private relief funds helped to provide enough cash for some of these people to continue their journeys to friends and relatives in the new world, if they had any. Even the White Star Line helped out. Those families that had lost their breadwinners and had nobody in America prepared to take them in would be sent back to where they came from. One of the more generous organisations prepared to help out the survivors was the Pennsylvania Railroad, which provided a special train that would take any survivor, regardless of class, to Pennsylvania and points west.

The last of *Titanic's* survivors to leave *Carpathia* were the crew. Of the approximately 884 who had signed aboard, just 182 had survived. Curiously, 11 more crewmen, whose names do not appear on any crew list, also survived the disaster and came ashore at New York with the rest, long after all the other survivors and crowds had departed. These crew members were not allowed to leave the dockyard but were marched down *Carpathia's* aft gangway, along the empty pier and down a narrow stairway to where the United States Immigration Service tender *George Starr* was waiting. The *George Starr* took them northward for about six city blocks to pier 60, where they were disembarked at the pier's reception area. All harbour employees had been cleared from the area so there was hardly anyone around to see the crewmen marched across the reception area to pier 61, where they were put on board the IMM (Red Star Line) vessel *Lapland*. *Titanic's* four surviving officers were put into first-class cabins, but all the rest of the crew were assigned berths in the third-class areas of the ship. Somebody had taken quite a lot of trouble to make sure that *Titanic's* survivors had not had the chance to tell their stories to anyone, most of all the press.

Even then the people trying so hard to suppress information about what had really happened to the *Titanic* must have known that they couldn't keep a lid on it for ever. The press, both local and national, throughout the western world was clamouring for information and inevitably reporters would reach survivors who were prepared to talk. When they did, some of the stories they were told hardly fitted in with the version of events the White Star Line, and the British and American Governments, were trying to pass off as the truth. These stories told of chaos aboard the sinking ship, passengers and crew panicking, passengers being shot by trigger-happy officers and the inefficiency of the crew when it came to getting the lifeboats away. Some of these eye-witnesses had some equally horrific tales to tell of events aboard the rescue ship where, according to them, babies were left unattended and unclothed in freezing cold rooms and even such essentials as soap and toiletries were denied them unless they were prepared to pay exorbitant amounts of money for them.

Meanwhile, at New York, the liner's surviving lifeboats were being attended to. All identification marks such as numbers and *Titanic's* name were removed, supposedly to deter souvenir hunters. During this exercise a dockyard employee noticed that *Olympic's* name was cut into the boats, not *Titanic's*. He also noted that some trouble was taken to obliterate these incised names, which were quickly filled with putty and painted over. Within a couple of days the boats were taken out of the water and hauled up into a convenient loft where they remained for some time. Then they were taken to Lane's Brooklyn boatyard for evaluation, so that their value could be deducted from any insurance payout. Eventually most of the boats were taken back to Britain and were put aboard *Olympic* to comply with a new company and BoT policy, that there should be enough lifeboats on every ship to accommodate everyone aboard.

Curiously, even though there was a great shortage of available lifeboats at that time because of the new policy, which meant that all of the shipping lines were grabbing whatever boats they could get their hands on, one of *Titanic's* lifeboats was not placed aboard any other vessel. This lifeboat, *Titanic's* No 14, was left to rot at Southampton, where it remained for six years. Only after the Great War was anything done with No 14, when it was presented to a group of local sea scouts as a gesture of appreciation for the sacrifices made by former members during the recent conflict. By this time the lifeboat's paint had faded and was starting to peel, so the scouts decided to freshen it up a little. They stripped the existing paint away prior to refinishing the boat ready for use as a cutter. As they removed what remained of the old paint they found the word 'Olympic' or 'Olympus' carved into the gunwale. At that time *Olympic* was still in service (and would remain so for almost another 20 years), her decks cluttered with dozens of lifeboats. Clearly this particular specimen did not come from her. To further confuse the issue, the scouts' boat came with her cast identification plates showing that it was indeed from *Titanic* and it still carried White Star Line badges. These cast metal badges were carefully preserved by the sea scouts and for many years were used as trophies, being presented to either port or starboard teams on winning some in-house event such as rowing. (In recent years these badges seem to have disappeared, which, as they are of considerable monetary value, is not surprising.) The boat itself served the sea scouts for many years before eventually being badly damaged in a collision with the Portsmouth to Gosport ferry. After that it was taken by the Royal Navy to Haslar to be broken up. It remained there for years before finally vanishing completely. The story of this boat, with the incriminating name cut into its gunwale, was recorded by a Royal Naval admiral in a privately published account of Hampshire scouting. The book is extremely rare but not completely unobtainable.

Within days of *Titanic's* survivors reaching New York a Senate Inquiry into the disaster was begun. 'Inquiry' is not perhaps the right word to describe what was in fact a carefully choreographed cover-up carried out by the United States Government. Senator William Alden Smith headed this American farce and conducted a great part of the questioning. Throughout the proceedings he hardly asked a single pertinent question and studiously ignored any answers that did not tie in with the findings he had obviously predetermined to come up with. Smith did his job remarkably well inasmuch as he obscured the relevant facts and at the same time used the whole show as a publicity vehicle to further his own political ambitions. He also, by accepting as fact the demonstrably untrue statement of *Californian's* donkeyman Gill, provided a convenient scapegoat that diverted attention away from what had really occurred. As we have already seen in Chapter 17, *Californian* was much too far away from the sinking liner for any signals or lights to have been seen from her, and for anyone on *Californian* to have claimed to have actually seen *Titanic* is ridiculous. Nevertheless, that is exactly what Gill made out, that he had seen *Titanic*, and Senator Smith appears to have believed him. According to Smith the mystery ship visible from *Titanic* as she was sinking could be none other than *Californian*, and Captain Lord and his officers had committed possibly the worst crime any seaman could commit, in that they had seen distress signals and had failed to respond to them.

Senator Smith apparently believed that, had Lord gone to the rescue, many more, perhaps all of those lost with the liner, might have been saved. In one respect Smith was right. If *Californian* had been close enough and had seen the signals from *Titanic* early enough, there was no captain at sea who could have made a better job of taking off the liner's people. Unfortunately *Californian* wasn't close enough and her officers did not see distress signals, so she did not go to the rescue until it was too late. Captain Lord himself said that he had nothing to lose and everything to gain by rescuing the people from *Titanic*, so it seems hardly likely that he would have failed to go to the rescue if he had known there was a ship in trouble close by. As it was Lord became something of a pariah as a result of Senator Smith's single-minded determination to find him guilty of a crime for which he was never officially accused. Smith's pursuit of Lord also effectively diverted the attention of the American Inquiry away from the disaster and its causes and focused it on *Californian*, which, I suspect, was exactly what Senator Smith intended. Smith's election campaign had to a large degree been financed by J. P. Morgan, as had that of US President Taft, so it is hardly surprising that the American Inquiry didn't delve too deeply into what had really happened. The gold shipment was never mentioned at all and *Titanic's* route to disaster was glossed over.

The carefully selected witnesses failed to mention the chaos aboard the sinking ship, mainly because Senator Smith never asked any questions that might have brought it to light. No serious inquiries into the identities of the mystery ships in the area of the sinking at the relevant time were put in hand. Witness statements that might have pointed to a vastly different conclusion from the one Smith finally reached were ignored. The Inquiry did find that there was no real blame attaching to the owners, officers and crew of the *Titanic* except inasmuch as the ship was travelling at excessive speed under the prevailing conditions. Joseph Bruce Ismay, like Captain Lord, was singled out for special attention and pilloried for escaping the ship when so many others drowned. It seems that, according to Senator Smith, all of the Americans aboard behaved as heroes and gentlemen while he thought that everybody else, with the exception of the crew who were employed by the American owners of the ship, were nothing but a lot of cowards prepared to sacrifice anyone to save themselves. In short, the findings of the American Inquiry were completely useless in establishing the facts of what happened.

Once the American Inquiry was over *Titanic's* surviving crew members and the other survivors who had been detained in America were allowed to leave for home, where another farcical inquiry awaited them. The British Inquiry conducted by the Board of Trade and organised while the American one was still going on should have been definitive. It was to be chaired by Lord Charles Bigham, Baron Mersey of Toxteth, usually referred to as just 'Lord Mersey'. Mersey had served the British bench well for many years and it was usually upon him that the Government called when they needed a particular result from an inquiry. Lord Mersey had already been involved in the inquiry into the Jameson Raid, which had triggered the Boer War. As Cecil Rhodes's lieutenant, Jameson had led an armed raid into Boer territory supposedly to take control of South African gold and diamond resources for Britain. The whole affair appears to have been the brainchild of Rhodes, but the result was inevitable. The Boers took exception to being invaded, and resisted, giving the British the excuse to declare war.

The British were at the time all-powerful and expected to have no real trouble in overcoming Boer resistance and taking control of their country. However, as we already know the Boers were a much harder nut to crack than expected. The British people's sympathies were decidedly with the Boers, whom they saw as underdogs, and wanted to know why the mighty British Empire had gone to war with such a small and inoffensive country. There had to be an official inquiry, which, predictably under Mersey's guidance, eventually found the British Government innocent of any blame for bringing about the war. With the benefit of hindsight it is all too apparent that the so-called 'innocent' British Government had engineered the whole thing. Lord Mersey would later go on to chair the British Inquiry into the loss of the Cunard liner *Lusitania* in 1914, where he would again exonerate his Government of any wrongdoing. The simple fact that the British chose Mersey to head the *Lusitania* inquiry is reason enough for many people to assume that the findings were a whitewash. The British Inquiry into the loss of the *Titanic* suffered from the same predetermination to exonerate the Government from all blame as Mersey's other famous commissions.

The British Inquiry began on 2 May 1912. The assessors (effectively judges) had a list of 26 questions to which they wanted answers. The first eight related to events before *Titanic* had any warning that she might be approaching an icefield. The next six were about what ice warnings were received by the ship and what was done about them. Question 15 actually related to the collision itself, while questions 16 to 24 were about what was done to save the vessel and those aboard after she had struck the ice. Question 25 was about the general design and construction of the ship, and question 26 about the rules and regulations governing immigrant ships and whether they needed to be changed. In the main the same witnesses would be called as were questioned in America. Unlike the American Inquiry, which called no passengers, the British would call one fare-paying survivor, Sir Cosmo Duff Gordon. It will be recalled that Sir Cosmo had effectively hired his own lifeboat and seven crew members to make good his escape from the sinking liner with his wife, one employee and a couple of friends. (Sir Cosmo has, over the years, been accused of taking advantage of his status in saving the lives of himself and his friends. There has never, as far as I am aware, been any suggestion that others were kept out of the Duff Gordon boat by the use of firearms or any other force. Sir Cosmo only did what any other sane man should have done and saved what he could from the wreck. He was organised, which is more than can be said for the rest of the evacuation of the *Titanic*.)

Maritime engineers would also be called upon to give evidence together with the survivors, so we would expect to see a fair account of what went on and how perhaps the whole event could have been avoided or the loss of life minimised. Instead, the Mersey inquiry was another whitewash, perhaps more reprehensible than the American one because the British had more time to prepare, and appeared to have had access to more expert witnesses.

The British Inquiry was a farce. As soon as any witness started to say anything that flew in the face of Mersey's preconceived ideas they were stopped, or simply ignored. The outcome of the inquiry was never in any doubt. The findings were very much the same as the American fiasco. The British Government in general and the Board of Trade in particular were cleared of any blame. Captain Lord and the *Californian* were again found guilty of failing to go to the aid of *Titanic*, even though he had never been formally accused of any such thing. The only real difference between the findings of the American and British Inquiries was that the British gave Joseph Bruce Ismay a glowing testimonial.

With public attention again centred on Captain Lord and the *Californian* instead of the disaster itself, the cover-up was well under way. The outbreak of the Great War just two years later would more than just divert public attention - it would remove many of the witnesses and their friends and relations together with a large percentage of the public themselves. *Titanic* would be all but forgotten and would remain so for the next 40 years - forgotten by all except the British Government, which wanted its gold back, and a few others who had realised that there was a story crying out to be told.

Captain Lord, adamant that he was not guilty of anything, actually requested that he be formally charged with failing to go to the aid of another vessel after distress signals had been seen and reported to him. His request was denied. Lord would carry the stigma of allowing 1,500 people to drown for the rest of his long life and would never officially be given the opportunity to clear himself or even expose facts concerning what really happened that night. Late in life, incensed by the portrayal of himself and his actions in the film A Night to Remember, Lord did try to set the record straight but, despite repeated attempts to get the inquiry reopened, the BoT refused. Surely common sense tells us that Lord certainly had no doubts about his innocence or he would have let the matter rest in the hope that his part in the disaster would eventually be forgotten. Instead he repeatedly tried to bring the affair to the attention of succeeding generations of the public.

However, because of the British Government's refusal to formally charge him with any crime, Captain Lord never did attempt to explain why he had asked if there was any colour in the rockets seen from *Californian*. Nor was he ever asked why he did not go to bed that night, how enough fuel could be found for his ship when so many others lay idle, what was so important about a cargo of woollens, and so on. He never had to explain a remark he made to a newspaper reporter shortly after *Californian* reached Boston at the conclusion of that eventful voyage. The reporter had asked Lord for the position of his ship during the time *Titanic* was sinking. Captain Lord refused to answer the question on the grounds that the reporter was requesting 'state secrets'. That single remark from Captain Stanley Lord is evidence enough to indicate a conspiracy involving at least himself and the British Government.

As far as we know the only state secret involving the ships sailing under the British flag on the night of 14/15 April 1912 was the secret shipment of gold aboard *Titanic*.

Chapter 22

Conclusion

We now have a somewhat different series of events surrounding the loss of the *Titanic* from those usually associated with the disaster. The governments of the major European powers were preparing for war years before it actually broke out in 1914. The British, with most to lose, searched for short cuts to increase naval superiority over their most likely adversary, Germany, by investing in merchant vessels that could hopefully supplement the fleet. To some extent the Germans did exactly the same thing, which meant that the mighty Royal Navy never achieved what it considered to be a decisive advantage. That those controlling the Navy were more than a little worried about coming events is clearly illustrated by the Committee of Imperial Defence meeting, where they declared that in the event of war they would not be able to spare any ships to support the Army. Ships for that purpose would have to be found elsewhere.

The primary British-owned shipping line at the time, Cunard, had vessels built with the aid of Government subsidy that could quickly be converted into armed merchant cruisers, but this didn't help the Army. The Army needed troopships. The only other major line sailing under the British flag was the American-owned White Star Line. Again, with the incentive of subsidies White Star agreed to build some particularly large ships specifically designed for use as troop carriers in the event of war. Luckily for Britain the owner of White Star was the anglophile multimillionaire John Pierpont Morgan. Unfortunately, while Mr Morgan had a soft spot for the British, he was also a hard-headed and ruthless businessman, with a penchant for collecting religious artefacts and other works of art from around the world.

The Cunard liners, which entered service from 1906, soon proved worthless as warships, to the dismay of the British Government. They were much too fragile and far too costly to run. This must have set alarm bells ringing with regard to the other governmental project of producing cut-price troopships. Would they also turn out to be worthless? By 1911 the situation in Europe had deteriorated to the point that everyone in the know expected war to begin at any moment. They had to know if the new troopships worked or not.

The Agadir crisis brought everything to a head. Morgan began shipping home to America all of the art treasures he had been displaying in major British museums, leaving those museums looking a little bare, and embarrassing the Government with what it saw as his defeatist attitude. We know that the collision between *Olympic* and the cruiser HMS *Hawke* is unlikely to have been a complete accident. The most likely explanation for the collision is that it was a test of the viability of the 'Olympics' as troopships and a rap on the knuckles for Mr Morgan. Unfortunately, Commander Blunt on the *Hawke* overdid things and all but destroyed the liner.

White Star couldn't make an insurance claim to cover the damage to its ship because a naval inquiry had predictably found that the collision was the company's fault. It was left with a ship that was effectively beyond economic repair, a write-off, but it couldn't afford to simply scrap a new ship that had just cost a million and a half pounds to build.

Switching *Olympic* with her sister, which was nearing completion, was not a difficult undertaking for a shipyard with the resources and expertise of Harland & Wolff. That was the easy part of the operation. The difficulty would lie in subsequently disposing of the damaged member of the pair. Converting it into a reasonable facsimile of the second sister was no harder than the first part of the switch had been. Nobody was expecting a switch so they wouldn't be looking too hard at either vessel. Once the makeover was complete it seemed a simple matter to take the crippled liner to sea and stage a fake collision with an iceberg. There was no apparent reason for anyone to be hurt in the accident, and as the vessel would not really be any less seaworthy than when she set out there would be plenty of time to get everyone off, or so they thought. So the first sister, masquerading as the second, prepared for what should have been a maiden voyage.

It is not clear whether the intention was merely to pretend that the ship was very badly damaged, then claim on the insurance to actually put her right, or to sink her and be done with it. The second scenario seems the more likely, simply because the collision was supposed to take place in one of the deepest regions of the North Atlantic Ocean. It was inconceivable in 1912 that any vessel that sank in that location would ever be seen again, so once it had gone the chances of anyone finding out what had actually happened were negligible.

Because there shouldn't have been any real danger to the people on the ship, up to the time of the staged collision the voyage could be treated just like any other. A full load of passengers could be taken out together with a full, but hand-picked, crew. To allay any suspicions that might be lurking in the back of anyone's mind, it was made known that J. P. Morgan himself, and a load of his valuable ancient artefacts, would be aboard - not that there was ever any chance that he actually would be. The White Star Line was so sure that there was no real danger involved that, distracted by making sure that everything else was going to plan, it completely forgot the third party insurance on the passengers, crew and baggage. It was not until the day after the liner had foundered and about 1,500 passengers and crew had died that Harold Sanderson arranged the passenger insurance. Propitiously the insurance company favoured by White Star had its offices in the very building that the line had occupied until the end of the 19th century. The officers of the insurance company must have been well known to the higher management of White Star. Despite the fact that such an insurance deal is of itself fraudulent, the insurance company did pay out, not that it actually cost them anything. They recouped their losses by putting up the insurance rates across the board and charging all of the shipping lines a special premium, thus defrauding the shareholders of those lines.

It would appear that the British Government was fooled into believing that the ship was going all the way to America. It arranged to ship a load of gold on *Titanic*, as it believed the ship to be. Only the higher echelons of the White Star Line and almost certainly J. P. Morgan himself knew that the liner was only going as far as the Grand Banks. This privileged information presented the conspirators with a heaven-sent opportunity, which put them in a position where they thought they couldn't possibly lose. If they spirited the gold away before the ship sailed they would still be in pocket even if the insurance companies failed to pay up. If the insurance did pay, they stood to make a fortune. As we know, the British Navy has been searching the wreck for that gold since 1953 without any luck. They can't find it because it isn't there and hasn't been since around Easter 1912.

Ships were sent out to meet the *Titanic* when the staged collision took place in order to take off the passengers and crew. Most of these rescue ships were owned by the same company that owned the White Star Line, J. P. Morgan's International Mercantile Marine. A couple of outsiders were brought in, such as the Cunard Line's *Carpathia* and possibly a Canadian Pacific Line liner. Although they were notionally competitors, Cunard and White Star had been collaborating for years and would eventually merge. Canadian Pacific was owned by the American Canadian Pacific Railroad Company, and was therefore closely associated with J. P. Morgan. He had a lot of money tied up in the US railway system and actually owned all of the rolling stock on America's eastern seaboard, so he was well used to dealing with the railway companies.

The plan was simple and could easily have worked, in which case the *Titanic*, like so many other ships that have sunk in the North Atlantic, would now be forgotten. However, chance has a nasty habit of laughing at the most carefully thought-out plans of mere mortals.

The plan to dispose of the *Titanic*, and with her all of the evidence that things were not as they should be, worked fine until the night of 14 April 1912, when it failed utterly.

Californian made it to the prearranged meeting place in readiness to take off *Titanic's* people, and stopped to wait. Captain Lord informed the liner of his whereabouts by wireless. Captain Smith on the *Titanic* had chosen his target icebergs from an ice warning from *Mesaba* received earlier that day. The rendezvous would hopefully be within easy calling distance of *Californian*. Some little distance away to the southwards the *Carpathia* was also moving to within striking distance of the rendezvous. Whether by chance or design the Canadian Pacific liner *Mount Temple* had also moved into the immediate area.

Titanic's lookouts, Fleet and Lee, spotted the icebergs ahead of the ship at about 11.15pm and attempted to alert the officers on the liner's bridge, without any conspicuous success. It was a bitterly cold night and those officers were in all probability taking a short break in the chartroom where it was a lot warmer than out on the open-sided bridge. The officer of the watch, Chief Officer William McMaster Murdoch, obviously did not expect the ship to reach the ice quite so quickly or he would have been ready. As it was, there was nobody on the bridge to instruct the helmsman to alter course away from the iceberg that lay 10 or 12 miles away, directly ahead of the ship. There was still plenty of time to avert a disaster if only someone with some authority had heard the warnings from the crow's-nest, but nobody did.

The iceberg was only spotted by anyone in a position to do anything about it at the very last moment when Mr Murdoch returned to the bridge and went out onto the open wing. By that time the berg was probably slightly less than half a mile ahead of the ship. With her engines at full ahead there was still time for the liner to turn away from disaster, but Murdoch immediately ordered the engines full astern and the helm put hard a-starboard. Without the thrust from the central turbine engine, *Titanic's* ability to turn sharply was dramatically reduced. However, it still appears that Mr Murdoch's attempt to avoid the iceberg might have been successful, or at the very least reduced the collision to a minor scrape.

Unfortunately for those aboard the *Titanic* there seems to have been another obstruction ahead and slightly to the left of the ice. We cannot be sure of exactly what this other obstruction was, but it is unlikely to have been more ice. More probably it was another ship or perhaps a wreck, similar to the one *Olympic* had struck on 24 February, just 50 days earlier.

In view of what occurred later that night another ship is the more likely candidate. Whatever it was, it ripped open the forward part of the liner so badly that she could no longer remain afloat indefinitely. No doubt the life of the ship could have been extended if the pumps had been operational or not already fully occupied dealing with leaks that had been there since the vessel had left Southampton, or before.

In the event no effective measures at all were taken to keep the liner afloat for as long as possible, to allow rescue ships to reach her in time to take everyone off. Instead, many of the officers, crew and passengers panicked and prepared to abandon ship. Even at this point there was still a chance. The officers on the bridge of *Titanic* had another steamer in view about 5 miles away. Red, white and blue distress signals were sent up in an effort to attract the attention of the stranger but she ignored them. Mr Lightoller later said that he wished he had a 6-inch gun so that he could have put a shot into the mystery vessel to wake her up. I have no doubt at all that this mystery ship was already wide awake. *Titanic's* distress signals would have been clearly visible and audible to the stranger. It would have been all but impossible for the officers on her bridge and the lookouts in her crow's-nest to not have been aware of a large, brilliantly illuminated liner only a few miles away, firing distress rockets. Instead of coming to the rescue the mystery ship appeared to have hung around for a while, as if waiting for something, and then to have quietly made off. If this mysterious vessel had been there by design, like *Californian*, then perhaps her skipper had realised that things had gone wrong and decided that discretion was the better part of valour. Or perhaps they had spotted the all-white rockets that were seen from *Californian* and assumed another vessel was on its way and their services were no longer required.

As we now know, 705 survivors from *Titanic* managed to find places in lifeboats, one way or another - lifeboats that could easily have accommodated more than half as many again under normal circumstances. Conditions that night were anything but normal. The sea was as smooth as a millpond so, if they had been properly managed, the boats could have taken a great many more people than they were rated for. It is quite possible that instead of 1,500 people going down with the ship the same number might have been saved. We could have no better evidence of the panic that had gripped the ship during her final hours on the surface.

Over and above those 705 people from *Titanic*, we seem to have another 98 from some other source. Where but from another ship could these survivors have come? And, perhaps more importantly, where did they go? That both Captains Lord and Rostron saw too many lifeboats at the scene of the sinking also argues that there was another, unknown, vessel involved in the disaster.

Carpathia only picked up 13 of *Titanic's* proper wooden lifeboats even though, according to Captain Rostron, people had been from all 16 of them. We know from the record that some people who had not survived the night in the open boats were taken aboard the Cunard vessel and were later buried at sea, so the fact that there were corpses in a lifeboat was no deterrent to picking them up. We also know that *Californian* found lifeboats at the scene, but Captain Lord declined to recover any of them. Perhaps both skippers had realised that there were too many boats and didn't want that fact advertised.

Even as *Carpathia* was making her way back to New York to land *Titanic's* survivors, those very people were being sworn to secrecy about what had happened on the ship. A carefully prepared statement was drawn up exonerating both passengers and crew from any wrongdoing or incompetence. The statement, which purported to have come from surviving passengers, contained technical references and nautical terms that would only have been familiar to professional seamen. In short, it was written either by or with the aid of the surviving officers from *Titanic* and possibly the officers of *Carpathia* as part of a cover-up. Many of the assertions made in the statement can now be proven fictitious.

Once *Carpathia* reached New York and off-loaded *Titanic's* people and lifeboats, the public were kept well away from them. Passengers were whisked away, crew were detained incommunicado, and identifying marks were swiftly removed from the lifeboats. This proved to be a mistake, as it revealed the name of the ship for which the boats had been built - *Olympic*. A ship's lifeboats were built by Harland & Wolff specifically for each individual vessel and were usually constructed aboard the ship for which they were intended.

After the American Inquiry, which as we know was an incompetently handled farce, the crew of *Titanic* were returned to Britain where, once again, they were held incommunicado. When *Lapland*, the vessel bringing the surviving crew home, reached Plymouth, it was intercepted by a tender, the *Sir Richard Grenville*, which had brought out the two most senior White Star officials in Britain, no less that Harold Sanderson and E. C. Grenfell, together with a couple of other lesser White Star representatives. Also aboard the tender was a Mr Wolverstan from the Board of Trade, accompanied by four assistants, and Mr Woolven, representing the Receiver of Wrecks and the Customs & Excise. White Star and the British Government were not taking any chances that the survivors might not take seriously any instructions they were given.

The survivors were eventually taken ashore and confined within the walls and railings of Plymouth Dockyard, well away from the questioning press and relatives who had been awaiting their return. Then, one by one, the survivors were questioned and instructed to say nothing to anyone about what had occurred aboard the ship. They were then obliged to sign the Official Secrets Act, confirming the involvement of the British Government in the cover-up. Signing the Act meant that crew members were liable to 20 years imprisonment if they ever divulged what they knew. This debriefing and signing of the Act took a couple of days, so friends and relatives of the surviving crew just had to wait.

Then came the British Inquiry into the disaster where, in the main, selected witnesses answered carefully selected questions with well-rehearsed replies. Those of the crew who were in a position to know anything particularly damning were rewarded for keeping silent at the inquiry by being given jobs for life with the line at a time when jobs for life just didn't exist for ordinary crew members (they still don't). One important witness was awarded a sideways promotion when he was made a harbour master in South Africa, a far cry from being a mere helmsman. Of course, Robert Hitchens was in a position to know exactly what had been happening on the bridge of the *Titanic*, and who was there at any given time.

There were, as always, winners and losers. The British Government had its troopships. The vessel sailing under the name *Olympic* was by far the most successful troop carrier of the entire First World War, even if the price of £8,000,000-plus was a little on the steep side. *Olympic* went on to serve the White Star Line for 25 years, right up to the eve of the Second World War, as one of the most successful ocean liners ever.

The gold, it seems, has never been recovered, so whoever made off with it didn't do too badly out of the affair. Ismay and Pirrie both bought large houses shortly after the *Titanic* disaster, but they never exhibited any other signs of suddenly coming into a great fortune. J. P. Morgan's organisation continued much as usual, although Morgan himself died in 1913. It is unlikely that we will ever know where the gold went.

It also seems unlikely that we shall ever discover what became of the 98 extra survivors, who clearly did not come from *Titanic* but whose names were transmitted by *Carpathia*. One can only hope that they were allowed to continue their journey to wherever, although no trace of them has ever come to light.

The White Star Line, which had slightly over-insured the ship, recovered its money, not that it did the company a lot of good. The spectre of the *Titanic* haunted the line and it never truly prospered again. In 1927 IMM sold White Star to Lord Kylsant's Royal Mail group of shipping companies, which didn't improve matters at all. Just four years later Kylsant was jailed for publishing misleading statements in the 1928 Royal Mail prospectus. By 1933 White Star was in serious financial trouble, having lost £1,500,000, exactly what it had cost it to build each of the 'Olympic' class ships more than 20 years before. In 1934 the White Star Line and Cunard merged, forming Cunard White Star. The White Star part of the name was dropped shortly after the end of the Second World War.

There is one more curious chapter regarding a survivor from the *Titanic*, a humble fireman called Thomas Hart. Before *Titanic* left Southampton every member of her crew was checked out by the Board of Trade inspector, Maurice Clarke, to see that the details recorded in the Certificate of Continuous Discharge (effectively a seaman's service record and a licence to work) were correct. Thomas Hart's name does not appear on any survivor list from the White Star liner. He does not appear to have been picked up by *Carpathia*, or any other known vessel in the area when *Titanic* foundered. Nevertheless Hart turned up at his College Street, Southampton, home in late May 1912. He claimed that he had lost his Discharge book during a drinking bout in a public house shortly before *Titanic* sailed. His place aboard the ship must have been taken by whoever had found or stolen his papers. His story is palpably untrue. No fewer than 34 other crew members, who also worked in the boiler rooms of the *Titanic*, came from the same small area of Southampton as Hart. Some, if not all, would have known him and spotted an impostor right away - and remember that Clarke had checked everyone's papers. Nobody could have passed themselves off as Hart without the connivance of his shipmates. Either Thomas Hart was part of yet another conspiracy or there was a second rescue ship; after all, he couldn't have swum home. Where had he been for the two months since the sinking? It seems that officialdom failed, as usual in the case of the *Titanic*, to ask the right questions.

Back in 1912 the political situation in Europe continued to deteriorate and the threat of war pushed *Titanic* out of the public consciousness - there were other things to worry about. For more than 40 years the worst shipping disaster up to that time was all but forgotten, and so it would have remained. However, the *Titanic* had become a symbol, a part of the English language. Major catastrophes and disasters were, and still are, referred to as of 'Titanic' proportions. It appears that her name, as well as the ship herself, carried on well after the date on which she officially went to the bottom of the sea.

Appendix 1

The shipbuilders' scale models

Like most ships, the 'Olympic' class vessels were first given physical form as builders' half models. These are exact scale miniatures of the full-sized ship, but usually only one side of this 'working model' is actually built. In the case of the 'Olympics' a complete model of the finished class leader, *Olympic*, was also constructed.

In March 1910 the quarter-inch working model had been completed, but no name was painted on it. However, identification was provided on the background sheet of wood on which the half model was mounted - it said, '*Olympic* and *Titanic*'. In addition to the half models, a complete quarter-inch-scale finished model (ie a fully rigged replica) was also constructed, and this was also completed in the spring of 1910. Only the name *Olympic* appeared on the bow, however. There is no record of a separate *Titanic* model being built. The half model, which would later be sent to the British Inquiry into the *Titanic* disaster, weighed about 30 hundredweight, which means that it was the larger of the two.

According to Dr Alan Scarth, Curator of Ship Models, Merseyside Maritime Museum, the quarter-inch builders' scale model of *Olympic* and *Titanic* in the museum was completed some time between spring 1910 and 1911, and was wired up for internal illumination. This model, although obviously of *Olympic* and originally with that name on bow and stern, has *Titanic's* build number (401) written in pencil on the inside of several doors and other small fittings on its superstructure. Scarth, apparently without any provenance whatsoever, claims that after the *Titanic* disaster this same model, after being removed from its original display case, which declared it to be of both vessels, was then put into a somewhat more modest case with a nameplate indicating that it represented *Olympic* alone. Then, within about a year or so the model was substantially altered by the builders to represent the third sister, *Britannic*, and displayed by the White Star Line at the Anglo-American Exposition at the White City, London, in 1914. This is difficult to believe as these models were built accurately to scale, and *Britannic* was both wider and longer than the other two vessels of the 'Olympic' class.

The vessel known as *Olympic*, after doing sterling service as a troopship during the First World War, was refitted ready to return to civilian service between August 1919 and June 1920. At the same time the model was altered again, back to resembling just *Olympic*. However, this time the conversion was incomplete, not unlike that of *Olympic* into *Titanic* in 1911. The large screens of 41 windows on A Deck, the arrangement of windows on B Deck, and the decking over the aft well deck remained. Neither *Olympic* nor *Titanic* ever had any of these features. *Titanic* had 42 screens on each side of A Deck, while in reality *Britannic* only had 38. Then the model seems to have disappeared.

It next seems to have appeared with Wards of Sheffield, which broke up *Olympic* at its Albion works in 1937, although this might have been a different, smaller model altogether. The model next turned up in a hangar at Blackpool Airport, where it had been kept by the Lancashire Aircraft Corporation, Blackpool, with a view to its possible display at the airport restaurant. The LAC donated the model to Liverpool City Museums in 1951. How the model got to Blackpool is something of a mystery, but there is an unsubstantiated story that it was displayed as the *Titanic*, either at the Tower or Winter Gardens in Blackpool at some time in the 1930s. While it was in the tender care of the Liverpool Museum Service, between 1951 and the early 1970s, the model suffered greatly; its display case was disposed of, and a number of small parts disappeared. Then, at long last, it was thoroughly cleaned and partially repaired before going on display in 1974. In 1978 it was sent to Scale Model International Ltd of Crosby, Merseyside, for complete restoration. During this work, which was not competed until 1982, it was discovered that the model, in certain minor details, most resembled *Titanic*, rather than the other two vessels of her class, especially once she had been stripped down. (This is hardly surprising when one discovers that *Olympic* was really *Titanic* operating under her sister's name for all but about one year of her long life.)

'Finally, cost, time and ethical (sic) constraints weighed heavily against the major reconstruction of its superstructure, which would have been required to make the model accurate to any one of the three ships concerned at any time in its history. The compromise reached, therefore, was to have the model restored as a fairly accurate representation of the *Titanic* as she sailed, while accepting that certain features, notably the window arrangement on decks A and B, were those of the short-lived *Britannic* model of 1914. The most obvious structural change made was the removal of the decking over the aft well deck, which had never been a feature of either the *Olympic* or the *Titanic*.'

And that, according to Dr Scarth, is how the Liverpool Museum Service, between 1951 and 1982, managed to completely destroy the historical value of the shipbuilders' scale model, originally constructed by Harland & Wolff of Belfast, of possibly the most famous class of ships ever built, and of which one was certainly the best-known liner of them all.

Appendix 2

Titanic's insurance

The insurance situation with regard to the *Titanic* is, to say the least, difficult to unravel. The White Star Line habitually under-insured its ships by about a third of their value to save money on the premiums. *Titanic* had cost the line about £1,500,000 so, following the company's usual practice, she would normally have been covered for £1,000,000, which is exactly what has always been claimed. In truth the ship was insured for considerably more than just a million, or even her real value.

Willis Faber & Co acted as agents and sold £1,000,000-worth of insurance in relatively small parcels to a large number of insurance companies in Britain, none being in a position to accept such a large risk alone. Among the largest of the risks taken on in Britain was for £75,000 by R. T. Jones of the Commercial Union. More than 70 other companies were involved, accepting risks of between £1,000 and £75,000. The world's most famous maritime insurer, Lloyd's of London, does not appear on the document listing the names and amounts covered, although that list does show that the full £1,000,000 was covered. This insurance document, known as 'The *Titanic* Slip', is regarded as the definitive evidence that the ship was truly covered for only the £1,000,000 usually claimed. However, from other documentation it is apparent that Lloyd's did indeed carry a large piece of *Titanic's* insurance.

As late as 8 July 1912 Lloyd's appears to have been trying to distance itself from the disaster, even though as early as 17 April it had begun to liquidate assets to cover its commitment. The *Liverpool Echo* carried an article quoting from a letter written by Mr A. Scott, secretary of Lloyd's, to *The Times*:

'In view of the reports which have appeared in the press in connection with the inquiry into the loss of the SS *Titanic*, to the effect that the vessel was built considerably in excess of the requirements of Lloyd's Register, I am directed to say that these statements are inaccurate. On the contrary, in important parts of her structure the vessel as built did not come up to the requirements of Lloyd's Register for a vessel of her dimensions.'

Nevertheless, Lloyd's, unlike some German underwriters, honoured its commitment and eventually paid out almost £1,500,000.

As is already apparent, insurance cover for *Titanic* was not only arranged in Britain but another large sum was covered by European, Australian and American companies, again in many relatively small parcels. The Insurance

Company of North America carried $50,000 of the risk and Atlantic Mutual accepted double that amount. For American purposes the vessel was valued at $5 million, which was equivalent to £1,000,000 at the time.

Despite the generally held belief that *Titanic* was under-insured by as much as a third of her actual value, it seems that this was not the case. In fact, the vessel was dramatically over-insured by more than £1,500,000, perhaps more. The insurance situation with *Titanic* was so complicated that to the present day the file on the ship has still not been finally closed.

There is a clause written into maritime insurance of the day, and it may well still be included in more modern policies. This clause, known as the 'Sister Ship Clause', states that 'should the vessel insured come into collision or receive salvage services from another vessel belonging wholly or in part to the same owners or under the same management, the assured shall have the same rights under the policy as they would have were the other vessel the property of owners not interested in the policy.' This would explain why any vessels intended to be part of any rescue or salvage attempt would have to belong to the same owners as the victim and why vessels belonging to other owners would be discouraged from participating in any rescue, which is exactly what happened in April 1912.

On 16 April 1912, the day after *Titanic* foundered, the Liverpool & London Steamship Protection Association, an insurance company, agreed to provide the third party insurance covering passengers, crew and baggage aboard the ship.

Olympic had provisionally been entered onto the London & Liverpool's books at 45,000 tons at the committee meeting on 14 February 1911, but not on risk.

Titanic was provisionally entered at 46,000 tons at the committee meeting on 13 February 1912, but not on risk.

Olympic was entered onto the company books on risk at 45,324 tons at the committee meeting on 30 May 1911 to coincide with the ship's trials and transfer from H&W. The entry was backdated to 28 May to cover the sea trials. The backdating of insurance cover is fraud, no matter whether it is done with the best possible motives or not.

Titanic was entered on risk at 46,329 tons at the committee meeting on 16 April 1912. The entry was backdated to 1 April 1912 to cover the sea trials. Unfortunately this entry was made the day after the ship sank, and the committee knew this, which again is fraud.

To cover the insurance company's losses a special premium was levied on all of the other passenger-carrying lines insured by them, thus defrauding the shareholders and owners of those lines.

Clearly the Liverpool & London Insurance Company was prepared to bend the rules a little for the White Star Line. However, if the ship that sank on 15 April 1912 was really *Olympic*, she was legitimately covered by the insurance agreement entered onto the insurer's book on the previous 30 May.

Appendix 3

The Tutankhamun Deception by Gerald O'Farrell raises the strong possibility that Howard Carter and Lord Carnarvon had discovered and been removing articles from Tutankhamun's tomb for more than a decade before its official opening in November 1922. One of the chief beneficiaries of this looting appears to have been J. P. Morgan's Metropolitan Museum in New York.

The millionaire Theodore Davis had, during most of the first ten years of the 20th century, employed Howard Carter on his concession ground in the Valley of the Kings. Davis had in 1909 given artefacts to Herbert Winlock (later to become director of the Metropolitan Museum) to ship to New York. Winlock did not examine these closely until 1921 when he was amazed to find some of them bore the seal of Tutankhamun and the royal necropolis seal, proof that they had been interred in the Valley of the Kings. Some of the material recovered from the tomb appears to have been in the form of papyrus.

Some time in 1910 or 1911 Carter and Carnarvon appear to have recovered some papyrus scrolls from the Tutankhamun tomb. One of the scrolls tells how a group of disaffected Egyptians, together with their assorted multi-racial collection of slaves, left Egypt to preserve the religion founded by the heretic pharaoh Akhenaten, with his blessing and under the guidance of his trusted advisor Moses. In short, the Coptic scroll was a very early example of the second book of the Bible, Exodus, showing that the Jews were not God's chosen people but a mongrel race descended from Egyptians and slaves. Whether or not the scroll gave an accurate picture of history was immaterial. It was certainly ancient, which gave it credibility; and it was political dynamite. What stability there was in the Middle East was based on sectarianism, and anything that upset the delicate balance could easily set the whole area alight.

J. P. Morgan's focus of interest in antiquity and religion embraced how the Christians evolved from Judaic law and what the Jews had inherited from earlier civilisations in Egypt and Sumeria. He personally travelled great distances year after year, in discomfort, collecting any artefacts relating to the subject.

The scroll was first offered for sale to the British Museum, but it was unable to come up with the necessary cash to buy it. Obviously the British Museum did not inform the Government of the scroll's existence or that they had been offered it. If they had, the money to buy the potentially inflammatory document would undoubtedly have been found. After all, the British Government needed the oil from Persia (now Iraq) for its new battleships, so it had more than a slight interest in preserving the stability of the area.

In any event, in 1912 Morgan paid £80,000 for the Coptic manuscript that had first been offered to the British Museum. The sum paid tells us that Mr Morgan was well aware of both the intrinsic and political value of the old scroll.

Appendix 4

The Quitzrau affidavit

'DOMINION OF CANADA
Province of Ontario
City of Toronto

Dr F. C. Quitzrau, being first duly sworn, deposes and says that he was a passenger, travelling second class, on the steamer *Mount Temple*, which left Antwerp April 3, 1912; that about midnight Sunday, April 14, New York time, he was awakened by the sudden stopping of the engines; that he immediately went to the cabin, where already were gathered several of the stewards and passengers, who informed him that word had already been received by wireless from the *Titanic* that the *Titanic* had struck an iceberg and was calling for help.

Orders were immediately given and the *Mount Temple* course changed, heading straight for the *Titanic*. About 3 o'clock New York time, 2 o'clock ship's time, the *Titanic* was sighted by some of the officers and crew; that as soon as the *Titanic* was seen all lights on the *Mount Temple* were put out and the engines stopped and the boat lay dead for about two hours; that as soon as day broke the engines were started and the *Mount Temple* circled the *Titanic's* position, the officers insisting that this be done, although the captain had given orders that the boat proceed on its journey. While encircling the *Titanic's* position we sighted the *Frankfurt* to the north-west of us, the *Birma* to the south, speaking to both of these by wireless, the latter asking if we were in distress; that about 6 o'clock we saw the *Carpathia*, from which we had previously received a message that the *Titanic* had gone down; that about 8.30 the *Carpathia* wirelessed that it had picked up 20 lifeboats and about 720 passengers all told, and that there was no need for the *Mount Temple* to stand by, as the remainder of those on board were drowned.

Dr F. C. QUITZRAU

Subscribed and sworn to before me on this 29th day of April, 1912.

(SEAL)

WILLIAM JAMES ELLIOTT

Notary Public for the Province of Ontario.'

Bibliography

Newspapers

Daily Express
Evening Chronicle (Newcastle)
Independent on Sunday
Lloyd's Weekly News: Ginns P., *The Deathless Story of the Titanic* (1912)
New York Times
The Daily Telegraph
The Guardian (London)
The Independent
The Oxford Times
The Times (London)
Sunday Chronicle, 1953

Magazines

Reader's Digest: Great Mysteries of the Past
Journal of Commerce: 'Report on the British Inquiry into the Circumstances Attending the Loss of RMS *Titanic*', 1912 Oldham, W. J. *The Ismay Line*
National Geographic
Oxford Journal, Illustrated, 1912
Proceedings of the Institution of Mechanical Engineers, 1895
The Sunday Mirror

Books

Angelucci and Carcari *Ships* (London: MacDonald & Janes, 1975)
Ballard, R. D. *The Discovery of the Titanic* (London: Guild, Hodder & Stoughton, London, 1987)
Beesley, L. *The Loss of the SS Titanic* (Heinemann, 1912)
Boyd-Smith, P. *Titanic from Rare Historical Reports* (Southampton: Brooks Books, 1992)
Bryceson, Dave *The Titanic Disaster* (Patrick Stephens Ltd, 1998)

Cahill, R. A. *Disasters at Sea: Titanic to Exxon Valdez* (Century, 1990)

Coleman, T. *The Liners* (Harmondsworth, 1976)

Davie, M. *Titanic, The Full Story of a Tragedy* (1986)

Eaton, John P. and Haas, Charles A. *Titanic: Triumph and Tragedy* (Patrick Stephens Ltd, 1986)

   Titanic: Destination Disaster (Patrick Stephens Ltd, 1987)

   Falling Star: Misadventures of White Star Line Ships (Patrick Stephens Ltd, 1989)

Garrett, R. *The Titanic and Other Victims of the North Atlantic* (Buchan & Enright, 1986)

Gracie, A. *The Truth About the Titanic* (1913)

Harrison. L. *A Titanic Myth: The Californian Incident* (William Kimber, 1986)

Hobson, D. *The Pride of Lucifer* (Hamish Hamilton, 1990)

Hutchings, D. F. RMS *Titanic: A Modern Legend* (Waterfront Publications, 1993)

Jackson, S. *J. P. Morgan* (Heinemann, 1984)

Lord, W. *A Night To Remember* (Corgi, 1956)

   The Night Lives On (1987)

Lynch, D. and Marshall, K. *Titanic: An Illustrated History* (Hodder & Stoughton, 1992)

McCluskie, Tom *Anatomy of the Titanic* (PRC, 1998)

McCluskie, Tom, Sharpe, Michael and Marriott, Leo *Titanic and Her Sisters* (Parkgate Books, 1998)

McDougall, Robert *Titanic: The Solis Project* (2005)

   White Star Liners: Picture Postcards and Memorabilia (2002)

Marcus, G. *The Maiden Voyage* (New York: Manor Books, 1978)

Mills, S. RMS *Olympic: The Old Reliable* (Blandford Forum: Waterfront Publications, 1993)

O'Connor, R. *Down to Eternity* (Gold Medal Books, Fawcett Publications)

O'Farrell, Gerald *The Tutankhamun Deception* (Sidgwick & Jackson, 2001)

Pellegrino, C. *Her Name Titanic: The Untold Story of the Sinking and Finding of the Unsinkable Ship* (1990)

Preston, A. *History of The Royal Navy* (London: Hamlyn Bison, 1983)

Reade, L. *The Ship That Stood Still* (Sparkford: Patrick Stephens Ltd, 1993)

Report on the Loss of the SS Titanic (The Official Government Inquiry, HMSO, 1912.)

Rostron, A. *The Loss of the Titanic* (Westbury, Wilts: *Titanic* Signals Archive, 1991)

Shipbuilder: Ocean Liners of the Past: White Star Triple Screw Atlantic Liners Olympic and *Titanic* (Sparkford: Patrick Stephens Ltd, 1988)

Stafford, David *Churchill and the Secret Service* (John Murray, 1997)

Stenson, P. Lights: *The Odyssey of C. H. Lightoller* (Bodley Head, 1984)

Titanic Signals News (White Star Publications, Winter/Spring 1994)

Titanic - Reappraisal of Evidence Relating to SS Californian (Marine Accidents Investigations Board, HMSO 1992)

Wade, W. C. *The Titanic: End of a Dream* (London: Weidenfeld & Nicolson, 1979)

Wile, Frederic *Men Around the Kaiser* (Heinemann, 1914)

Woodroffe & MacDonald *Titanic* (London: MacDonald & Co, 1989)

Videos

Secrets of The Titanic (National Geographic, 1986)

Titanic (W. H. Smith, 1993)

Titanic (The Way We Were)

Lusitania (Network First)

Index